7291

LEARNING RESOURCE
CENTRE

**HAVANT
COLLEGE**

New Road
Havant
Hants PO9 1QL

Tel: 023 9271 4045
Email: LRC@havant.ac.uk

POLITICS AND THE MASS MEDIA IN BRITAIN

R. NEGRINE

London and New York

DEDICATION
To Ruth, David, Peter, Alice and Eileen

First published 1989
by Routledge
11 New Fetter Lane, London EC4P 4EE
29 West 35th Street, New York, NY 10001

Reprinted 1991

Typeset in 10/12pt Baskerville Linotron 202
by Columns of Reading
Printed and bound in Great Britain by
Biddles Ltd, Guildford and King's Lynn

British Library Cataloguing in Publication Data

Negrine, Ralph
Politics and the mass media
1. Mass media. Political aspects
I. Title
302.2′34

Library of Congress Cataloging in Publication Data

Negrine, Ralph M.
Politics and the mass media in Britain / R. Negrine.
p. cm.
Includes index.
ISBN 0–415–01529–4   ISBN 0–415–01530–8 (pbk.)
1. Mass media—Political aspects—Great Britain. I. Title.
P95.82.G7N44   1989
302.2′34′0941—dc19

HB 0–415–01529–4
PB 0–415–01530–8

CONTENTS

PREFACE

This book examines the political role of the mass media in contemporary Britain. It covers the main features of the press and television in Britain and, with the extensive use of examples, it develops an analysis of their relationships with 'politics' and political and social institutions and the implications of those relationships.

The definition of politics adopted throughout this book is a broad one, namely, that 'politics creates and conditions all aspects of our lives and it is at the core of the development of problems in society and the collective modes of their resolution'.[1] The reason for adopting such a broad definition is that politics and political discourse infuse all aspects of our lives and the mass media play a key role in this process of political communication. Thus, the study of the mass media and elections sits alongside the study of pressure groups' use of the modern means of mass communication.

Although the book deals with a broad definition of politics, it adopts a more restricted register of mass media. The two most often cited sources of information about the world – television and the press – take pride of place in this book. And within those two media, attention is mainly focused on those aspects of the media which are overtly political – either in content or in their implications. Thus, for example, television news and current affairs feature prominently while light entertainment does not; similarly, more attention is paid to 'political' stories in the press than to stories which highlight the sexual peccadillos of television superstars.

The decision to focus on these areas should not be taken as a dismissal of the other output, nor of their classification as 'non-political'. In their own, and very important ways, the entertainment format, the James Bond film, and the representations of the life and loves of Samantha Fox, are steeped in political implications. Our concern, however, is with the processes, relationships and structures of political (mass) communication.

This orientation towards the more traditionally defined 'political' content of the mass media also explains the absence of any discussion of women's magazines, pop music radio stations or popular films. Again, it is not the absence of 'political' implications that has ruled them out but the specific perspective adopted here as well as the author's limited resources and time. The emphasis is, as Seymour-Ure has recently reminded us, on the means of communications that are 'for' politics.[1]

There are other omissions which the careful reader will note. There is no discussion of the laws which restrict the media in one way or another. The D Notice System, the Official Secrets Act, the law of contempt, the Prevention of Terrorism Act, and matters of libel, are all absent from the following pages. There are two major reasons for the decision not to cover them. First, they are well and extensively documented elsewhere and a discussion here would not further our knowledge of them or of their operation. Second, when grouped together they illustrate a fairly simple but vitally important fact about the nature and extent of secrecy in Britain, namely, that the mass media operate within a structure of government that is highly secretive, that is extremely protective of its interests and that will do its utmost to retain control of information which it deems to be of national interest. Such is the everyday context of the mass media in Britain.

In this last decade the power of government and the force of the law have brought even greater pressure to bear on the enterprising journalist. The roll-call is frighteningly lengthy: Peter Snow during the Falklands campaign; *Real Lives: At the Edge of the Union*; Kate Adie over the reporting of the American bombing of Libya; Duncan Campbell over the Zircon Spy satellite programme, and the BBC Radio Four programme *My Country Right or Wrong* on the Secret Service. The fallout from Peter Wright's *Spycatcher* memoirs has affected the press in a way previously unimaginable and there is no sign that the Government is intent on giving up its fight to muzzle the press.

But it is not only the journalist who has suffered from the effects of a secretive and powerful centralized state machine. Individuals interested in protecting civil liberties and natural justice have also suffered. The two cases which rocked the 1980s testify to this: Sarah Tisdall was imprisoned for leaking documents, though the jury cleared Clive Ponting.

These incidents are separated by many things – different contexts, actors, situations – but they have one thing in common, and that is that they symbolize the lack of freedom of information which Britain enjoys. It is in this atmosphere that day-to-day journalism operates and whilst not all journalists are touched by these incidents they are bound to have a damaging effect on morale and investigative fervour.

If the journalistic backdrop is one of secrecy and legalistic oppression, the journalistic 'stage' comprises a politically committed newspaper industry which does not allow for a range of views to be aired fairly. These two factors, by themselves, restrict the ability of the 'honest, enterprising and responsible' journalist – if he/she exists – to do their work adequately for the purposes of informing the community. Whether there can be a reform of the system so as to make such a role more realistic is touched upon throughout the book. It is not explored specifically and in detail because the experiences of past debates on the subject have never got beyond the academics' pages. More important for the future are those philosophies of liberalism and deregulation which appear to be having such an enormous impact on this (Thatcher) Government's thinking about the restructuring of the means of mass communications. These are explored in great detail.

The book, therefore, covers a variety of related ideas, practices and organizations. Although some of the chapters can stand on their own, others benefit from being seen in the broader context which is set out in the first two chapters. The first chapter, Politics and the Mass Media, is a review of current thinking about the place of mass communication in politics as well as an assessment of the media's political 'impact'. It also establishes a number of propositions which are explored in later chapters. For example, the relationship between political actors and the mass media which is set out in this chapter is examined in greater detail in the study of pressure groups and the mass media (Chapter 8).

Chapter 2 focuses on contemporary 'theories of the mass media'. After a brief historical review of the development of such theories, this chapter raises questions about the adequacy of these theories in the present day. The position adopted here is that such theories have failed to take into account the extent of social, political and economic change which has overtaken the world and which has had an enormous impact on historically derived, and sometimes preserved, theories of the mass media. It explores both the reasons for the inadequacy of these theories and some proposals for reform. This chapter also includes a discussion of the neo-liberal philosophy with its calls for a deregulation or liberalization of the airwaves and the institutionalization of a form of 'electronic publishing'.

Chapters 3 and 4 concentrate on the British press. The first of these two chapters examines the political history of the press, whilst the second concentrates on the economic development of the medium. Clearly, the separation is, to some extent, for purposes of clarification of the argument, and there is considerable overlap between the two chapters. For an understanding of today's press one needs to read both chapters.

Just as two chapters are devoted to the press, two are devoted to broadcasting. Chapter 5 gives a broad analysis of British broadcasting and of its development within a particular socio-political milieu. Chapter 6 develops the argument further with specific reference to the more political aspects and relationships of the broadcasting organizations. This chapter includes not only case studies but also a review of the pressures and problems of the Independent Television sector *vis-à-vis* political broadcasting.

Chapter 7 focuses on the study of news. It considers the importance of news values as they affect the content of the mass media before turning to the context of news production. This chapter also explores the question of television 'bias' by referring, albeit somewhat briefly, to two studies: the Glasgow University Media Group's *Bad News* and the more recent study of *The Television Coverage of the Miners' Strike*. The last section of Chapter 8 looks at contemporary examples of news management by focusing on a study of lobby correspondents.

Chapter 8 takes issue with a number of propositions set out in Chapter 1. It looks at the ways in which pressure groups make increasing use of the mass media. It considers not only why they attempt to make use of the mass media but also whether this has any effect on the policy-making process. The pressure group examined here is CLEAR (Campaign for Lead-Free Air).

Chapter 9 reviews the literature on the role of the mass media in general elections. It combines a number of different aspects of this enormous area: the 'impact' of the mass media on voting behaviour, the study of broadcasting practices, the organization of Party Political and Election Broadcasts, newspaper practices, the content of electoral coverage in both the press and broadcasting. Extensive use is made of data from recent elections, including the 1987 election.

The last chapter focuses on the future. It includes a discussion of the 'new media' of cable and satellite television, and attempts to give a coherent and comprehensive account of these new media as well as of the legislative and regulatory framework within which they are being rapidly developed. The focus of this chapter is the direction of future change as well as the implications of that change for existing broadcasting organizations. Instead of setting out remedies, *it asks whether it is possible to set out remedies.* Drawing on recent interest in the question of 'media policy' or 'media policies', it concludes that all such policies are fundamentally about the sorts of societies which we desire and, following on from that, the sorts of means of mass communications which service those societies. In this respect they are neither rational nor value-free, but political.

The book is intended for the general reader even though it is, at times, very detailed. The area of mass communications is an ever-expanding one and this book only touches the surface. The careful and keen reader is therefore recommended to turn to the many books referred to here. These will not only broaden the readers' knowledge but also highlight the continuous debates and differences of political perspectives that populate the field.

The author and publishers are grateful to the following for permission to reproduce Figures: Audit Bureau of Circulations, as reported by P. Clark in *Campaign*, 16 October 1981 (Figs 4.1 and 4.2, pp. 68 and 69); and the Mirror Group Newspapers Ltd, 1, 10 and 11 June 1987 (Figs 9.1–9.3, pp. 203–5). All other sources, where applicable, appear below the figure/table or in the Notes at the end of the book.

Chapter One

POLITICS AND THE MASS MEDIA

INTRODUCTION

Empirical research has long confirmed that for most people the mass media are the major sources of information about world events (Table 1.1) and about political affairs (Table 1.2).

Table 1.1 Sources of most world news[1]

	1980 %	1983 %	1985 %
Television	52	60	62
Radio	14	10	14
Newspapers	33	28	23
Magazines	0	0	0
Talking to People	1	1	1

However, despite television's growing importance as a source of information, regular readers of newspapers continue to attach a great deal of weight to the print medium (Table 1.2(b)). Non-readers show a greater dependence on television for political information.

Both tables conceal significant variations in responses between readers of 'quality' and 'tabloid' newspapers (Table 1.3)[2]: the former remain wedded to their preferred medium, using it much more extensively as a means of surveying the world in depth, whilst readers of tabloid newspapers rely more heavily on television and also tend to attach greater credibility to it as a source of news (Table 1.4).[3]

1

Table 1.2 Voters' major sources of political information[4]

	(a) % citing source:			(b) % citing sources in top 2 media sources amongst:
	as most important	in top 2 sources	readers	non-readers
TV	63	88	88	85
Newspapers	29	73	80	35
Radio	4	14	11	29

These tables confirm the centrality of the media for the public. They are the means by which the public acquires information about the world and, more importantly, through which the public derives its knowledge and perceptions of current political and social problems and of the means to their resolution.

The approach to the study of 'politics and the mass media' adopted here is inevitably much broader than that usually found within political science. Traditionally, the study of politics and its relationship to the mass media has focused on institutions and bona fide political actors. Governments, politicians, departments or voting patterns have usually been the political scientists' fodder. When married to an interest in the mass media, the result has been an over-concentration on institutions, structures and the political élite. While this remains of importance, this sort of approach overlooks the part the mass media play in generating public perceptions of political and social change as well as of policies and decision-making processes. The political significance of the mass media goes far beyond such questions as 'who controls the media?' and 'how do people get elected?'; even concerns over 'bias' and

Table 1.3 Regular readers of:

	Telegraph, Times, Guardian or FT	Express or Mail	Mirror, Sun or Star
Main source of news	%	%	%
television	32	62	65
newspapers	57	28	24
radio	25	14	14

Table 1.4 Regular readers of:

	Telegraph, Times, Guardian or FT	Express or Mail	Mirror, Sun or Star
Most believable source of news	%	%	%
television	30	59	66
newspapers	35	13	11
radio	20	16	13

'objectivity' are too narrow to take in the full significance of the mass media. Politics and the political infuse all aspects of our lives, our attitudes and our behaviour. And because the mass media are at the heart of the processes of communication through which 'problems' and their 'resolution' are framed and discussed, they deserve extensive analysis.[5]

THE NATURE OF 'MEDIATED' KNOWLEDGE

This broad approach to the political significance of the mass media is reflected in many contemporary writings. These emphasize the media's role in providing information – both images and texts – which forms the basis of public perceptions and responses to events. The media provide, in Blumler's words, 'the informational building blocks to structure views of the world . . . from which may stem a range of actions'.[6] Although these 'informational building blocks' combine with a multiplicity of political and social factors to direct an individual's action, they determine the limits of our knowledge and of our perceptions of events and their causes.

The growing interest in exploring the 'stored information about . . . objects held by individuals'[7] – sometimes referred to as cognitions – marks a shift away from the view of the media as of great importance in the formation of individual and specific attitudes or opinions. An individual may not acquire a specific attitude – on how to vote, about race or trade unions – from the mass media, but he/she will derive information from the media which will contribute something to each of these individual areas.

It is therefore conceptually useful to distinguish between what

3

the mass media tell us to think about – this is signalled by the events they cover – and what specific attitudes or opinions we have to adopt towards those events, though clearly these distinctions may be difficult to uphold in practice. A television or press report of an event, for example, will consist of a selection of information and that particular selection will inevitably inform as well as contribute towards, rather than directly form, specific attitudes.

This distinction between cognitions (the informational building blocks, the stored bits of information) and specific attitudes or opinions is critical, for it not only emphasizes the public's growing dependence on the mass media for information but it also draws our attention to the consequences of such a dependence. Because only a small handful of events can ever be experienced by individuals at first hand, we inevitably rely on the mass media to inform us about events beyond our immediate grasp. But the mass media select which events to cover and they take decisions about how those events will be presented; they therefore not only inform us about (a small selection of) events but their presentation of those events will also consist of their explanations and interpretations of those events. To paraphrase C. Wright Mills, '. . .men [and women!] live in second-hand worlds. . .The quality of their lives is determined by meanings they have received from others. Everyone lives in a world of such meanings'.[8] As the influence of other agencies of socialization and knowledge transmission such as the Church, schools, and political parties declines, the mass media become even more central in the creation of the 'images in our heads of the world outside'.[9]

What sort of information do the mass media select and how is that information presented? Analyses of 'news values' suggest that the information chosen is not simply a random selection of events. There is a clear pattern; a pattern which indicates a hierarchy of seemingly important events and individuals. Elite groups, nations and individuals as well as large-scale, dramatic events dominate the news (see Chapter 7). Thus, the news values and news judgements which determine the content of the media not only direct our thinking to specific areas which the media define as 'important' but, conversely, direct our thinking away from other 'unimportant' areas. In this way they contribute to our mental maps of the world. In the realms of politics 'they define – and also define away – opposition '.[10]

News values and considerations of newsworthiness also prioritize events and they describe, establish and reinforce images and relationships of order and power in our society. The prominence accorded to certain political actors, institutions, and practices is not simply an outcome of judgements of what is, or is not, somehow intrinsically important. News judgements contain within them an implicit understanding of the nature of our society, where power lies and how it is or should be exercised. For example, 'the very notion of "élite persons"' – a key category of newsworthiness – has, according to Hall, 'the "routine knowledge of social structures" inscribed within it'. In order to communicate, the mass media must 'infer what is already known, as a present or abstract structure. . . but [this structure] is a construction and interpretation about the world'.[11] It is not a mere reflection of it; the media do not simply report the world for us in any 'neutral' or 'objective' sense, they interpret the world for us.

Furthermore, the items selected will usually have rich meanings within specific cultural contexts. So within specific cultural contexts, the mass media are able to employ existing cultural referants because, like coins of exchange, they are comprehended by all. In this way, there is a reciprocity between the mass media and society/culture. They draw upon past and present political/ social and cultural referants but, at the same time, they also contribute to these. This allows for cultural continuity as well as for cultural change.

A good illustration of this is the way in which today's images and meanings of the monarchy have been successfully layered onto the more popular and spectacular historic traditions – so ignoring less popular and controversial republican ones – and, at the same time, given a contemporary appearance. Members of the Royal Family have long been aware that to remain in the public conscience requires coming to terms with, and feeding, the needs of the media. The Royal Family has thus judiciously assented to this and so has participated in the creation of its own image; in the process, it has ensured that the monarchy, as an institution and as a symbol, retains a cultural past, present, and (crucially) future. It goes without saying that both sets of institutions have benefited enormously from this symbiosis: the former from its continued popularity and support and the latter from a continuous stream of royal copy which appears to ensure increased sales.

The media also perceive some institutions as more 'important' and hence more 'newsworthy' than others and they perpetuate that perception by locating themselves within or near those institutions. Political institutions, the judiciary, and the police, for example, are considered 'newsworthy' and become natural sources of information for the mass media. Consequently there is a 'bias towards authority'[12] ever present in media work.

The very presence of the media also tends to alter the relationships between the political and social institutions which they link up. The mass media form a web of communications across institutions and their existence and practices impact on those institutions and their relationships to each other. The mass media have become an integral part of a complex network of institutions and they contribute, and give meaning, to the relationships between institutions and groups in the political system.

This is true in at least two senses. In the first place, the mass media are 'so deeply embedded in the [political] system that without them political activity in its contemporary forms could hardly carry on at all'.[13] Few contemporary political strategies are conceived without considerable attention being paid to media considerations. This is particularly so during election campaigns, though one can easily cite numerous other and different examples (see Chapter 8).

Beyond this accessible and easily comprehensible illustration of the 'impact' of the mass media and the extent to which political activity is a by-product of the existence of the mass media, there is another, more elusive, but just as significant aspect to the media's role in contemporary society: the nature of political practice and the contours of the political system are, to an extent, derived from the work of the mass media. To quote Gitlin at some length,

> the texture of political life has changed since broadcasting became a central feature of American life. The very ubiquity of the mass media removes media as a whole system from the scope of positivist social analysis; for how may we 'measure' the 'impact' of a social force which is omnipresent within social life and which has a great deal to do with constituting it?[14]

The contours of the political system cannot be seen as something external to the mass media, something on which they have an

6

'impact', since they play a part in its determination by, for instance, giving meanings to events, by setting the agenda for debate and by shaping the political climate. The recent coverage of environmental issues illustrates this point.

By giving substantial coverage to environmental issues, the mass media call attention to them. Publicity forces policy-makers to respond. Those lobbying on behalf of the environment may also gain a legitimate place within the policy-making process and the character of their organization may change as a consequence. All these changes fall well within the observation that 'political activity in its contemporary form' owes a great deal to the existence and practices of the mass media.

Media activity gives shape to the ill-defined contours of the political system: it brings new players and issues into the political arena, it leaves others out and it rearranges positions and placings. Such activity goes beyond the granting or withdrawing of legitimacy. In a real way, the mass media give political systems their contemporary form and operational concepts within the political system their contemporary flavour.

But the mass media do not single-handedly give shape to the contours of the political system. Much recent research has focused on the degrees of co-operation and collusion between the mass media and those with the power to impress their own definitions of the world onto the practices of news organizations. This would suggest that the study of politics and the mass media needs to take account of the relationships between the media and those in positions of power; it also needs to focus on specific and recognizable instances of 'impact' and 'effects' as well as the deeper level of perceptions of politics and of the political system.

THE MEDIA, THEIR 'POLITICAL IMPACT' AND 'THE QUESTION OF "REALITY"'

Although it is plainly easier to examine the narrower conception of the media's political impact by exploring specific case studies, long-term and fundamental changes in the public's perceptions of the political world must not be overlooked. These two dimensions of the media's political influence can be illustrated by briefly comparing two contrasting, albeit complementary, approaches to the study of the role of the mass media within the political system.

(1)   Political 'impact' as changed relationships:
the work of Colin Seymour-Ure

Seymour-Ure's detailed study of the part the mass media have played in British politics contains a considered summary, and clarification, of the concepts of 'effect' and 'impact'. Though he often poses specific questions when exploring individual case studies, he nevertheless adopts a fairly wide-ranging conception of 'effects' since his orientation is towards such broad questions as 'effect of what kind upon whom or what?'[15] and 'How far and in what ways are the political relationships and individuals affected by the communication between them?'.[16]

In adopting this approach, Seymour-Ure avoids the idea of the mass media having a universal and unitary effect on all members of the audience. The 'impact' of the mass media will, according to his analysis, differ depending on the context of the communication and the actors concerned. He also distances himself from approaches to the study of media 'impact' which conceive of them in a fairly narrow way. Instead of using the Lasswellian framework for the study of the media's effect on, say, individual voting preferences – namely, what is 'the effect of the media on the election' – Seymour-Ure suggests that one should rephrase the question as follows: 'What is the function of media in the electoral process?' This would avoid the *'assumption that the effect of the media is limited to the potency of their messages'.*[17]

The suggestion that the media can have a multiplicity of 'effects' on a variety of different actors is developed fully in his examination of the meaning, and nature, of media 'effects'. 'At its broadest', he writes, ' "effect" is defined . . . .as any change within the political system induced directly or indirectly by the mass media.'[18] These can vary in intensity: the media may be the cause of something or, at the other extreme, merely a catalyst. In essence, though, 'all political effects are initially upon individuals. They consist in increments of information, which may or may not modify attitudes which may or may not modify behaviour'.[19] At the most basic level, an 'effect' would consist of an individual's changed 'relationship with at least one other individual'.[20]

Such effects could take place at a number of different levels within the political system: an individual's relationship to another could change as a result of the media just as an individual's

8

relationship to an institution could change as an outcome of media work, and so on. Seymour-Ure sets out five such possible levels of 'changed relationships', with appropriate examples:

- political system/individual e.g. Enoch Powell's 1968 'rivers of blood' speech had an enormous 'impact' on British politics;
- political system/institution e.g. the entrenchment of the monarchy;
- institution/institution e.g. the relative strengths of the political parties;
- institution/individual e.g. resignations of individual politicians;
- individual/individual e.g. the televised Kennedy/Nixon debates in the early 1960s worked to the former's advantage.[21]

An interest in 'the relationships that the media affect' means, in effect, that one can legitimately explore an enormous field of activity; no field is precluded since the media are omnipresent. The areas that the political scientist will explore will, however, most likely depend on the sorts of 'effects' and relationships they are interested in.

(2) Television and 'the question of "Reality"': the work of Kurt and Gladys Lang

Whilst Seymour-Ure's approach is focused on individual case studies, he hints at but does not examine a range of important, but empirically not easily verifiable, effects of mass media in general, and of television in particular: effects which may be both cumulative and long-term. Such studies are rare since they require an examination of media practices and content as well as a critical assessment of the media's presentation of the 'real world' – an assessment which takes it for granted that the media do not reproduce 'reality' in a pure form; their use of language and images as well as the working practices of journalists inevitably refract 'reality', so 'distorting' it.

Probably the best example of this type of approach to the study of the mass media is the Langs' classic study of MacArthur Day in Chicago in 1952.[22] This study set out to examine television coverage of a procession in Chicago in honour of General MacArthur, who had had a distinguished military career in the Far East, and to contrast television's 'unique perspective' with the

9

direct experiences of actual participants amongst the crowds. The study has often been used to illustrate the way television deals with events and constructs meanings around those events. Although the coverage provided by television is by no means neutral or impartial, television's 'bias' is seen as the product of routine practices and is, therefore, a form of unintended or unwitting bias.

The study also provides a wealth of information which points to the way television, and by extension the media, alter relationships within the political system. The Langs observed that

> the most important single media effect. . .of MacArthur Day was the dissemination of an image of overwhelming public sentiment in favour of the General (MacArthur). This effect gathered force as it was incorporated into political strategy, picked up by other media, entered into gossip, and thus came to overshadow immediate reality as it might have been recorded by an observer on the scene.[23]

Thirty years later, in a review of their own earlier work, the Langs reaffirmed their original conclusions and added some important insights. These brought to centre stage their concern with media 'reality': the public is dependent on what the mass media disseminate 'yet under no circumstances can the picture replicate the world in its full complexity'. 'Media reality', according to the Langs, constitutes 'a symbolic environment. . .super-imposed on the natural environment'. The public plays no part in this 'social construction', it can do 'little more than accept or ignore what is transmitted'.[24]

The 'public definition of an event' is therefore no more than the outcome of a struggle to control the 'flow of information to the public about such an event'[25] and these struggles are themselves part of politics. Television's 'cumulative effects' are thus related to the ways in which it 'transmits reality and affects the imagery of politics and political figures'. Such effects, they concluded, extend 'to the shared experience of politics provided by television to which individuals, political actors and institutions somehow accom-modate'.[26]

In recent years, there have been several examples of governments excluding or controlling television cameras in order to control the 'flow of information' and so minimize the political impact of the medium. In the early 1980s the South African Government restricted television's movements in the townships and more recently, in 1987–8, the Israeli Government imposed restrictions on television's movements in Gaza and the occupied territories. These examples have their parallels in Europe; Britain did not let television loose during the Falklands campaign. Whether these attempts at control have been successful or not is, in many ways, irrelevant. The central point is that by controlling the moving pictures of dissent, governments believe that they can not only minimize the dissent itself but also completely remove the major source of criticism. As will be argued more fully below, for many television 'reality' is political reality and so by negating the former one is controlling the latter.

THE MASS MEDIA IN POLITICS

There can be little doubt that the mass media are a vital part of the political system. Political strategies now usually incorporate media strategies as well; indeed, the two are no longer separate. Perhaps the best recent example of this, and of the media's growing significance in overtly political activity, can be seen in the Labour Party's strategies in the period immediately preceding the 1987 general election. Throughout 1986 and 1987, the popular press created and reinforced the image of 'the loony left' and 'the militant left' in Labour politics. Stories of alleged 'loony left' politics became a standard feature of their political coverage: the apocryphal 'baa baa white sheep', 'black rubbish bins' and the true or false antics of Labour Party candidates or spokespersons entered the public consciousness.

Stung by these allegations, the Labour Party reappraised its strategy. In the short run it attempted to detach itself from its 'extremist' wing – more properly, those sections of the Labour Party which the right-wing popular press considered extreme – on the grounds that the 'loony left' cost it electoral votes. In the long run it was to create a new 'image' of itself which was purposely devoid of politics, as well as left-wing politics. The Labour Party's obsession with distancing itself from anything which the right-wing media could pick up and exploit as 'extremist' is well described by Wainwright in her account of a Labour Party election rally. The (significantly titled) Labour Family Fun Day in Islington, London – an American-style political convention with a well staged show –

was a well policed event. To test the atmosphere, Wainwright purposely bought a copy of *Socialist Worker*. 'Slipping it under my arm', she writes,

> I returned to the hall. When I came to be searched, an earnest young man asked me: 'Please could you leave the paper on one side and pick it up afterwards?' 'Don't be ridiculous,' I replied laughing. 'Why should I do that?' 'Please,' he pleaded, 'it will embarrass Neil Kinnock' [the Labour leader].[27]

The Labour Party's insecurity in the face of the press continued into the election. It nevertheless managed to run a good (television) election campaign. In this respect, it behaved as others who have political power, money, or status do: it manipulated the media in order to create favourable impressions and images. Mikhail Gorbachev achieved the same goal during the 1985 Geneva Summit meeting with Reagan. The Russians changed their 'style' in order to capture Western media attention, in order to transform their image. As one reporter remarked, 'the success of the Soviet pre-summit public relations effort . . .has infuriated the Americans who are used to dominating the media without even trying'.[28]

Media presentation has now become such a critical feature of the process of negotiations and public image-making that those who do not give it its due credit are likely to find their credibility in question. It is possible to detect a similar set of concerns in accounts of the NUM's handling of the media in their year-long dispute with the Coal Board over pit closures.[29]

Sometimes, however, the media cannot be so easily deployed by political actors and the media may, in consequence, exert an indeterminate and sometimes capricious effect on the doings of political institutions and actors. In the 1985/6 Westland Affair two political opponents deployed the media as part of their armoury but, in the event, both were forced to resign as the affair gained a momentum of its own.[30]

Undue concern with presentation can also create contradictions between media reality and the substance of events. This problem is most acute when the individual (or group) courting media attention seeks to placate different and conflicting audiences, for example an international/foreign audience and a home one. A good contemporary example is the meeting between President Sadat of

Egypt and Prime Minister Begin of Israel in Jerusalem in 1977. This superbly staged meeting between the two heads of state did little to further the peace process in the Middle East. In fact, it did much to disguise Sadat's unpopularity at home and his break away from the other countries of the Middle East. Those aware of his unpopularity and unilateralism had little difficulty in comprehending the motives of his assassins. In contrast, those abroad, notably in the West, who were fed the diet of stage-managed events, found his assassination both momentous and incomprehensible.

Two significant points emerge from the above examples and both need to be considered in the context of a model of political communication. The first relates to differences between political actors and groups in their abilities to use, influence or indeed manipulate the media; the second to the political consequences of these actions.

Few attempts to change public perceptions are achieved easily, nor can they be performed by all members of society. Those without power or legitimacy lack the resources necessary to capture the mass media. The planning and organization required to lead the media and so define the 'real' issues and their meaning are outside the scope of 'powerless' individuals. Members of the general public usually only respond and react to media content: they are rarely in control of media work. In such ways political actors, aided and abetted by the mass media, help construct images of 'reality'.

At the same time, however, leading actors find themselves confronting, and responding to, those very same images that they help create. Such images or representations can possess great power. Their visibility, achieved on account of the mass media, forces them into the public and political domain. At times, these images may be so powerful as to demand an immediate response. 'The winter of discontent' of 1978/9 played just such a powerful role in British politics because it was composed of extremely powerful images. Those images of chaos and of a nation purportedly tearing itself apart – despite much evidence to the contrary – demanded an immediate political response. Government simply had to act; not to do so would have amounted to avoiding a problem that was 'evident' and 'plain' to all, particularly those who watched the news on television! The Prime Minister's (Callaghan) dismissive attitude towards those in the media who emphasized the critical state of affairs in Britain – an attitude condensed into the apocryphal 'Crisis? What crisis?' statement – may have been, in his eyes, a rational assessment of the situation and the media's tendency to exaggerate, but it ignored and misjudged the impact of media imagery and, consequently, the public's desire for reassurance and for the problem to be 'resolved'.

In the long run, such images become coins of exchange along with pickets, football riots, and urban disturbances; they populate our consciousness and can be recalled intact by the sheer mention of a single word or by a brief news clip from the past. But, importantly, they cannot be ignored nor can they be dismissed easily as irrational fabrications. As Labour Party politicians and trade unionists found out to their cost in the year-long miners' dispute, one could not dismiss comments about 'picket violence' as untrue and mere fabrications. The television viewing public had seen images of violence and expected political leaders to acknowledge them and to respond accordingly and responsibly. Not to do so amounted to a dereliction of duty in the same way that Callaghan's statement misunderstood the political content of media imagery.

The images the media present of 'reality' are, for many, accounts of 'real' events and not fictional ones. The veracity of the media account may be questioned but few doubt that the events reported took place in some way. To question the 'real-ness' of the events reported, as Callaghan did, is to strain one's credibility since it demands the viewing public to ignore or disregard media imagery. Callaghan's mistake may have derived from his own inability to grasp the significance of media images irrespective of how closely they did or did not correlate with some other version of 'reality'. It may be that for the public gallery, media 'reality' is political reality.

TOWARDS A MODEL OF POLITICAL COMMUNICATION

As with other models, our model (Fig. 1.1) is not comprehensive but only attempts to emphasize and closely examine a small section of the mosaic of mass communication. It incorporates a number of points which are critical to the analysis of the processes of political communication:

- that different content reflects different sets of relationships between the mass media and the major actors/events being reported. A media event such as a 'walkabout' portrays a media subservient to the political actor. Other events/reports will reflect different relationships.

- that different actors have different degrees of power over the creation of media content. In their interactions with the media, political actors pursue their own goals and do frequently dominate media content. The public at large, though it may be politically literate, is usually the recipient of media content. Its power to change content is minimal.

It may be argued that relegating the audience to a passive role in the mass communication process misrepresents their part in the production of television (and media) content. It is undoubtedly true that the audience plays no *active* part in the production of content and that audience feedback is minimal but, as some have pointed out, the communicators' image of the audience can affect the content of mass communication. The intervention of the audience is through the communicators' perceptions and images of the unknown audience.[31] The intervention of the audience, in this context, is of a metaphysical quality, implicit rather than explicit. However, at the other extreme, say, in the case of advertising where considerable audience testing and piloting is undertaken, audience intervention takes place *prior* to the process of message construction and mass communication. In fact, some of these practices have also been applied to political communication; an election broadcast or a staged political event is constructed in such a way as to elicit a pre-determined and desired response. Thus the process of message selection and presentation encapsulates the notion of audience feedback.[32] The careful 'packaging' of Mrs Thatcher by Gordon Reece from the mid-1970s onwards was designed to create a different image of her in the minds of the public, an image which was felt to elicit a more positive response on the part of the public. That which was known to be disliked – for example, the voice – was changed to one which was softer and not shrill.

- that there is not one single audience but different audiences for mass communication. The public or audience of the *Financial Times* is not the same audience as that of the *Sun*. Such differences may explain differences in content as well as the nature and distribution of power in British society.

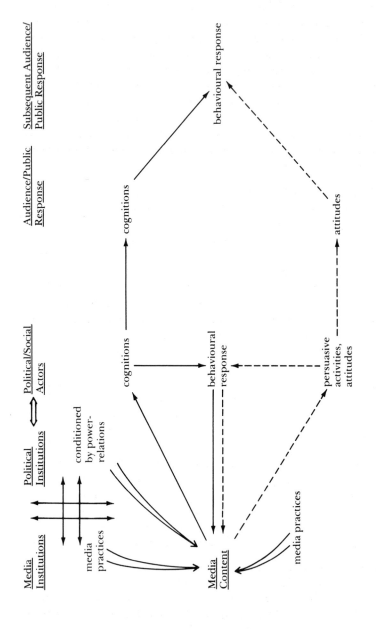

Figure 1.1 A model of mass communications (after Becker *et al.*)[35]

- that the process of news-making involves a degree of interaction or strategic bargaining, as between the sources of news and the news media. Each feeds off the other, each informs the other and the subsequent reactions are reciprocal and continuous rather than unilinear and in one direction. The product of this interaction or bargaining is the media content to which the public at large attend. Examples are again useful. Chibnall has observed the close proximity between crime reporters and Scotland Yard[33] and Cockerell *et al.* have described lobby practices in British political reporting.[34] Proximity to sources is suggestive of collusion rather than adversity, though elements of both probably co-exist.

The model partially retains the traditional distinction between a political élite and a mass public. But rather than simply using this for the purpose of political comment in a static model of the communication process, the rationale behind its retention here is that there are real and important differences between these two groups and their relationships, and work, with the media. The examples above have already indicated this: politicians, officials, even trade unionists, work closely with journalists. Such a relationship – symbiotic, advantageous to both, and biased 'towards authority' – is not one that is open to the public.

However, the public is by no means an empty receptacle responding uncritically and unquestioningly to the sayings and doings of those in power. Indeed, the public's reception of mass communication content remains an academic problem since there is as yet little substantive evidence which directly links public perceptions, actions, and reactions *purely and simply* to media content. Other social and political factors intrude into the flow, and reception, of communication and these may be quite powerful in influencing public perceptions of events reported by the media. This corrective to assertions of media omnipotence can be found in a recent study of a major political/industrial story, the 1984–5 miners' strike in Britain. After analysing all the major news reports broadcast during the year-long dispute, the authors observed that

> despite television being overwhelmingly the major source of news for the general public, audience perceptions of the news and as to what the strike was all about differed considerably. In other words while the public may have all watched the same news they didn't all see it in the same way.[36]

17

[C]onsistent differences in public perceptions of the news [were] associated with people's (political) predispositions.[37]

The contradictory nature of these statements – media omnipotence and the barrier to it in people's predispositions – merely confirms the difficulty of examining a process as complex as that of mass communication. The problem is, however, that to examine their 'impact' on the (differentiated) public requires a long-term culturally and historically informed analysis that is far from easy.

It is for these reasons that many of the relationships between media content and public perceptions remain at the level of supposition and assertion. Sometimes, though, there is substantial support for the view that the media are important in forming public perceptions; one can find evidence for this in studies of 'agenda-setting',[38] 'race and the mass media',[39] 'reporting the welfare state',[40] as well as studies of 'moral panics'.[41]

Our model of political communication does not presuppose a view that the mass media are omnipotent. However, it does emphasize the extent to which the public relies on the mass media for information about the outside world even though, in the final analysis, their understanding of those events may differ, particularly along political lines.

THE MASS MEDIA AND CONCEPTIONS OF SOCIETY

The model set out above relates the mass media to 'power relations' but, at the same time, retains core elements of the 'fourth estate' concept, namely, that the media can, and sometimes do, act autonomously and are not completely subservient to the state or political institutions. This perspective avoids both general statements and general conclusions about the mass media and favours an approach which highlights the richness of the relationship between the mass media and politics.

Such an approach treads a thin line between the traditional pluralist and Marxist divide in media studies. The major differences between the two positions – and they are at times crudely drawn – focus on:

- the extent to which the mass media are autonomous in determining the content and form of their messages,

- the nature of the relationship between political institutions or the state and the mass media, and
- the nature of the media 'audience'.

Generally speaking, pluralists accord the media varying degrees of autonomy both with regard to their relations with other institutions and with regard to their work in the production of content and meaning. One prominent analysis of this maintains that the interaction between political institutions broadly defined and media institutions is one of 'dependence and adaptation'. 'Political communication', the authors claim,

> originates in mutual dependence within a framework of divergent though overlapping purposes. Each side of the politician-media professional partnership is striving to realize certain goals *vis-à-vis* the audience: yet it cannot pursue them without securing in some form the co-operation of the other side.[42]

Other factors in this relationship – the roles adopted by the two groups, their shared culture, the ground rules and the mechanisms of conflict management – highlight the complexity of the mechanisms of political communication. '[T]hey badly need each other's services and dependability; but as a result of their conflicting purposes, roles, and definitions of politics, they are periodically buffetted by upsets and strains.'[43] The partners in the relationship may not always confront each other as adversaries but occasionally their different responsibilities in relation to the public may push them in opposite directions. Unfortunately, in the competitive struggle for dominance, both partners often overlook or forget the needs of the public.

In this conception of the social and political world, the established order is not permanently fixed. Institutions and groups compete for power and there is, consequently, a plurality of power centres rather than a concentration of power. Through the competition for political power, change – both positive and negative – can take place. In effect, individuals and groups can have an impact on the political and social order. Moreover, the ensuing change is likely to be of a gradual nature and not a radical rearrangement of the political or social order. Thus, fluidity, continuous change, and an evolving social order are the characteristics of this conception of the political and social world.

In contrast, Marxists emphasize the established and fixed nature of the distribution of power in society. Power is centralized within a handful of institutions – sometimes collectively referred to as 'the state'[44] – and those with economic and political power – a ruling class – guard it jealously and use whatever mechanism is available, including the mass media, to retain their power and to ensure their continued monopolization of power. Those without economic or political power – the working class – are, therefore, excluded from sharing in, amongst other things, the economic wealth of a country.

In a very important sense, then, both the pluralist and Marxist positions *vis-à-vis* the media are derived from an understanding and analysis – at times implicit, at other times explicit – of the nature of power, and its distribution, in society.

The pluralist description of the social order with its myriad political institutions, groups, and actors all competing, albeit unequally, for power treats the media as a set of institutions which may act independently in society but which may also be deployed by powerful groups. This position is readily dismissed by Marxists. For them, the social order is structured and not composed of discrete and shifting groups: there are real and deep inequalities between classes which cannot be easily eliminated or resolved by recourse to a competition, by groups or individuals, for political power. The location of (class) economic power is beyond the arena of political competition so admired by the pluralists. The mass media are thus integrated into an already structured and unequal society and, more importantly, those systemic inequalities are not self-sustaining but require agencies such as the mass media, the education system, and the Church to maintain and reproduce them.[45]

But unlike those Marxists who conceive of the mass media as no more than relay systems working on behalf of the dominant classes, some have forcefully argued that systems of maintenance and reproduction do not necessarily operate smoothly;[46] there are contradictions, there is social and political dissent and there is political struggle. One cannot therefore ignore historical and contemporary struggles between the state and the mass media; nor can one reduce diverse and complex social, political and economic processes to simplified and simplistic accounts.

Recent commentaries on the mass media derived from within the broad Marxist tradition have attempted to move away from the simplistic view of the mass media as mere relay systems; a view which implicitly suggests that the study of the mass media is not problematic since their ownership (usually by large corporations) pre-determines the nature of their work. There is now a general acceptance of the belief that the work and context of the mass media deserves deep analysis and that processes of maintenance and reproduction, of manufacturing consent and consensus, are by no means simple or closed. Political leadership over the whole of society depends 'not only on the expression of the interests of a ruling class but also on its acceptance as "normal reality" or "commonsense" by those. . .subordinated to it'. Consent must be won; although the ideas consented to may 'in fact express the needs of a dominant class'.[47] Here again, the media are heavily implicated. 'Relations of domination are sustained by a mobilization of meaning' largely, one must assume, via the media.[48]

But the media carry a rich variety of messages which are open to different interpretations by a differentiated audience (rather than a coherent class). There is room for a struggle over meaning and, more significantly, there is also the possibility of developing 'counter hegemonic projects',[49] that is, for alternative and subordinate views to gain dominance. The media are thus also transformed into the site of such struggles.

It may therefore be difficult to accept unquestioningly the notion of unidimensionality and the unproblematic production (and reproduction) of a subservient mass by the capitalist mass media. Subordinate classes are granted a degree of power to make meanings, to negotiate meanings and even to reject meanings. Such a perspective also undermines any analysis which sees the audience or classes as uncritically receiving the content of the mass media. Even the idea that the mass media's power resides in their ability to keep 'important' issues off the agenda[50] fails to take into account the diversity of media – magazines, journals, books, radio – which allow for an enormous amount of information to find its way into the public domain.

Inevitably though, different interpretations of the role of the mass media in society will continue to be informed by contrasting analyses of society. Those works derived from the broad Marxist tradition will pursue the theme of domination in capitalist societies, whilst pluralists will still shy away from generalizations, preferring detailed empirical work. Furthermore, they will still resist drawing conclusions about the proximity of the mass media to state institutions despite the fact that, as in the case of Blumler and Gurevitch (see p. 19 above), it is only a short step away from their analyses and conclusions.

Nevertheless, there has been some crossover of knowledge between these two camps, with each benefiting from the fertilization that has followed. Pluralists, for example, may now be more willing to examine in much greater detail the relationships between state institutions and the mass media, just as Marxists may be more prepared to consider empirical and detailed case studies.[51]

This book attempts to sustain a detailed analysis of the mass media based on the fruits of this cross-fertilization. It will draw from a wide range of perspectives in its appraisal of the mass media and it will be based on both contemporary case studies and theoretical analyses of the media. At its core is a model of the political communication process which is multi-layered, complex, and differentiated – and those differences do impact on the political work of the mass media.

Chapter Two

THEORIES OF THE MEDIA

Of all the existing means of mass communication, it is only the press that has spawned a set of 'theories' to explain and to justify its actions and its purposes. Means of communication that have developed since the inception of the press in the 17th and 18th centuries – notably, television and radio – have tended to adapt these theories to suit their own special requirements. In some cases, even the notion of 'the freedom of the press' has been transposed into other contexts and used to defend practices in radio and television. Yet the press has gone through many significant changes since ideas about 'press freedom' were first discussed well over 200 years ago. New forms of journalism have developed, there have been changes in printing techniques, changes in ownership, and even changes in perceptions of the role of the newspaper within society. Furthermore, the press is now only one medium amongst many. Radio, and later television, have usurped some of its duties.

Despite the enormity of these changes, and the social, economic, and political transformation of the societies within which these changes have taken place, the concepts most often used to justify the existence, and role, of the press – and latterly, the media – today still retain significant elements of 19th century (and sometimes earlier) political thought.

Discussion of the roles and duties of the media in the contemporary scene must inevitably go beyond earlier and rather limited comments on the press. Nevertheless, one must not underestimate the importance of earlier ideas about press freedom, nor must one underestimate the extent to which these ideas still reside within more complex statements about the mass media. The

1986 Peacock Committee, for example, considered the future of television in Britain by invoking parallels with the press and the abolition of pre-publication censorship in 1694.[1]

Such ideas, and lessons of history, are clearly of fundamental importance and should not be dismissed out of hand. Can they, however, satisfactorily incorporate the changes in societies which now determine the existence and practices of the present media? How do they help us understand developments in the media?

FREEDOM OF THE PRESS

In 17th century England, the state exercised enormous control over the press. It exercised powers of regulation and censorship on the grounds that press freedom was a threat to the security and stability of the state. Statements in favour of the 'freedom of the press' and the 'freedom to publish' – from Milton's *Aeropagitica* of 1644[2] onwards – were, therefore, intended as replies to those who maintained that granting the press its freedom would pose threats to the stability of the state. They were part of a broader argument against the powers of the state over what could and could not be published and what ideas could and could not be tolerated.

Milton's views in favour of freeing the press from state, or any other forms of, control were based on the idea that the censorship and control of ideas inevitably resulted in a loss of an element of truth. Individuals could only choose between truth and falsehood if they had access to both; ultimately, 'reason and virtue are predicated upon the freedom to choose'.[3] Decades later, both Bentham and de Tocqueville were to add their support to these essentially libertarian ideas by arguing that total freedom was very much preferable to any form of suppression.[4]

Other writers expanded on, and embellished, earlier statements on the 'freedom of the press', its role in society and its practices. The press acquired an educational role and the role of 'watchdog': it was the 'fourth estate' taking governments to task and protecting the public interest as well as representing public opinion; and it could also help create a politically literate society. In all these intricate ways, the press became the channel *par excellence* through which political debate was to be conducted and political society came into existence and survived. The nature of political representation and the meaning of 'public opinion' would all change as a consequence of the existence of the press.[5]

These arguments in favour of, or against, granting the press its freedom continued well into the 19th century. Whereas the American Constitution guaranteed that 'Congress shall make no law. . . abridging the freedom of speech or of the press' as early as 1791, the British State continued to regulate the press through a variety of taxes on paper and advertising until the mid-1850s. The repeal of the 'taxes on knowledge' in the mid-1850s is, therefore, an historical and political watershed; it ensured that individuals and groups could voice opinions and circulate those opinions via the press without risk of prosecution.

In practice, few of the conceptual embellishments of the idea of the 'freedom of the press' proved to be any more than occasional glimpses of what an ideal press ought to be like. It could no more act as a 'watchdog' than a critical examiner of the actions of politicians or government because it was closely and inextricably tied to both. As Boyce has pointed out, the credibility of the press 'lay in its apparent independence from the political party machine' even though its natural position 'was that of being part of the political machine'.[6] (See Chapter 3.) The newspaper was anything but an 'independent', 'responsible', 'oppositional/adversarial' force in society; it was a politically committed and attached organ.

The practices of the press were to further undermine its credibility. Almost inevitably, the press sought out the centres of political and economic power both as a major definer of the social and political terrain and as a source of information. Consequently, it began to offer a 'top-down' interpretation of processes and problems in society. The detachment of the press from political parties after the turn of the century – a result of economic rather than ideological factors – did not lessen the importance of those with political and economic power. In fact, the 'state' became very adept at using the press as a means of perpetuating its own (sometimes precarious) existence. 'The government [of 1918]', according to Middlemass,

> clearly intended to create a public distinction between good and bad trade union behaviour, in advance of the bargaining over post-war reconstruction. . .Tory Ministers. . .could be found . . .asking editors to show their patriotism 'by refraining from attacks on the capitalist class'.[7]

Newspapers were thus (intentionally) failing to fully represent public opinion. The BBC was no better; its 'Byzantine mentality' created an approach which 'remained synonymous with the nineteenth century parliamentary constitution'.[8]

Despite these very significant shortcomings, the idea of the 'free' press remained (as it still remains) a real and vital concept. That the press in the 19th and 20th centuries chose to attach itself to political parties and also chose to abdicate its responsibilities towards its publics by identifying itself too closely with the interests of the state in no way reflects upon the notions of the free press. It does not wholly undermine the principle though it does leave it somewhat tarnished. To quote Bentham, 'The liberty of the press has its inconveniences, but the evil which may result from it is not to be compared to the evil of censorship'.[9]

The concept of the 'freedom of the press' must, therefore, be appraised with reference to *the structural and organisational independence* of the press from the state. Other criteria such as the press's preference for orientating itself to the state, to political parties, or to economic interests are important but secondary considerations. The essence of the concept must, as it were, be detached from the practice. Milton's ideas, for instance, were developed in an age when the state exercised enormous controls over intellectual and cultural life. In that environment, the idea of seeking 'freedom' from the state had a real and concrete point of reference. Though it no longer has the same resonance, it remains an important criterion.

Though it is structurally and organizationally outside the control of the state, as an institution the press daily confronts pressures and constraints which *limit* its freedom. Like all other institutions, it cannot enjoy *absolute* freedom. No editor is absolutely free to do what he/she desires. Their working contexts impose certain limits on what they are able to do; for example, on how many journalists they can employ and on how much news space they have on the paper. Such 'limits' on the freedom of the press are often overlooked yet their consequences may be just as severe as those which the state can impose.

Similarly, a newspaper owned by a forceful press magnate may be under heavy pressure to adopt a certain political line in its columns. Such pressure is often regarded as improper and undermining editorial sovereignty and responsibility; undermining, in other words, 'press freedom'. But newspapers, and their editors, can face other constraints. The editor of a newspaper owned by a Trust will be 'forced' to carry on the newspaper's tradition. Like their counterparts on privately owned newspapers, they will have to take note of the restrictions on space which advertising forces on the paper. As Curran[10] has forcefully shown, advertising also plays a part in shaping a newspaper and so the needs of advertising to some extent determine the nature of the newspaper. Finally, no editor has a limitless source of funding, no editor can ignore the readers and their needs and wants, and no editor can safely depart from established news practices. Editors must, then, exercise a choice and exercising a choice inevitably involves ignoring certain options. So that even if a proprietor or advertiser does not exert undue pressure, there are other forces that impinge on the 'freedom' of an editor and a newspaper.

It could be argued that economic and organizational 'pressures' are qualitatively different from the sorts of constraints that governments or 'states' are able to impose. In reality, though, there is no rational basis for making a distinction between 'proper' and 'acceptable' pressures – the former – and 'improper' ones – the latter. Both sets of pressures involve restrictions of one sort or another. To some, state or proprietorial interference may be deemed 'improper' interference but to others an editor's pursuit of the liberal-middle ground may be an equal misuse of hierarchical power.

If, however, press freedom is never absolute, there can be no real way of *guaranteeing* that the mass media will represent a wide range of views. For as soon as a news organization is established within a competitive economic system, it has to exercise choices about what sort of medium it is, what it does and for whom it does it. These choices inevitably narrow its vision and place it in a certain niche in the media market.

The short-lived 'left-of-centre' *News-on-Sunday* (1986–7) provides a good example. The original intention was to publish a radical, investigative, and hard-hitting tabloid. Many of its ideological touchstones – anti-sexist, anti-fascist, anti-racist – were contained in a published charter. Despite this ideological coherence (or inflexibility?) numerous disputes raged within the editorial board even prior to its first edition. With the departure of some key figures, the paper appeared to change its intended style and its original objectives. To its critics, it became a mild tabloid and a very pale imitation of what was originally intended. When it failed to attract substantial readers, it faced a financial crisis which forced it to curtail some of its journalistic efforts. The foreign desk was, for example, closed down as journalists were sacked. As the financial crisis deepened, the ownership of the paper changed. This led, in turn, to a re-definition of the nature of the paper and eventually to its closure.

Throughout this period, the *News-on-Sunday* changed as both internal and external pressure challenged its very survival. Its intentions were not borne out, perhaps could not be borne out, because it attempted to find a niche within a competitive industry without engaging in the sort of competition which guaranteed its rivals' success. By contrast, *Sunday Sport*, a soft-porn-tabloid also launched in 1986, eschewed the high moral ground and went for the marketplace, seeking to satisfy the insatiable (British?) appetite for 'all tits and no balls'.

The ideological, economic and structural problems that confronted the *News-on-Sunday* provide many lessons for those who believe that establishing newspapers is an easy task. More critically, it highlights the nature of the constraints on press 'freedom': one simply cannot do what one 'wants'; the exigencies of the market determine what is, and is not, possible.

If there can be no way of *guaranteeing* the full representation of all views, is it possible to create structures which lessen or remove restrictions on press 'freedom'? Before exploring this question in detail, we turn to an appraisal of the 'theories of the press'.

THE PRESS IN THE AGE OF THE MEDIA

Despite the changing circumstances within which the press now operates and much evidence with which to discredit its own claims to legitimacy as 'the fourth estate', there has been no serious attempt to reconsider the theories of the press and the media generally as they relate to the remaining decade of this century. The press today lives alongside the power of television and competes with it for allegiance and influence. Yet the ideas used to justify the existence and work of the media, such as the 'freedom of the press', are ideas whose true meanings are but a memory of past struggles in very different circumstances. We revert to these distant ideas when discussing the press and the media instead of attempting to recast the core concepts in the context of today's society.

There has been no significant advance on the theories of the press as set out by Siebert *et al.*[11] in the mid-1950s when television was still in its infancy. Their discussion of what the press 'should be and do' reflects an East–West Cold War divide and they set out ideal, polar positions so as to highlight differences. On the one hand, one finds the libertarian and social responsibility models of the press in those states where 'freedom to publish' and the 'freedom of the press' are established; on the other hand, where there are no such freedoms, one finds the authoritarian and Soviet models of the press.

The libertarian model is identified with the struggle for a free press. As this model had some rather obvious shortcomings in that it identified the freedom to publish with individual property rights of purchase and sale of newspaper titles, it was necessary to overlay the libertarian (*laissez-faire*) position with an element of social conscience. As a result, the social responsibility theory was born; newspapers remained the property of their owners, they could still be bought and sold in the marketplace, but owners and newspapers were now credited with obligations to society – obligations to provide information, to allow a diversity of views to be printed, to encourage the best and most professional of journalistic activity so as to pursue truth and knowledge (Table 2.1).

Faced with the reality that newspapers (and television stations) were no more than private organs for private gain, commentators

Table 2.1

	Libertarian	*Social Responsibility*
Chief purpose	to help discover truth and to check on government	to raise conflict to the plane of discussion
Essential difference from others	instrument for checking on government and meeting other needs of society	media assume obligation of social responsibility; otherwise, someone else must see that they do

could only hope that private ownership would be tempered by a social conscience.

It is not difficult to be critical of these propositions. Even Siebert *et al.* noted that the press was falling into too few hands to allow for a proper 'marketplace of ideas' to operate. The authors were, however, satisfied that once the press assumed obligations to society, there would be a greater likelihood that all sides of events would be fairly represented and that sufficient information would be available to the public.

Severe criticism of these ideas did little to detract from the belief that even a sickly press was preferable to the Soviet and authoritarian theories outlined by Siebert *et al.* These contrasted the Western models with the sorts of restrictions that could and were applied to the media in other political systems: the media were not free to publish, the expression of opinion was controlled, the Party/government could dictate the content of the media, and the essential freedoms associated with the Western models were obviously absent.

These four theories of the press have featured in numerous discussions about the role of the press. Although these theories could not easily be deployed in the 'real' world, they did serve a valuable purpose as condensations of patterns of thought about the media. On the one hand, they proposed the creation of a press/media where no regulations restrained freedoms and, on the other hand, they pointed to the undesirable nature of regulations. One of the curious anomalies that this gave rise to was the difficulty of placing an institution such as the BBC into their scheme of things. Was the BBC 'owned by the government' or not? Was a regulatory framework inevitably anti-libertarian? In this respect, the European tradition appeared at odds with the American one.

More recently, and as a direct outcome of shortcomings in the original four theories, two 'new' theories have been proposed. The first of these, the 'development media theory', is 'appropriate to the media situation of developing countries'.[12] Developing countries have their own specific economic, political and social requirements and it is often felt that the media should 'carry out positive development tasks'; that they should accept restrictions if the state so desires and that they should be subordinate to the needs (economic, cultural, political) of a developing state. Instead of being critical, adversarial or even sceptical, the media should bow down to the needs of the country so as to encourage development across all sectors. Instead of being 'destructive' the media should be 'constructive'.

Superficially attractive and officially, if implicitly, condoned by UNESCO,[13] this theory has come in for severe criticism from Western media interests and journalists. Some of this criticism is based on the fear that Western interests might be endangered: access to the country and its resources might be restricted or journalists might not be allowed to operate freely but be directed in their work. Other objections to the theory reflect the old libertarian argument of the 16th century, namely, that any control of the media, however benevolent, might be censorious. The 'development theory' made it too easy to claim that a state's interests were at stake at the first sign of legitimate criticism. Indeed, anything could be proclaimed as being against state interest.

The 'development media theory' has generated a far more vigorous debate than the second of the new theories. The 'democratic-participant' media theory is also the result of recent debates on media issues though this theory is 'difficult to formulate, partly because it lacks full legitimation and incorporation into media institutions and partly because some of its tenets are. . .to be found' elsewhere. 'It favours multiplicity, smallness of scale, locality, deinstitutionalization, interchange of sender-receiver roles, horizontality of communication links at all levels of society, interaction.'[14] It is, in brief, a reaction to all the evils of the present media and the existing processes of communication. More importantly, it reiterates the belief that '[t]he organisation and content of media should *not* be subject to centralised political or state bureaucratic control'.[15]

This belief in 'independence' is well entrenched in the West and it has developed out of a general mistrust of centralized political power and of power that had historically not tolerated the free expression of dissenting views. Whether one interpreted this from the perspective of a 16th century Milton or that of a 20th century anarchist, the outcome was still the same in its condemnation of restrictions on the free expression and dissemination of opinions. This strong attachment to a hard-won freedom can neither be denigrated, nor eradicated from consciousness. It is at the heart of contemporary conceptions of what the media do and ought to do.

31

Media theories for the present must, therefore, make the absence of state control their cornerstone. Likewise proposals for the reform of the media must pay due attention to it. There are, however, two other fundamental problems which cannot be so easily resolved. First, proposals for reform – such proposals will be discussed more fully below – ultimately fail in their intentions because they do not take into account the social, economic and political nature of today's society and the way that important relationships have changed. For example, few proposals examine the impact of the welfare state on the relationship between the individual and the state or the ability of the individual to select their own media from an enormous range of national and increasingly international outlets. In other words, the proposals are framed in a political and social void which does not engage with the sorts of social, political and economic changes that have recently been experienced by all.

Second, proposals which only address (and seek to reform) the structural changes that have afflicted the media, e.g. conglomeration, but fail to note changes in the processes of news-production and journalistic work, are incomplete solutions.

What are these changes and how do they affect media theories?

Four major areas of change need to be considered. Some describe trends in society, others identify changes in media practices. Each of these areas impacts directly or indirectly on the structures and regulations surrounding the media, on the work of the media, and on its degrees of freedom. Moreover, because each of these areas has changed the relationship of the individual to the state, the media are also forced to re-evaluate their roles *vis-à-vis* the individual and the public interest/public opinion. As the parameters within which the media operate change, so too must media theories.

The four areas are:

(a) the national and international media context
(b) the coming of the interventionist (welfare) state and the growth of the state bureaucracy
(c) the realignment in British politics since 1945
(d) media coverage : 'representations', 'forgetting' and the 'destruction of memory'.

(a) The national and international media context

The changes in media ownership since 1945 have been well documented. Briefly, the mass media in Britain form a part of an international media scene with multinationals in charge of broadcasting and newspaper interests. The prime example of this is undoubtedly Murdoch's News International with its Australian-American connections. This pattern suggests that individual media institutions are unlikely to survive either in isolation or as independent (national) trading units. It is worth noting, for instance, that all the new titles coming out in the United Kingdom in recent years have had substantial backing from a variety of sources: finance corporations, industrial interests, media interests, and so on. Media enterprises – newspapers, radio or television services – now need such large sums of capital that they cannot afford *not* to turn to outside (sometimes foreign) interests. This trend is most noticeable in relation to the 'new media'.

The economic internationalization of the media – a process which reaches its apotheosis with satellite broadcasting – has another side to it, and that is the use of media output, notably television output, e.g. *Dallas*, internationally. The cultural impact of this has been well researched and extensively commented upon elsewhere.[16] It describes a process where national media find it cheaper and more advantageous to broadcast foreign/non-national material. Such fictional programmes will be joined in the very near future by internationally available news output. America's Cable News Network (CNN) is the prime example here. Its output can now reach separate continents and subscribers will, in the future, have access to different interpretations of news events (see Chapter 10). Internationalization of content has the effect of questioning established national media practices. Adhering to such notions as balance and impartiality may be justifiable in a national context, although even this is increasingly suspect, but in the international context these notions and their attendant practices are meaningless.

Media theories, as developed in the past, are uniquely national and ethnocentric. They have never been reformulated in such a way as to incorporate the consequences of the internationalization of media ownership and content. Such a reformulation would not only call for a reassessment of traditional notions and practices –

balance, impartiality, objectivity, ownership, editorial sovereignty – but would also require the media to improve upon their present performances in explaining events in the world.

(b)   The Welfare State and the state bureaucracy

Since the end of the Second World War, state institutions have extended their influence over a whole range of activities which touch individual lives. The state determines the amount of money individuals have available via direct and indirect taxation as well as social benefits; it regulates vast areas of our lives, e.g. via health and safety regulations; it subsidizes foods and housing, for example, and it provides a range of services such as health and education.[17]

There are two consequences which follow from this and both impact on the work of the media. First, the state is now in charge of vast amounts of administrative and political information which is of direct relevance to individuals. This information – and it is of enormous diversity and emanates from all governmental departments – does not often find its way into the media. The dominance of long-standing and still influential 'news values' militates against such information surfacing with any degree of frequency, particularly in the popular media. The result is that the media, by and large, do not play what could be an important part in informing the citizen. The role of the media as information providers is often overlooked by those who emphasize their overtly political functions.

Second, because governments and ministers still retain political objectives and motivations, they will attempt to guard jealously information within their purview and to use it in such ways as to influence and direct public opinion. As Norton Taylor points out, 'administrations have always attempted to present their policies in the best possible light; to avoid public relations pitfalls; to coordinate information policy; and to counter bad news they can do little about. . .'.[18] While this is a continuing habit of government it is worth pondering whether governments have become more adept at doing this and whether they have encouraged the growth of a machinery with which to co-ordinate media policy generally. It is also crucial to ask whether the media are able to cope with this growth in information and whether they can do anything to counter the efforts of governments to manipulate it for their own ends.

(c)   The Realignment in British politics

With the realignment in British politics, it is no longer satisfactory
to consider that a 'left-wing newspaper' will tip the balance
towards some notional idea of equality or fairness in Fleet
St/Wapping. If one abandons a crude Marxist version of the
composition of classes in society and the class struggle, then one
similarly abandons any pretence of being able to reproduce that in
the media. The results of the 1983 and 1987 general elections were
pointers to this problem. With the national vote split three ways,
what positions should the press and broadcasting take up? It is
insufficient to call for a simple 'left-right' divide of media power
since the traditional 'magnetic poles' of ideology no longer attract
so strongly.

Furthermore, structural reforms which simply aim to bring a
balance to political representations in the media fail to address the
broader question of which particular set of views need to be
represented. Is it merely a matter of reproducing party political
views and, if so, of which political parties? Is it more appropriate to
reproduce cross-cutting sectional views? In other words, how does
one determine which views are 'significant' and also ensure that
these views are represented?

(d)   Media coverage: 'forgetting' and the 'destruction of memory'

In the prologue to his book on the harrowing contemporary history
of Cambodia, William Shawcross[19] makes several references to the
part the modern means of mass communication play in creating
and recreating national and international events. In brief,
Shawcross suggests that the means of modern mass communication
bombard us continually with images and information about world
events and specifically about natural and man-made disasters, for
example, wars, famines, floods, etc. The effects of this are two-fold.
First, it can create a feeling of impotence as one disaster succeeds
another without any suggestion that earlier disasters were in any
way ameliorated. Second, and to Shawcross more important, the
effect of continuous, albeit concentrated and short-term, reporting
of disasters destroys 'memory':

> the bloody massacre in Bangladesh quickly covered the memory
> of the Russian invasion of Czechoslovakia; the assassination of

Allende drowned the groans of Bangladesh; the war in the Sinai desert made people forget Allende; the Cambodian massacre made people forget Sinai; and so on and so forth, until ultimately everyone lets everything be forgotten.[20]

Such a roll-call can easily be updated: Iran, Lebanon, Afghanistan, Poland, Ireland, Ethiopia, and so on. The capacity of the means of mass communication to convey these images of destruction and suffering cannot be doubted, but there are two fundamental issues of broad political concern that remain unresolved. The first is whether we tend to accept too readily the veracity and accuracy of media reports. Often, the media convey a fairly complete picture of the events in question. This is certainly true when they deal with stories near home. At other times, however, the media are only able to report snippets of information, incomplete fragments of a complex situation. They can even become unknowing agents of propaganda. This is particularly true of foreign stories. We are therefore exposed to incomplete explanations of events: we know of the famine but cannot comprehend its causes, we are made aware of problems but cannot fathom their resolution.

The second issue, and it is closely related to the first, is whether the succession of images – and they succeed each other with alarming frequency – enables us not only to remember past events but to learn from our past mistakes. Shawcross raises these questions within the context of disaster relief but they have a broader setting. The mass media, particularly the national mass media, pursue stories with great intensity for short periods only. A 'good' story may run for four or five weeks, after which the media and the public tire of it. Another story then takes over. Significantly though, the media do not retrieve the information at some later date for the public's benefit. This is evident in a number of situations. The Ethiopian famine of 1984–5 was a more severe relation of the Ethiopian famine of the 1970s yet the latter was consigned to a memory which is rarely mined for information and for the lessons of history.

THE NEED TO REFORM MEDIA THEORY

Traditional media theory fails to provide any intellectual coherence, because it does not consider the changed circumstances within which the media function and it does not review the impact of a competitive, international, media system. A media theory for the 21st century needs to consider these changed circumstances and, more fundamentally, whether we have come, or been led, to expect too much from means of mass communication which are so obviously and primarily economic enterprises with too few available resources to tackle the range of issues that occupy today's citizen. Put differently, and more provocatively, can the means of mass communication modelled on the 19th and early 20th century models of what a newspaper must, can, and should do, retain any validity today and in the future? How does one deal with a *Sun* newspaper or a Sky Channel? Furthermore, do the recommendations for reform presently advocated come anywhere near improving the present situation?

It is worth recalling, briefly, the source of current dissatisfaction with the media, and particularly the organization and structure of the press. According to either the libertarian or social responsibility theories of the media, the means of mass communication should not be controlled by the state. In addition to the absence of state control, the ownership of the press, and indeed the media, should not be concentrated in too few hands. Although there are no specific 'injunctions' against this, the theories imply that concentration of ownership is undesirable. The failure to achieve many of these desired objectives has been apparent. Ownership is heavily concentrated and the majority of newspapers are politically partisan. Also, a section of the press has abandoned any pretence at providing its readers with 'politics'. These shortcomings are clearly compounded by the difficulty of creating new titles. It is, therefore, difficult to believe in the transition of the newspaper from the libertarian model to the social responsibility one.

This pattern and economic and other pressures make it unlikely that the media will acquire 'duties and obligations' to society unless they are *forced* to acquire obligations. Much of what is often praised in broadcasting is there because of a regulatory structure which encourages diversity in programming. A deregulated – libertarian – environment would allow the market to determine the content and quality of the service.

However, such regulatory mechanisms have always been anathema to the newspaper industry. Although the 1977 Royal Commission[21] was forced to acknowledge the shortcomings of the liberal theory of the press based on proprietorial freedom, it drew back from suggesting any departures from the status quo. It sought to defend and protect proprietorial freedom yet it 'seemed to be defining press freedom as a wider, collective freedom of all journalists working in the press'. As Curran and Seaton observed, the Commission wanted to 'transplant the public service rationale of broadcasting to the press. . . but was opposed to the framework of public regulation that underpins it'.[22]

Their own proposals for reform are aimed at restructuring the British press but it can be argued that even they fail to come to grips with the sort of major 'shortcomings' of the press (and media) identified above. Altering the structure does not necessarily tackle *practices* and the more fundamental issues of how the media should treat and explain the complexity of contemporary social problems or how they should act in the face of the increasing ability of governments and other authorities to control and manipulate information.

More significantly, they seem to be locked into a caricature of British politics. Their solutions to the dire state of the press are to be found in the labour movement, the Labour Party and the Campaign for Press and Broadcasting Freedom. The 'new approach' they propose, is 'a programme consciously directed towards broadening the ideological and cultural content of Britain's mass media so that it is more representative of the spread of interests and views within the community'. They propose a series of anti-monopoly measures and the promotion of ideologically different mass, local, and community media. This latter recommendation is tied up with the setting up of a Media Enterprise Board which would provide funding – funding derived from an advertising levy – for all newly established media. The Board's task would be to help fledgling media and in particular media with extensive readerships but whose inability to attract advertising support, perhaps because of their politics, puts them in constant danger of closing down.[23]

However, their idealism is tempered with realism. They suggest that not all attempts to start up new newspapers should be funded. The MEB should provide support to proposed new media enterprises *'providing always that these appear likely to succeed'*.[24] There is, in other words, no guarantee that the Board's meagre attempt at overcoming the *laissez-faire* economic approach will be any more successful in creating diversity. Would the MEB, one dares to ask, have funded the *News-on-Sunday* or *Today* and what criteria would it have used to justify its support?

Their discussion of broadcasting reform is equally unsatisfactory. In order to improve the broadcasting system and make it better able to resist political pressure – a prime duty of the libertarian/social responsibility media – they favour a wider range of representation on various broadcasting boards. Such a reform would be welcome indeed and would remove the existing bias towards 'the great and the good' but would it enable the broadcasting authorities to be *more assertive*[25] in their dealings with governments? There are many reasons to doubt that.

James Curran and Jean Seaton's strategy is premised on a series of structural changes which are intended to mitigate the 'undesirable' effects of the marketplace and produce a more 'responsible and representative' media. But there is a view, which is gaining political support, that suggests that the best way to guarantee a 'responsible and representative' media, especially with regard to broadcasting, is to *remove* all regulatory mechanisms altogether: for broadcasting to follow in the footsteps of the 'free' press. In that way, the public will be able to exercise a true choice rather than be forced to exercise a choice within an imposed framework.

REGULATION OR DEREGULATION: THE FUTURE OF THE BRITISH MEDIA

'The market in broadcasting'

A vocal exponent of the need to create a free market in broadcasting is Samuel Brittan.[26] Although he has often made references to this in his writings, he developed his argument more fully whilst a member of the Peacock Committee.[27]

His position is in stark contrast to that of Curran and Seaton. Whilst they are of the belief that regulation *encourages* diversity and underwrites artistic freedom,[28] Brittan maintains that regulation is no different from censorship. It is, in effect, a form of control. Although the term censorship is usually applied to instances of government interference in programme making, Brittan uses it much more broadly to include such structural and institutional constraints as the IBA's power to withdraw franchises and its right to vet schedules and programmes. As he later recalled, 'I was indeed disturbed (but not surprised) that liberal minded scholars and businessmen did not share my instinctive revulsion from "regulation". . .'.[29] This 'instinctive revulsion from regulation' is the foundation of his libertarian heritage and it gives rise to a particular vision of how broadcasting should develop and what its purposes should be.

The fundamental aim of broadcasting policy, according to Brittan/Peacock, is to enlarge 'the freedom of choice of the consumer and the opportunities to programme makers to offer alternative wares to the public'.[30] The free market principle and consumer sovereignty – that viewers and listeners are the best judges of their own interests and what they want to consume – are, therefore, the cornerstones of this particular approach to broadcasting. Consumers of broadcasting must themselves decide what they want and the price they are willing to pay. Their choice should always remain supreme: 'no one person or group, or committee, or "establishment" can be trusted to make a superior choice'.[31]

The belief in the broadcasting market is not without its difficulties: how can a multiplicity of channels be introduced so as to allow for consumer choice and how does one overcome the possible detrimental consequences of the market mechanism?

(i)   The introduction of multiplicity

The Peacock Committee recognizes that a full market strategy cannot be adopted unless there is 'full freedom of entry for programme makers, *a transmission system capable of carrying an indefinitely large number of programmes*, facilities of pay-per-view and a satisfactory charging mechanism'.[32] With the advent of subscription as a means of payment for television programmes and the introduction of many new channels of communication as a result of the new media, consumers would be better able to exercise their individual choices. But one would still need regulations or policies 'to prevent monopolistic concentration' and a 'common carrier' obligation imposed upon owners of transmission equipment.[33]

(ii)   The 'problem' of consumer choice

Under market conditions, would consumer choice eventually lead to a reduction of diversity or a lowering of quality as 'the worthy' is replaced by 'the popular'? Would the cheap American import drive out the expensive one-off play, for example? Is there a 'Gresham's Law' of broadcasting? The answers given by Brittan and the Committee are in the affirmative, if only implicitly. They therefore recommended that a body, the Public Service Broadcasting Council (PSBC), be created to oversee and encourage public service commitments in broadcasting. Herein lay a paradox: the PSBC was 'patronage [good], that is, supporting projects of merit and quality', whereas 'paternalism' [bad] referred to institutions, such as the BBC, which believed they knew what the public needed. Given its rather élitist duties, it is not surprising to note that the PSBC would be funded out of taxpayers' money and rents paid by ITV contractors and not by the (few) consumers of its products.

The case for *regulation* and public funding in order to create the PSBC is (perhaps paradoxically) matched by strong arguments for the *deregulation* of broadcasting and the introduction of consumer sovereignty. As the Committee reminds us, 'prepublication censorship (i.e. today's broadcasting regulation). . . has no place in a free society. . . .'[34] and there cannot be any justifications for imposing limits on what should or should not be published or printed. As long as the laws of the land were not broken, there should be a free market in information. Just as there are no restrictions on who should publish newspapers, there should be an equal openness in broadcasting. The broadcasting market 'will enable people to choose among broadcasters as they already do among newspapers'.[35] Furthermore, *individual consumer* choices, when aggregated, will have beneficial effects on broadcasting as a whole. Instead of diminishing the richness of broadcasting, the 'fully developed broadcasting market' would bring about a wider 'range, quality and penetration of the best'.[36]

The analogy with the press which is so often used by the authors to justify the liberation of broadcasting, e.g. as in 'electronic publishing', is only superficially attractive. It ignores the real history of the press in Britain and so it paints a naïve picture of a conservative and debased medium which offers little real choice. Whether these 'difficulties' with the analogy – or the impossibility of achieving a transmission system capable of an *indefinitely* large number of channels – would force an advocate of 'electronic publishing' to change their positions is very doubtful. They are too wedded to a consumer-driven philosophy.

Yet because they are aware of the nature of market forces, they are willing to consider *regulations* which would prevent anti-competitive practices and restrictions on access to the means of communications. The 'sophisticated market system', therefore, imposes its own regulatory requirements. Some, like the PSBC, are there to ensure that 'public service' programming does not disappear; others, such as the 'freedom of entry', 'common carrier obligations. . .' and the 'policy to prevent monopolistic concentration', are there to guarantee openness. Taken together, they produce not a free market but one *regulated* to allow for freedom!

Contrasting philosophies: Brittan/Peacock and Curran and Seaton

Although both sets of authors make recommendations for the creation of a broadcasting (and media) system to cater for the British public and its needs and wants, they differ enormously in their interpretations of what those needs and wants are. They also differ in the nature of the system which would deliver that which is desired.

The Peacock Committee strongly believes in the need for individuals to determine their own needs and wants. Such choices would not be guided nor would they be limited by the work of other institutions. Consumers should have a choice to 'buy' what they want. Similarly, producers would be able to make what they want and offer the products to the public at a price. Together, consumers and producers would come to arrangements which, in their consequences, give rise to a market in broadcasting. 'Public service' programming would exist, again at a price, but unlike the present system there would be no obligation on producers (IBA, BBC) to produce these and consumers would be free to avoid them.

Whether Curran and Seaton would agree with the principles that lie behind the above proposals is very doubtful. Market forces are usually to the detriment of 'quality' programming and they lessen diversity as producers chase the same audiences. Mechanisms and institutions need to be created to guide both the market and the consumer. Such institutions would also need to encourage diversity in output rather than simply encouraging the 'artistic and the worthy'. Only with diversity of output can there be real choice.

The idea that consumers should determine the fate of media by their exercise of economic choices would not be readily accepted by the 'left'. Not only would they point to economic forces which limit those choices but they would also point out that the resultant individual choices lead to an impoverishment of products, to the *Sun* and not the *Independent*, to *Sunday Sport* and not *News-on-Sunday*. This would reinforce their belief in the need to help the latter group of newspapers rather than simply leaving them to market forces.

Finally, whereas Brittan and Peacock would perceive nothing untoward in biased programming so long as consumers are free to exercise consumer choice as they do with newspapers (sic), Curran and Seaton propose that broadcasting and the press should be more representative of all political shades.

The two very different sets of recommendations discussed above offer some guidance for the development of a more appropriate and contemporary media theory. They are united in the emphasis they place on the need to avoid all forms of censorship or control over cultural workers. This freedom – to publish, of the press, of the media – should remain intact so long as laws are not broken. One also needs to be wary of the inequalities that market mechanisms bring in their wake. We do need to ensure that a broad range of views are truly represented even though we may not be able to force individual citizens (consumers?) to acknowledge these. At the same time, however, we have to consider the possibility that members of society (consumers?) may not care about 'representative-ness': setting up, say, a left-of-centre paper is a considerably simpler task than making people read it.

Both sets of recommendations, unfortunately, only deal with structural changes, with reforms which will alter the balance between producer and consumer or between the 'right' and the 'left'. They do not deal with the practices of the media; practices that are, in themselves, real obstacles to the development of a politically literate public. For example, journalists should perhaps consider redefining traditional concepts of 'newsworthiness' and 'news values'. So long as these remain at the centre of any newsgathering institution, then the risk of episodic and trivial coverage increases. To abandon 'news values' as the sole criteria of the media would not necessarily lead to a dereliction of duty. The media would still be able to cover current stories but within a longer-term, in-depth perspective so that Ethiopia or the Lebanon,

Westland or nuclear disarmament do not simply occupy a few weeks' worth of front page/main bulletin coverage per year.

By ignoring the vehicles in which politics is communicated, both sets of recommendations overlook obstacles to communication which are just as real in their consequences as structural ones.

To call for the reappraisal of what the media should do goes beyond questions of diversity or anti-monopoly legislation. Although these are of critical importance, it is not particularly obvious how either a free market in broadcasting or ideological diversity in the media would make us any the wiser about Iran, Iraq or the Lebanon. If the ultimate aim is to create a politically literate society, then the means of communication ought to strive to meet those objectives. They would be helped enormously if other agencies of enlightenment, particularly the schooling system, contributed to the task. In the end, it is naïve to expect the media to single-handedly change centuries of established ways of thinking about the role of the individual/citizen/consumer in the political and social system.

Chapter Three

THE BRITISH PRESS

In an era when the press displays its more ruthless, competitive and combative urges, it may seem curious to begin a discussion of the current state of the British press by delving into its history and, more particularly, its political history. What, one may ask, is the relevance of such an historical exhumation? What is its purpose? What lessons does it teach us?

An examination of the historical pattern of change serves four main purposes; purposes which take on great significance in the context of contemporary debates concerning the proper representation of all political opinion and the nature of bias in the press. First, an historical analysis reminds us that the press in the last century was not monolithic, that it displayed a rich diversity of styles, content and political positions. Different types of newspaper co-existed comfortably and their problems were not dissimilar from those experienced by their heirs. As Koss reminds us,

> [T]he remarkable thing about the British press, as it entered the twentieth century, was its resemblance. . .to the press of mid-Victorian times, in some respects to that of pre-Victorian times. The problems. . .had grown tremendously in scale; but they were fundamentally the same.[1]

Indeed, the problems he cites – the commercialism of the press, the effect of advertising, the trend to sensationalism, concentration of ownership, and the reduction of political coverage – have a contemporary ring to them.

Second, to better understand such ideas as 'press freedom', one needs to relate them to their original context. Third, an historical analysis also serves to illustrate how a narrow section of the press –

the political or quality press – has had a continuing fascination with, and attraction to, the centres of legitimate political power and those who exercise it; moreover, the relationship between the triumvirate of politicians, proprietors and editors – namely, those who exercise political power and those who seek to bask in the afterglow of the exercise of that power – was never fixed. It changed, and still changes, as political fortunes and circumstances change. And this had consequences for the press:

> The question of the sort of relations between journalists and politicians which could be considered proper was to remain of great importance in determining the changing role of the press.[2]

Why that relationship 'remains of great importance' touches on the final purpose of the historical analysis. Newspapers and political parties have 'an affinity'.[3] There has been a tendency for newspapers to represent both existing political parties and emergent ones. Newspapers, therefore, are the media through which political parties can establish and/or sustain themselves in the minds of the public. The newspaper is the channel through which a political party can transmit its ideology and advertise its programme.

This affinity or linkage has real historical roots though its importance and character has changed in recent decades. However, the disappearance of organizational links between the press and parties has not affected the manner in which those linkages continue to be *perceived*. In political systems where there is free electoral competition between political parties for power, 'one might expect to find a connection not only between individual papers and parties but also a correspondence, or parallelism, between the *range* of papers and the *range* of parties'.[4] Such a correspondence would ensure that no political party exercises undue influence and control over the means of communication or that the means of communication do not overwhelmingly support one political party. An absence of correspondence, by corollary, would be an indication of the 'skewness' of support within the means of communication.

It is with this 'ideal' of 'parallelism' in mind that one embarks on an analysis of the biased nature of the British press, its 'unfairness' to the Labour party and its 'infatuation' with the

Conservative party. The 'ideal', therefore, forms the benchmark by which we judge the efficacy, honesty, and impartiality of the press in contemporary Britain.

The absence of 'parallelism' – an issue discussed more fully below – can also seriously affect the political power of a party in opposition. While it is the task of oppositions to oppose, the veracity of that opposition is dependent on the mass media, just as public judgements about the competence of that opposition rely on information derived from the mass media. 'An out-party sometimes forgets that the power it exercises as an opposition is to some extent in the hands of journalists';[5] the more supportive the press is of the opposition party, the more pressure it can bring on the party in power.

Over the last two centuries, the relationship between the press and the political parties has gone through many changes. In his work on the history of the 'political' press – namely that section of the press that exercised political influence – Koss identifies three broad historical phases. The first of these is characterized by state control of the press and its eventual emancipation from such controls. It corresponds, more or less, with the era of the pre-Victorian press. In the second phase, one can find evidence of the press's gradual 'emancipation from the political controls, diverse and sometimes imperceptible, that replaced [state control]'.[6] This phase corresponds to the mid-Victorian press and was to end at the turn of the century with the confirmation of the marketplace and commercialism as the key determinants of the press. The third, and contemporary, phase emphasizes the dominance of the marketplace and the lessening importance of politics for much of the national daily press.

This chapter will concentrate on these 'historical sketches' as a way of illustrating in general terms the pattern of 'de-alignment' or the loosening of ties between the press and the political parties which has taken place from the mid-Victorian period onwards. It also considers the implications of this process. One important lesson which one can draw from this historical analysis is that it may not be possible to predetermine the nature of the proper relationship between politics and the press: each era spawns different sets of relationships which are closely linked to particular configurations of social, political and economic forces.

A POLITICAL HISTORY OF THE PRESS: A BRIEF REVIEW

The pre-Victorian press

The pre-Victorian press was subservient to the state and to state interests. In addition to punitive legal and financial restraints, governments and officials ensured that preferential treatment and a steady stream of funds kept the press in check. As the 18th century turned, governments and officials had less to offer and newspaper publishers found advertising more lucrative as a form of revenue. Although this represented a growing separation of the press from the state, the latter still exercised immense control over the press through the taxes and duties which it imposed upon it.

These duties – often referred to as the 'taxes on knowledge' –

Table 3.1 Newspapers published in Britain, 1900–1987

		1900	*1914*
London	Morning	21	27
Dailies	Evening	11	7
	Other	440	434
Provinces	Morning	70	42
	Evening	101	77
	Others	1304	1326

	1921	*1947*	*1975*	*1987**
National Dailies	12	9	9	11
Provincial Mornings	41	28	17	16
Provincial Evenings	89	75	78	64
Provincial Weeklies*	–	1307	1097	359
Nat. & Prov. Sundays	21	16	12	4 Prov. 9 Nats.

	1976	*1986*	*1987*
Freesheets (mostly weeklies)	169	903	965

*Figures exclude N. Ireland. Figures kindly supplied by Audit Bureau of Circulation and relate only to those organizations that are members of ABC.

48

were designed to limit the growth, circulation and distribution of the press in general and of the radical press in particular. In the 1830s, for example, every newspaper publisher was required to pay a duty on each newspaper published, a duty on each advertisement, as well as a small paper duty. The combined effect of these 'taxes' was to make the stamped press an expensive commodity, thereby restricting its circulation, and to make the 'unstamped' press, i.e. those newspapers which refused to pay the duties, illegal and so subject to punitive measures.[7]

Though the duties were reduced throughout the first half of the 19th century, they were not finally abolished until 1861. Their abolition marked the beginnings of an enormous growth in the number of titles published as well as a reduction in cover prices: in 1855, most of the metropolitan dailies were priced at 5d, by 1870 prices ranged from ½d to 3d, with one at 4d.[8] The growth in titles was also significant. There were some 43 English provincial titles published in 1868 but 138 in 1886.[9] This growth was to continue into the 20th century (Table 3.1).

Three features of the *pre-Victorian* press have a contemporary significance. In the first place, the press was controlled and constrained. Arguments in favour of freeing the press stemmed from a real experience of repression. It is perhaps because of this that there is so much opposition to any form of state involvement in today's press. Second, and more specifically, it was 'daily journalism that counted politically, if only by dint of its opportunity for reiteration'.[10] The Sunday press, the weekly press and the provincial press paled into insignificance in the light of the metropolitan press which replayed daily the myriad Parliamentary political scene in print. Even the radical unstamped press, which achieved remarkable sales in the early 19th century, failed to achieve this continuity and regularity of production. With its sights set against the established social and political order, it was further estranged from those newspapers which were able to participate in the reporting and gossip of metropolitan politics. Thus, as the political centre grew in importance, those who ignored it were unlikely to gain legitimacy as political newspapers. Finally, the politically important and influential newspapers were not the newspapers with the greatest circulation but the small circulation, élite (political) newspapers as exemplified by *The Times*.

The press in an age of rapid change: 1855–1945

The emancipation of the press from direct state control freed it into the arms of eager politicians, though both groups of interest benefited from the close, *voluntarily* established, affinity which was to develop in the mid-Victorian decades. Each political faction 'considered it imperative to secure prominent, sympathetic, and reasonably accurate publicity for its own views. . . [J]oined to political agencies,. . .[newspapers] augmented their own status. . . they were invested with a new validity, and an implicit authority.'[11]

As a result of this close relationship, the *mid-Victorian* press became overtly partisan. Freedom of the press in the context of emancipation from the controls of the state meant 'the freedom to *make* a political choice..'.[12] In this period, the press and the political parties experienced their most intimate relationships: newspapers were closely allied to the many political factions which dominated late 19th century politics. This was true of both the English metropolitan and provincial press. All the metropolitan dailies published in 1855 as well as in 1870 were committed to either the Liberals or the Conservatives; the same was also broadly true of the English provincial daily press. Between 1868 and 1885, only about one-fifth of all English provincial titles were *not* politically committed to the Liberals or to the Conservatives or to a combination of both.[13]

Why did such a close and intimate relationship develop? Part of the answer lies in the press's eternal fascination with those who wield political power. For the 'political' press this is self-evident since their *raison d'être* is the reporting of politics, but even other sections of the press inevitably turn to political affairs to confirm their claims to seriousness. For those involved in politics, the press was to become a medium for furthering political debate and education, for defining and defending party political positions, and for formulating political programmes. Within a small political élite – and 19th century politics was conducted in a restricted political arena – the press could thus play a significant communicative role even though this role might appear alien to the majority of the public. Inevitably, then, the two spheres of politics and journalism converged: those active in both spheres were engaging in similar activities by constantly exposing themselves, their ideas and their work to public scrutiny.

One way of illustrating the 'natural' affinity between these two spheres *as well as its continuing relevance* is to identify the overlap between the two occupations. Though precise historical data relating to the mid-1850s is hard to come by, Lee has estimated that before 1880, there were six or fewer newspaper proprietors in the House of Commons. In 1880, that figure more than doubled to 14 and continued to rise. From 1892 to 1910, there were between 20 and 30 newspaper proprietors in the Commons.[14] Interestingly, in the late 20th century there are no newspaper proprietors listed as members of the Commons: this reflects both the changing role of the press *vis-à-vis* politics and the changing nature of its ownership. By contrast, the professions of journalism and politics continue to be closely allied. In the period 1892 to 1910, there were between 28 and 41 journalists in the Commons. Journalists also represent a fertile field of would-be Parliamentarians: in each successive general election since 1959, over 100 of the candidates standing for all three major political parties have been journalists.[15] In the 1979 Parliament, there were 52 MPs whose main occupations were listed as 'journalists and authors' and 5 listed as 'publishers'.[16] In 1983, of the 116 'publishers and journalists' standing only 45 were elected: 30 of the 71 defeated candidates had stood for the SDP![17]

One outcome of this 'natural' affinity was that newspaper editorial offices and political parties were often populated by the same people; newspapers were sometimes funded by political parties and, in line with their 'freedom to make a political choice', they espoused certain political ideologies. These very real linkages contrasted with the theoretical separation between the two spheres which is contained in the notion of the 'fourth estate'. Whilst the theory of the 'fourth estate' placed the press in an antagonistic and inquisitional role to the state and its institutions, in practice in the 19th century, the press was 'a part of the political machine'.[18] The two spheres of politics and newspapers were 'to all intents and purposes. . .concentric'.[19]

The commercialization of the press

With time, the intimate relationship described above was to go through periods of stress and change. Three major causes account for the ensuing periods of upheaval which culminated in the establishment of a less formal relationship between the press and the political parties in the late 20th century:

- a more commercial approach to newspapers;
- an aversion to maintaining newspapers for political reasons only. As costs of newspapers escalated this reason became even more important;
- an aversion to political affairs content in the 'new journalism' of the late 19th century.

The 'industrialization' of the press[20] (see also pp. 67–78) transformed it into a commodity and an industrial product. As newspaper costs escalated and as the nature of the commodity changed politicians and political parties saw their financial grip over newspapers being prised open; by the late 19th century, newspapers had become such costly ventures that they were beyond the reach of politicians. Not only were the funds difficult to find but it was becoming increasingly difficult to justify such expenditure on newspapers. As newspaper proprietors showed a growing concern for profitability, politicians became more wary of 'servants who postured as masters, and whose allegiance was, in any case, problematic'.[21] For the press, the loosening of the relationship with politicians produced a dilemma: it aspired to greatness as the fourth estate and as an institution for political enlightenment yet it had to pursue the mass audience in order to survive commercially. The press in the 19th century (and to this day) had 'its head in politics and its feet in commerce'.[22] This gave rise to a

> struggle between two conceptions of the press: the one of a Fourth Estate, with proprietorship a form of public service and journalists a species of public philosophers; the other of the press as an industry, with proprietors as businessmen and journalism a trade or craft.[23]

Although that struggle brought about changes in the formal relationship between the press and politicians, it did not fundamentally alter the natural attraction that these two spheres had for each other. Politicians were still able to use their 'authority' and status to get their own way. They were primary sources of information, some became newspaper leader-writers[24] but, perhaps more significantly, they also 'contracted an assortment of interlocking alliances with editors, leader-writers, and proprietors, all of whom were expected to do their bidding'.[25] But despite these manoeuvres, politicians and political parties gradually became marginalized. One way of illustrating this is to explore the ways in which economic pressures led to changes in the content and style of the newspaper.

The 'depoliticization' of the press in the 19th century

The political press, directed as it was to a small, literate and politically informed public, did not aim to capture its readers with an entertaining and interesting package. It was, by all accounts, set out in a 'dull and severe style'. Other sections of the press, for example the Sunday newspapers, had always shown less interest in politics and devoted considerably less space to the staple diet of the ideal 'fourth estate' newspaper.

By the end of the 19th century, there was steady pressure towards a more 'business-like' attitude to newspaper publishing: newspapers, like all other commodities, would have to succumb to the market and the logic and practices of business enterprises. This change in attitude to the newspaper had many important repercussions. Newspapers and journalists were now much more aware of the needs of the market and of commerce. Critics of this process of commercialization often pointed to the way that it made journalists less concerned with 'the old style of principled journalism'. For them, the 'golden age' of journalism was being superseded by a more questionable set of practices and principles. But this pattern was not unique to Britain and it merely confirmed the strength of the economic forces which were coming to' determine the development of the newspaper industry and of the newspaper itself.[26]

This process of change can be seen in the growing importance of the 'new journalism' of the 1880s. Changes in content and style – 'news' was now moved to the front pages, there were briefer stories, news stories grew in importance as 'opinion and commentary' lost favour, different typographical styles were used to attract readers and make newspapers less severe – reflected much more than a mere process of 'modernization'. The newspaper was undergoing a redefinition of its role and place in society. The relationship between paper and reader was thus being changed from the ideal one of a tutorial and intellectual nature, to one of a market character. Both qualities had always been there. . . but there does seem to have been. . . a change in the balance of the two.[27]

One consequence was the downgrading of 'political news'. In the 1860s, 1870s, and even in the 1880s, the pride of the 'old journalism' would be replete with leaders and the texts of politicians' speeches. But the drive to increase sales and to provide more entertaining material in a different form – both products of the commercialization of the newspaper – directly challenged the place of the political speech and the political leader in the newspaper of the late 19th century. The verbatim reproduction in print of the political speech was an expensive exercise which was not usually rewarded with increased sales and so, by the 1900s, the political leader and the political speech had been replaced with shortened accounts and by a flood of 'news' stories. The 'new journalism' meant 'less politics. . .more "sensation" and more "sport", the staples of the popular 19th century Sunday press'.[28]

The changing relationship between the newspaper and its readers and the changing content of the newspaper had one other important impact on the long-term development of the press: it fundamentally altered the newspaper's expectations of its readers. Although not all newspapers were affected to the same degree, the trend towards more 'sensation' and more 'sport' suggested that the 'reader was expected to be intellectually more passive. . .attracted less by the prospect of greater wisdom than by that of "Elevated" status, and he was now appealed to in a shrill capitalised format'.[29] It is this turn to 'passivity' which remains critical to this very day; today's tabloid press can only be reinforcing a process which began well over a century ago.

The declining fortunes of explicit political content is illustrative of long-term processes which have left the press open to (perhaps) 'undesirable' commercial influences and considerations. That such considerations have always existed should not blind us to their 'undesirable' effects; however, that they have always existed also suggests that there may be no 'ideal' to which the press should aspire or indeed revert. Each period had thrown up a different set of relationships, different influences and different pressures on newspapers. The press in the late 19th century thus illustrates a point of transition from one set of dominant relationships to another.

Power without responsibility

Despite the growing independence of the press from political parties, vestiges of 19th century practices remained as politicians persisted in summoning newspapers to their side of the political battle by whatever means possible. For example, '*The Observer, The Standard, The Globe,* and *The Pall Mall Gazette* were each receiving aid from the Unionist funds, sometimes as much as £10,000 a year' in the 1910s.[30]

The outstanding example of politicians seeking to gain press support through the acquisition of newspaper titles in the 20th century is the purchase of the *Daily Chronicle* in 1918 by supporters of Lloyd George. Lloyd George sought to obtain regular press support through the direct means of ownership. In the event, most of the purchase money (£1,650,000) came from 'wealthy admirers'.[31] This transaction 'exposed the myth of the Fourth Estate' because it confirmed in a stark fashion the well established close connections between the press and politics. To many, acknowledging the existence of the 'concentric circles' meant abandoning the pretence that the press was 'the fourth estate'. Yet politicians persisted in propagating the myth and continued to draw attention to the supposed independence of the press. Asquith's criticism of Lloyd George's actions played upon the myth that

> the press should be a free press, criticising the government, and [that the public] wished the government to be an independent government, not disregarding the criticisms of the press, but nonetheless responsible only to Parliament.[32]

Paradoxically, the 'surreptitious alliance between the press and the government' which Asquith was criticizing was the norm and not the exception what he implied it was.

In fact, any attempt by the press to act as a free oppositional/adversarial press was itself likely to generate some form of criticism since it confronted governments with powerful adversaries, a situation which governments (and Parliaments) did not, and still do not, appear willing to tolerate. So long as newspapers remain in awe of political authority, they are beyond criticism; once they challenge that authority, they suffer the full force of its reaction. Herein lies the significance of the actions of the press barons – Beaverbrook, Northcliffe and Rothermere – in their dealings with politicians in the 1920s and 1930s.

The press barons – in particular Beaverbrook (who owned the *Express*) and Rothermere (who owned the *Mail*) – had amassed their vast power through their industrial holdings and/or their ownership of large circulation, and profitable, newspapers. It was a power which was ultimately independent of either their (parliamentary) political standing or political favours. Both newspaper proprietors decided to use their newspapers to pursue a political philosophy and policy – the Empire Crusade – which differed in important respects from the policies of Stanley Baldwin's Conservative Government. The *Express* and the *Mail* saw the Empire Crusade as a means of uniting the Empire by encouraging free trade within it and both newspapers gave publicity and financial support to those by-election candidates who promised to uphold that line in Parliament.

In adopting this crusade, the press barons were also directly challenging Baldwin's leadership of the Government and of the party. It was perhaps this, more than the policy of Empire Free Trade *per se*, which lay behind their actions. Such a challenge could not go unheeded, particularly as it departed from the usual array of Parliamentary or constitutional procedures.

The affair came to a head in a series of by-elections in the early 1930s in which the press barons gave their support to Empire Crusade candidates in their fight against the official Conservative central office candidates. By supporting their own candidates, they were challenging Baldwin's authority and leadership even though he had been given a vote of confidence by the Party in 1931. In the St George, Westminster, by-election in March 1931 the Empire Crusade candidacy seemed to exacerbate the divisions in the Conservative party which the press proprietors had initiated. As the London *Times* reported:

> The present campaign [against Baldwin] is prompted by influences outside of the Conservative Party, which refuse to accept the expressed decision of the party itself. . . .The choice of leader and the policy of the Conservative, or indeed, of any

organized political party, are the responsibilities of the party: and members of the party are responsible to their constituents. . . . Those who control great engines of publicity are responsible to no one but themselves; equally their methods are their own.[33]

This theme was echoed in Baldwin's now famous attack on the press when he accused the proprietors of the *Mail*, *Express* and *Herald* of wanting

power, and power without responsibility – the prerogative of the harlot throughout the ages. This contest is not a contest as to who is to lead the party, but as to who is to appoint the leader of the party. It is a challenge to the accepted constitutional Parliamentary system.[34]

Baldwin's speech sets out the boundaries within which the press must operate: it can act as an adjunct of the political parties, it can be the mouthpiece of the parties or politicians and it may even criticize governments in power, but it cannot transgress the real line which marks off dependence on, from independence of, the political parties. It can ask things of politicians but it cannot make demands of them.

Beaverbrook and Rothermere had tried, in their own ways and using their own particular methods, to dislodge the 'concentric circles' by establishing another focus of power – themselves and their newspapers – that would generate a circle of press power of equal strength and significance to that of the political circle. They failed to achieve their objectives and, in a sense, they were bound to fail because their power, based as it was on financial and propagandist resources, was no match for established constitutional and democratic procedures. Broadcasters were to find that their challenges would be met with a similar response.

The vehement reaction to what was a unique challenge to accepted procedure has ensured that the basic pattern of newspapers working hand-in-hand with political parties and politicians continues to thrive. Newspaper support of political parties is nowadays *volunteered*, it is not commanded. 'Freedom from party control, as distinct from party commitment, is now so much taken for granted that it requires no affirmation.'[35]

The contemporary press, 1945 –

One key influence in the loosening of the relationship between the press and political parties was the decrease in the number of titles published and, in particular, of evenings and provincials (see Table 3.1). This decline was significant because it 'reduced the opportunity for the reflection of nuances of debate about policy and personalities within the parties'.[36] Whereas in the 19th century each political faction prided itself on having its own newspaper, the steady decline in titles narrowed the available range and, inevitably, displaced political considerations as proprietorial and editorial attention turned to questions of commercial survival.

The process of commercialization and industrialization in the newspaper industry which began in the 19th century thus continued to have an important effect on newspapers in this century as newspaper costs escalated, as new methods were developed to tap new audiences, to reach new readers, and to increase sales. Again, it is the combination of all these factors which is important. Two sets of examples illustrate these trends. Until the launch of the *Independent* in 1986, no new national quality daily newspaper had been launched for 113 years. As for the tabloids, additions to the range of publications have either been arm's-length extensions of existing publishing groups (*Today*, 1986–) or born out of existing publishing houses (*Mail on Sunday*, 1983–, *Star*, 1978). In all these cases (and this is the central point) the costs of launching and maintaining each of these publications are in excess of £20m. Such sums are not obtained without some sort of commitment to success which, in contemporary terms, means circulation and advertising rather than a blind commitment to a political creed.

It is also extremely unlikely that today's political parties or their backers would have either sufficient funds or the desire to use such large sums of money for purchasing newspapers. Past experiences were not encouraging. In the 1910s and 1920s, some newspaper proprietors seemed willing to continue to subsidize their newspapers on political grounds, but the mounting losses incurred in this process – Pearson spent £¾m keeping the *Westminster Gazette* going, the TUC had spent £½m on the *Daily Herald* between 1921 and 1928 but only saw profit once in the early years – increased the reluctance of the politically committed to get involved. Neither the

Morning Post (Conservative) nor the *Daily Chronicle* (Liberal) found willing *political* saviours in the mid-1930s. Similarly, when the left-wing *News-on-Sunday* faltered in 1987, it was not a political institution that came to its, albeit temporary, rescue but a Northern businessman, Owen Oyston. Subsidy 'in a party interest – and particularly *by* parties – seems to have stopped by the outbreak of World War 2'.[37]

After the War, only two newspapers – the *Daily Telegraph* and the *Daily Herald* – continued to retain formal party links. Although other newspapers were allied to political parties, that alignment was an 'essentially' voluntary and/or historical one. It was not a case of a new breed of non-political owners coming to the fore but of ownership tempered by financial considerations and a changed attitude to the role of the newspapers in the 'reconstruction' of Britain. One example of this changed attitude to the role of the newspaper in the post-War period was the readiness of some newspapers to treat all political parties with equal respect. This was not common practice but it reached its apotheosis in the 1945 general election when the *Observer* completely detached itself from the political parties and carried articles by representatives of each of the main parties. Today, such a practice would not be considered particularly unusual; in the context of 1945 it was novel, more so since the *Observer* had been purchased in 1911 to keep it as a 'Tory organ'.[38] That newspapers had come a long way in the interim period was beyond doubt; that they were to travel even further was to be confirmed by the manner in which the Cadburys disposed of the *News Chronicle* in 1960. A paper long allied to the Liberal tradition had been allowed to be taken over by the right-wing *Mail*.

Another confirmation of the transformation of the press was its proneness for take-over for financial rather than political ends. The failure of the Liberal party to save the *News Chronicle*, and perhaps of the TUC and Labour Party to save the *Daily Herald* or to originate a paper of their own, only confirmed the lack of financial power which political institutions exercised. The real power behind newspapers shifted to those who, like the Canadian Roy Thomson or the American Rupert Murdoch, acquired newspapers for their business empires.

Although Thomson and Murdoch may be unusual with respect to the vastness of their empires, other contemporary publishers have also tended to treat newspapers as part of the financial and commercial landscape. They undoubtedly relish the prestige and the political power it (reputedly) gives them but their commitment to the newspaper world is ultimately a business one. The sale of the Express Group by Fleet Holdings (ex-Trafalgar House) to United Newspapers in the mid-1980s, the sale of the *Telegraph* to the Canadian Conrad Black, the re-launch and closure of the *Evening Standard* (1987), the launch and demise of the *London Daily News* and the purchase of *Today* by Murdoch (1987) amongst other recent changes, have all the appearances of companies engaging in long-term strategic planning rather than political machination on behalf of any specific political faction. These proprietors retain the potential to exercise political power: indeed, they have used their ownership to chart the political direction of their newspapers, but they have stopped well short of using their newspapers to make demands of the political system in the manner of the press barons of the 1930s. Possibly the last attempt at such a use of newspaper power – Cecil King's 1968 'Enough is Enough' article in the *Mirror* which called for Harold Wilson's resignation as Prime Minister – resulted in the dismissal of the 'abuser' of power, Cecil King himself. It may be 'accidental that there is no Beaverbrook or Rothermere'[39] but it is more likely that they would encounter an enormous backlash if they trespassed into the formal world of politics. Because they are only accountable to themselves and to their shareholders, they would leave themselves exposed and vulnerable to those who do not take kindly to being dictated to by 'outsiders'. Accusations of having 'power without responsibility' would thus ring equally true in the 1990s.

The newest breed of newspaper 'proprietor' – Whittam-Smith of the *Independent* – would probably abhor the prospect either of alignment with a political party or of dictating demands to a political party. The *Independent*, launched in October 1986 with venture capital, seeks to be independent of political party dogma. It seeks to give fair coverage to all political viewpoints and to treat all views with a degree of respect not always found in other serious newspapers. Despite its low circulation (hovering around 380,000 in mid-1988), the *Independent* marks the furthest point away from the description of the political press in the 19th century with which this discussion began. It is as if the 'social responsibility' theory of the press had been translated into real newspaper practices. What is equally interesting is that the journalistic profession has clasped the promising idea of the *Independent* to its bosom. Not only did journalists flock to join it – so giving it, at a stroke, a solid and respectable 'roll-call' – but it was rewarded with the 'What the Papers Say' Newspaper of the Year award in 1986.

That very same spirit of 'social responsibility' was to flicker, albeit very briefly, even in the *Daily Mail*. During the 1983 election, *Mail* journalists objected to the newspaper's coverage of the Labour Party and demanded that it be given a fairer representation.[40] It may be that such moves towards a willingness to detach comment from political allegiance and dogma is a passing fad but it does also suggest that many journalists are uneasy about blind, albeit volunteered, political commitment.

These changing patterns of allegiance can be analysed within the broad concept of 'parallelism': a concept which explores the extent to which newspapers reflect or fail to reflect the breadth of the party political discourse. A newspaper 'paralleled'

> a party if it was closely linked to that party by organisation, loyalty to party goals and the partisanship of its readers. A press system can be defined as paralleling a party system when such links exist between each newspaper and a party. . . Complete

---

Organizational links: the nature of links between pary and press

Strong links	*Weaker links*	*No links*
e.g. party ownership	informal links	
	affiliated to party	

Party Goals: does the press subscribe to party goals?

Extreme loyalty	*Independence*
e.g. *Morning Star*	e.g. *FT* or *Guardian*

Readership: do all press readers vote for the party?

All readers loyal to party	*Few readers loyal to the party*

Figure 3.1 Parallelism: press and political parties

parallelism would exist if every newspaper was linked extremely closely to one or another party. . .and when, in addition, the number of newspapers in the system was distributed between the parties in proportion to each party's strength.[41]

A close examination of the three primary links between press and party – by organization, loyalty to party goals, and the partisanship of its readers – reveals the range of possible relationships (Fig. 3.1).

Contemporary national newspapers display a number of different positions at all three levels. The ever loyal *Daily Telegraph* would come closest to paralleling the Conservative Party though even here its organizational links with the party are weak and may be getting even weaker as a result of its new Canadian ownership. The *Financial Times*, on the other hand, which is the City paper and which has a solid Conservative readership (see Fig. 4.3b, Chapter 4), prides itself on its critical edge in pursuing a business ideology which might, and often does, go against the Conservative Party's views.

Even the *Morning Star* which is the paper closest to a political party (the Communist Party) has shown itself to be anything but a servant of its political masters. In the early 1980s, the editorial board of the *Morning Star* adopted a philosophy which allied it closely to the Soviet Union. This went against the Communist Party's well known. Euro-Communist stand. In the ensuing power struggle over the right to dictate the newspaper's political position, the newspaper's editor was dismissed and replaced by the Communist Party's own adherents. Whilst this example is unique, it does serve to remind us that those who are editorially in charge of newspapers are sometimes, though perhaps not for long, able to lead the paper in directions which its masters do not always support or follow. Their abilities to do so seem to depend, and are related to, the organizational structures within which they operate and whether the owners of the paper are able to exercise their power speedily or not.

In general, then, newspapers do usually align themselves with certain political parties and do show their support for political party programmes and policies in a variety of ways, some stronger than others. This support is rarely total but undoubtedly some newspapers, e.g. the *Daily Mail*, *Sun*, are more ready than others to support wholeheartedly the political party of their choice. Such a connection between newspapers and political parties is only to be expected; newspapers have traditionally wished to play a part in the political system and have never been reluctant to express a view ('The *Sun* says') on the ways of the world.

Recently launched titles – *Today*, the *Independent* and the *News-on-Sunday* – neither confirm the historical trend nor disprove it. Both *Today* and the *Independent* originally eschewed political partisanship. Their intention was to treat each case on its merits rather than reproduce the traditional left-right divide in British politics. Once *Today* moved into Rupert Murdoch's News group it changed its politics; its neutral stance and its support for a middle-of-the-road SDP government in the 1987 general election gradually gave way to a more Conservative outlook. The *Independent* has remained independent from political allegiances though it too favoured a middle-of-the-road political outcome in the 1987 election. The interesting points to note for both papers are that they emerged at a time when the SDP, a party of the middle-ground, was in the ascendant, and that neither moved to the 'left', not even the social democratic 'left', in the 1987 election.

The journalism of 'neutrality' may therefore be no more than a reflection, and an acknowledgement, of the arrival of a new political force in Britain and a response to the existence of a market as evidenced by the SDP's success in the political and electoral arena. No newspaper would be brave enough to alienate prospective SDP members (readers?) amongst its readership and this must surely explain the overwhelming welcome the SDP got from Fleet St.[42]

CONCLUSION

The processes of commercialization and industrialization which have affected the British press have reduced the overall number of titles. They have also led to a narrowing of the range of political views represented in the press; as newspapers which voiced liberal and social democratic/Labour views (*News Chronicle, Daily Herald*) have closed down, the dominance of the Conservative press has become more pronounced. Whereas just under 50% of the adult population read a Labour paper in 1964, by 1983 only 24% did (Table 3.2).

Table 3.2 Penetration of Conservative and Labour daily papers, 1964–83[43]

	1964	1966	1970	1979	1983
% adults reading					
Cons. paper	60	61	54	66	75
Lab. paper	49	51	52	29	24
% working class					
reading Cons. paper	–	53	44	64	74
reading Lab. paper	–	59	61	34	30

Although it is possible to interpret 'freedom of the press' in such a way as to include within it the 'freedom' to make a political choice and to volunteer one's support, it does seem that political parties of the left are rarely favoured by newspapers. In a few cases, the continued support for a political party can be explained by reference to an historical connection. The *Mail*, the *Express*, and *The Times*, for instance, have always preferred 'conservative' parties. But even when that linkage has been broken by the entrance of a new press owner – Conrad Black, Rupert Murdoch, David Stevens – the newspapers in question have either maintained or reasserted their commitment to the political right. As a result the Conservative Party continues to enjoy the favours of those newspaper owners who are embedded in the present structures of power and of wealth generation.

One immediate, short-term outcome of the disproportionate distribution of political support is that political parties which propose radical, particularly left-wing, change will find it increasingly difficult to argue their case in public. This problem does not seem to afflict the radical right in the same way; since the early 1980s the Thatcher Government has been able to implement radical change without alienating its newspaper support. Those on the left who have dared not to act in moderation – the Hattons, Grants and Livingstones – have been violently pilloried, whilst their counterparts on the right – the Tebbits, the Brittans – have usually been seen as pioneers of reform. A longer-term effect may be that the national press will cease to act as a focus of left-wing radicalism and political challenge to established processes.

Can structural reforms 'improve' the situation by increasing diversity and lessening the adverse consequences of concentration? Authors of such reforms believe that greater diversity could be achieved by imposing restrictions on rules of ownership, by imposing levies on advertising revenue so as to create a pool of funds for alternative publications, and generally by controlling free-market forces. Such reforms would either completely displace existing rules derived from the Fair Trading Act and monopolies legislation or they would refashion them so as to make them more meaningful in the era of multi-media ownership. One example of such reforms is Curran and Seaton's proposal[44] that no group or individual should own more than three national newspapers; another proposal is to limit cross-ownership of media. The effect would certainly be to 'unscramble' existing media interests.

The weaknesses of the above proposals are fairly evident. In the first place all they would do would be to redistribute ownership (probably) amongst existing groups. These proposals would not necessarily increase the political diversity of the press. Diversity can only be increased through a body set up with the specific task of creating and sustaining new media. Whether such a body would succeed would depend on its organization and funding and whether it was able to create vehicles which could survive in the market-place and be purchased by the public. The other major weakness of the proposals is that they do not properly identify the nature of the problem. One aspect of the problem is, undoubtedly, the economic structure of the newspaper industry which makes it difficult to start newspapers. Another aspect is the apparent difficulty of getting radical or even social democratic ideas into circulation. Is the absence of a left-wing press therefore related to the structure of the industry or is the public, for whatever reasons, not receptive to such ideas?

It is impossible to resolve these problems since there is no information which would allow us to pass judgements on them. Attempts to create vehicles of left-wing opinion have not succeeded; both the *News-on-Sunday* and the *East End News* failed miserably. Part of the reasons for their failures are related to managerial and organizational considerations but these cannot account for everything. Until the nature of the problem can be identified, it is unlikely that adequate solutions will be proposed.

Structural reforms of any sort are unlikely under this present

Conservative Government. The press serves it too well for that to happen and so the problems which have taxed the left for so many years will continue to haunt it in the future. Unfortunately, proposals for change will become less likely as the lessons of the recent attempts to break the mould of Conservative journalism sink in.

Chapter Four

THE BRITISH PRESS: OWNERSHIP, CONTROL, ADVERTISING, AND RESTRUCTURING

INTRODUCTION

The 19th century saw two significant changes in the newspaper industry which were to have considerable impact on future developments. These were, first, the growing importance of advertising revenue for individual titles and, second, the development of the large circulation daily press.

Advertising has always had a place in the newspaper; some of the earliest newspapers were essentially means for communicating notices of events, such as the arrival of ships. In the 19th century, advertising and, more importantly, advertising revenue, became a vital ingredient in the make-up of the newspaper. It contributed to the newspaper both in terms of content and also in terms of much-needed revenue and so helped newspapers in their struggles to survive. This connection between advertising, advertising revenue and the profitability of newspapers could be found early in the 19th century in Britain[1] and in the USA.[2]

In the United States, however, that connection was given a unique twist when in 1833 a new mass circulation tabloid, the *Sun*, was published and sold at one-sixth of the cover price of other papers. The expectation was that the losses sustained by the low cover price would be more than made up by the larger circulation and by advertising. This was the same formula that Harmsworth (Lord Northcliffe) used when he launched the *Daily Mail* in 1896.

Harmsworth was one of many – others include Marconi and the pioneers of the film industry – who were at the forefront of what Briggs has called 'the development of the mass entertainment industry'[3] at the turn of the century. They greatly benefited from certain 'economic conditions' during the period – namely, the existence of a large and concentrated urban population, the rise in real incomes and an increase in leisure time – which made the 'mass entertainment industry' possible.

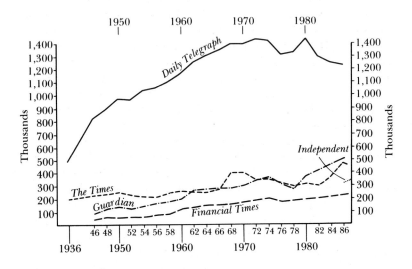

Figure 4.1 'Quality' national daily newspaper circulations

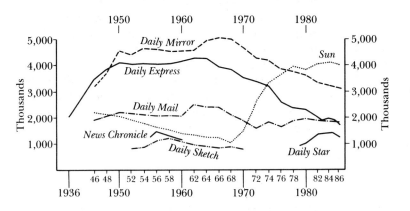

Figure 4.2 Popular national daily newspaper circulations

Newspaper titles such as the *Daily Mail* and the *Daily Mirror* were started up to exploit these economic conditions and the everpresent demand for 'reading and entertainment'.[4] These newspapers were unlike the 'political press' that served the political élite – their readers were substantially different, the content of the newspapers was also different, as was the relationship between the newspaper and its readers – but they were enormously successful. The *Daily Mail* sold well over 200,000 copies daily in its first years and reached half-a-million sales after three years. Such newspapers were to sell over 3 million copies each during the great press battles of the 1920s and 1930s: sales of such magnitude that they easily dwarfed the circulation of the dailies of the late 19th century.

The process of expansion which the press went through in the late 19th century did not continue beyond the First World War. In fact, there has been a steady decline in the total numbers of titles published since then. Not only are there fewer titles published today but the process of decline has also led to monopolies within large cities. For a brief period in the Spring of 1987, London was the only English metropolitan centre with more than one evening daily paper – it had three – having endured five years when only one, the *Standard*, was published. In 1900 it had nine!

By the late 1980s, the division between the small circulation 'quality' press and the large circulation 'tabloid' press had also become well established (Figs 4.1 and 4.2) and each sector appealed to different types of readers (Fig. 43a and Fig. 43b). Such trends accompanied many others, including the concentration of press (and media) ownership, the increasingly important role of advertising, and its effect on the 'political' content of the press. In the last few years, two new concerns have featured largely. These are, first, the restructuring of the national daily press within the East End of London and away from Fleet Street and, second, the brief resurgence of interest in new publications. Each of these issues will be dealt with in this chapter.

1. THE OWNERSHIP AND CONTROL OF THE PRESS

Concern about the concentration of ownership of the press is not of recent origin. There have been many periods in the past when the

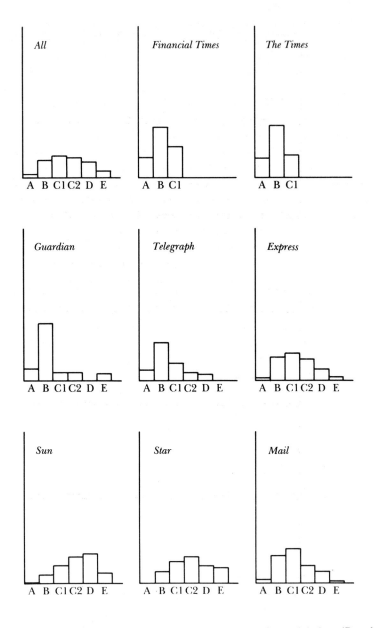

Figure 4.3a Readership of daily national newspapers by social class (Based on *British Social Attitudes*, 1985.)

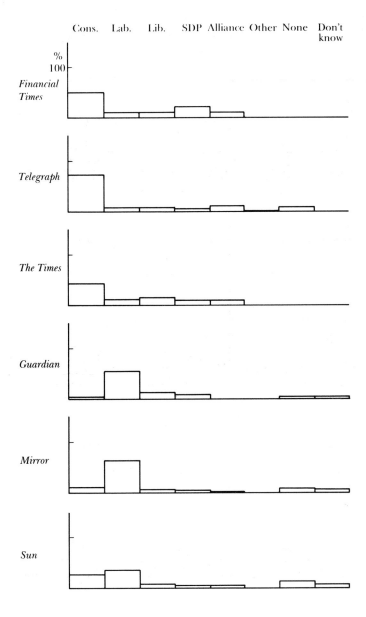

Figure 4.3b Party identification of newspaper readers (Based on British Social Attitudes, 1985.)

71

Table 4.1 Concentration of ownership by circulation in the metropolitan press, 1910[6]

	% of total circulation Morning	Evening
Northcliffe		
(*Mail,Mirror,Times*)	39	31.3
Morning Leader Group		
(*Express,Standard*)	15.5	34.5
Pearson		
(*Leader,News*)	12.4	16.8
Total	66.9	82.6

Table 4.2 Percentage of circulation controlled by. . . .(Jan-June 1987)*

	DAILIES Pops.	Qualities	*SUNDAYS* Pops.	Qualities
GROUP				
News International**	35.3	11.6	33.4	45
Mirror Group	25.6		40.2	
United Newspapers	24.5		15	
Associated	14.4		11.4	
Telegraph		43.2		26.5
Financial Times		10.5		
Independent		11		
Guardian		18.5		
Observer				28.5

*Figures exclude *Sunday Sport*.
**Has a 20% stake in Pearson's, the owners of the *Financial Times*.

degree of concentration has been significantly large (Table 4.1) and when such degrees of concentration have generated calls for inquiries. The 1947 Royal Commission on the Press[5] was, for example, established specifically to examine the degree, and the consequences, of concentration of ownership.

A glance at a table of ownership of the British press in 1987 (Table 4.2) confirms that concern is still with us. The reason for such concern can be found in the 1947 Royal Commission Report; it asked *whether such concentration as exists is on balance disadvantageous to the free expression of opinion or the accurate presentation of news*.[7]

Although the Commission was concerned with, broadly speaking, the effects of concentration of ownership on the diversity of content, it was inevitably drawn into a discussion of the links between owners and the views propagated in their particular newspapers. In this sense, it was interested both in the narrowing of the range of views presented in newspapers and the likelihood that newspapers could be used for political ends. Its findings – that concentration was not a particular problem and its effects not particularly harmful – have been heavily criticized ever since.

One such group of critics has been especially prolific. Graham Murdock and Peter Golding,[8] like other Marxists, take it for granted that there is a relationship between 'ownership and control'. However, their task is to explore the nature, and the consequences, of that relationship. They focus on three propositions:

1. control over the production and distribution of ideas is concentrated in the hands of the capitalist owners of the means of production;
2. as a result, their views . . . receive constant publicity and come to dominate the thinking of subordinate groups; and
3. this ideological domination plays a key role in maintaining class inequalities.[9]

These propositions raise key questions concerning

(i)   the relationship between ownership and control,
(ii) the processes through which dominant ideology is translated into cultural commodities, and
(iii) the dynamics of reception and the extent of adoption of the dominant ideas.[10]

(We are concerned here primarily with proposition (1) and question (i). The other issues deserve their own extensive studies though they are referred to in passing elsewhere in this book.)

The evidence for arguing that newspaper – and media – ownership is concentrated in a few hands is fairly abundant (see Table 4.2) but this does not, of itself, provide material for analysing the extent to which 'this *potential* for control is actually realized in practice, how exactly it operates and in whose ultimate interest (it is). . . .'.[11] In the absence of detailed empirical data with which to substantiate the process by which 'ownership' translates into 'control', such propositions can only be deemed 'assertions'.[12] Anecdotal evidence does tend to support the view that owners exercise control but these instances are anything but the basis for generalizable statements across fields and decades. Furthermore, it is highly unlikely that the same pattern of control will be in evidence across diverse organizations and forms of ownership. A publicly funded, public service organization such as the BBC would need to be treated differently from a privately owned quality paper or a Trust-owned *Guardian*. Although there may be common ground between them there are also likely to be enormous, and significant, differences.

Nevertheless, it is probable that ownership does contain within it the *potential* for direct and indirect control. Messrs Murdoch, Maxwell and Rowland, amongst others, are known to have attempted to exercise control over editorial content. Such instances are not typical of their managerial system of control for it is unlikely that a single individual would be able to oversee a widely dispersed media empire. Moreover, such forms of control are necessarily direct and crude and mask a range of other means by which results can be achieved.

Proprietors do appoint editors and chief executives; they decide budgets and manning levels and they put their imprint on the total organizations. In consequence, editors (and journalists) work within already defined structures and processes. Decisions about the allocation of space, funds, and resources are often not the editor's responsibilities. In fact, newspaper editors sometimes do not even exercise control over large sections of their newspapers. Executives may play a major part in the running of the paper.[13]

It is through the setting of objectives and the process of resource allocation that control can be exercised on branches of the media and that control remains with the proprietors. However, it is unlikely that such proprietorial power will be exercised without reference to commercial considerations or marketing considerations. In an increasingly cut-throat environment, purely political, or ideological, considerations may be important, albeit secondary.

Such an argument would apply to most, if not all, media enterprises irrespective of type of ownership. The *Independent* newspaper, the BBC, the *Guardian* (owned by a Trust) and the *Sun* are all concerned about their positions in the market-place. Their measures of success are not ideological purity but profitability within their chosen sectors. Newspapers exist in a competitive market-place and have to employ whatever means possible to survive in that market-place; overtly political packaging and purity may be incidental to that objective.

Table 4.3 Newspaper interests in radio, television and the 'new media' (end 1987)

	Commercial Radio (5% + holdings)	ITV	Cable Operators	Satellite Programmers
TOTAL	25	15	22	8
News UK Ltd.				1
Mirror Group Newspapers[1]	3	1 (20%)	3	3
United Newspapers	1			
Associated Newspapers	5			
Telegraph				
Financial Times (Pearson)		1 (21%)[2]		
The *Independent* (Newspaper P.PLC)				
Guardian and *Manchester Even. News*	1	1 (5.1%)		
The *Observer* (Lonrho)				
British Telecom			7[3]	3

[1]Interests held via Pergamon, Scottish Daily Record, British Cable Services or Maxwell Communications. Also includes ownership in two operations via SelecTV in Bolton and Daily Record in Clyde.
[2]Via PL Publishing Ltd.
[3]Either in the construction or management of the system.
Commercial Radio and ITV Information kindly supplied by the IBA, Summer 1988.

The general validity of the argument concerning the allocative power of ownership is in no doubt. There are, however, grave doubts about its extension to include the statement that 'the owning group continue to constitute an identifiable capitalist class with recognizable interests in common'.[14] This statement is too general to be meaningful. In fact, if one was to query the evidence on the concentration of media ownership, as Tunstall[15] does, then its validity is further undermined. Tunstall's main thesis is that the evidence for concentration of ownership is very *weak* if one charts ownership across all media fields rather than simply restricting it to the press, radio and television. Whilst this does provide a picture of greater diversity of ownership (and thus competition) (Table 4.3), it also highlights aspects of concentration.

How valid is it, then, to suggest that the owners 'constitute an identifiable capitalist class with recognizable interests in common' and what does it mean apart from something general pertaining to a concern for success and survival? Does private/commercial ownership produce a 'business bias'? Is it the basis of 'conservatism' in the media? Do the views of the owners receive constant publicity? All these questions (and there are others) imply that media workers are but ciphers and that they transmit the views of others. Unfortunately, the evidence which would enable us to arrive at firm conclusions is by no means straightforward.

Although journalists are 'the people who operate much of the power of the press as usually understood'[16] and they can exercise a measure of freedom in their choice of stories,[17] anecdotal evidence supports the view that the real power within the press is rarely 'shared between its owners and the journalists'.[18] In recent years, some newspapers have become vehicles for the pursuit of certain positions and ideologies and consequently less open to their ideological opponents. By abandoning any pretence to 'social responsibility', they have turned their backs on discussion and argument. In this real world of politics and journalism, there can be little room for the devolution of newspaper power to journalists.

A good example of this can be found in the newspaper coverage of the 1984–5 miners' strike. Specialist labour or industrial correspondents usually exercise a degree of autonomy in their selection and presentation of stories and some accept the need to balance their accounts more than others. But during the strike, owners and executives saw little reason to balance accounts.

Editors of those newspapers which supported the objectives of the NCB and the Government were generally favoured by Ministers and were given regular briefings. Although there is nothing particularly unusual in this degree of favouritism, it had two serious consequences:

- since most newspapers favoured the Government's position, it was not possible to get a 'balanced' view of the dispute;
- a 'balanced' account was ruled out because those editors also worked hard to exclude 'balanced' accounts. The BBC's radio correspondent, Nicholas Jones, admits that 'stories that gave prominence to the position of the NUM could simply be omitted, shortened, or submerged into another report. . .'.[19]

The hierarchical nature of news organizations – both as a chain of command and as an information processing organization – ensured that the power centre remained well removed from the specialist correspondents. Editors were in control of news output and had no qualms about 'manipulating' news content. Even as experienced, and senior, a journalist as the labour editor of the *Sunday Times* would find his copy altered without his knowledge and in ways which changed the substance of that copy. His only 'power' was to request that his name be removed from the story. Yet the editor of the *Sunday Times* explained his paper's coverage and position in a way which begs more questions than it answers. The *Sunday Times*, he wrote

> took a firm editorial line: for *the sake of liberal democracy, economic recovery and the rolling back of union power*. . .Scargill and his forces had to be defeated, and would be. . .*Our views, however, were kept to where they belong in a quality newspaper: the editorial column.*[20]

Journalists do sometimes react against the excesses of newspaper partisanship but even on these occasions it is proprietorial and editorial power that emerges unscathed and victorious. An attempt by *Daily Mail* journalists to broaden the paper's political coverage of the 1983 election was rejected on the grounds that only the editor was responsible for content and that outside pressure, if only from an organization's own journalists, amounted to interference in the running of that organization. It also implied that journalists, even experienced journalists, should not attempt to challenge the guidelines of those who edit or run newspapers.[21]

Not all news organizations display this pattern of behaviour, nor are all journalists mere interchangeable ciphers in the propaganda battle. The pursuit of the newsworthy, the move to more collective forms of journalism, and the ever-present desire to get copy into the papers, forces all journalists in one direction and towards that which will be interesting and a 'good read'. In this scenario, newspaper proprietors and editors do not always need to play an active part in order to ensure that continuity and similarity across, and between, newspapers is the norm.

In recent years, the evidence for proprietorial interference has become even more weighty. With Murdoch's acquisition of the *Times* Group of newspapers and the *Today* newspaper, and Maxwell's of the *Mirror* Group, the market is dominated by self-styled publicists who are not afraid of exercising their power as proprietors. The former had little difficulty in removing Harold Evans from the editorship of *The Times* despite the elaborate system of guarantees that surrounded the editor's post.

The power of proprietors – whether as individuals or as representatives of conglomerate ownership – remains a critical influence on the character of newspapers. Another, much less visible, influence on the style and character of newspapers (and the media) is advertising.

2. ADVERTISING AND THE PRESS

Though advertising revenue freed the press from direct political control, it introduced its own form of constraints on an expanding press in the 20th century. In effect, without the support of advertisers the British media would be in a poorer and much truncated form: advertising revenue accounts for some 40% of the popular press's total revenue and some 70% of the qualities' total revenue; advertising revenue also finances the commercial television channels, countless commercial radio channels and a sizeable proportion of the new cable and satellite channels. Without this extensive support, many of our newspapers, for example, would either cost much, much more or cease to exist.

With such a powerful presence, it would be difficult to argue that advertising revenue, and therefore advertisers, do not play an important role in deciding the future success of a particular medium. But what is the nature of that influence and what are its consequences?

Advertisers form part of the competitive commercial and capitalist context within which media operate, and their decisions reflect that context. They have clients who wish to sell certain products and services and their task is to enable their clients to reach as many potential customers as possible and at the lowest possible cost. In this sense, advertisers are not interested in readers or viewers as such, but in readers/viewers who are able to buy products. They are thus willing to pay several times more for the wealthy readers than they are for the less wealthy or poor. One effect of this is to force the quality press 'up market' so as to serve the wealthy reader. The popular tabloids, on the other hand, charge considerably less for their advertising space per thousand readers than do the qualities and this forces them to try to maximize sales. The resulting polarization 'caricatures'[22] and magnifies the divisions in British society based on education and class.

Sometimes, though, the outcome of the advertisers' work has surprising results. As Curran commented with respect to the 1920s and 1930s, 'developments in the process of media selection and market analysis, combined with important market changes, *positively fostered the development of a left press*'.[23]

Advertisers 'rediscovered' the working class since its combined weight was formidable. The decisions of advertisers also benefited important sections of the left press in the 1950s and 1960s.

> Crude advertising discrimination has tended to be directed at the socialist rather than social-democratic press, thus *exempting* the mass-circulation, *pro-Labour papers* that have flourished;. . .small circulation publications further to the left *which have tended to be poor advertising media, judged by the commercial criterion employed by advertising agencies*, have probably also suffered as a consequence of overt political discrimination.[24]

If advertisers cannot be faulted for using mainly 'commercial criteria' rather than ideological/political ones in their decisions, it is nevertheless true that the outcome of those decisions in their totality have enormous implications. They tend to favour those media which have audiences with (usually) high purchasing powers as against media which have readers or viewers with limited purchasing power. This power of 'patronage' imposes its own requirements on the nature of the press and ensures that the press, as well as other commercially funded media, continue to sell in order to sell readers to advertisers. Newspapers and television programmes are essentially means of packaging readers and viewers (more appropriately, consumers) for the benefit of advertisers.

Some of advertising's other influences are easy to identify. Advertising structures the newspaper into distinct categories and sections. Editorial space is, in practice, the space left over after advertising has taken its share of the newspaper. Furthermore, certain stories, e.g. travel, motoring, fashion, only exist because of their ability to bring advertising with them. The extreme example of such practices is the supplement with its focus on banking (with banking advertising) or cities/countries (with appropriate advertising). Such 'advertorials' blur the distinction between editorial content and advertising and so shift control over content to the advertisers and away from news organizations.[25] Few travel or motoring correspondents would wish to be overly critical of the holiday or car so lavishly provided by their respective sponsors.

In addition to imposing its own needs on the medium, advertising has immense ideological implications. It creates a 'dream' world. '[I]t mystifies the real world and deprives us of any understanding of it'; 'we become part of the symbolism of the ad world; not real people but identified in terms of what we consume.'[26] It therefore masks and distorts real relationships of power and dominance.

Despite the importance of the above influences, it is the impact of advertising on the structure and politics of the British press that has received closest attention. Two general critiques stand out. First, that 'the search for the affluent reader' distorts the make-up and content of the British press and, second, that the 'patronage' of advertisers favours some (the middle class) and not other (the working class) types of readers – it freezes out the working class reader and the working class newspaper. Both critiques have substantial analytic support.

According to Hirsch and Gordon[27], the quality press focuses on those issues which interest and reflect its middle and upper class readership. As this agenda spreads to other sections of the press, to radio and to television, it produces a 'self-enforcing conformity' whose importance 'lies not in the nuances of attitude taken on different items on the political agenda, but rather in the common agreement on that agenda itself. . .'.[28]

Examples abound. In the 1950s and 1960s, the authors claim, there was a neglect of the question of wealth and poverty in British society. More recently, one can point to the ways in which the press covers industrial relations news or news about welfare. In both these cases, there is a conformity in coverage which takes for granted a certain perspective on these issues. Industrial action, for example, is usually seen as reprehensible – 'the pressure exerted by trade unions. . . becomes a threat to democracy rather than part of it'[29] – whilst the pressure exerted by business is overlooked. Indeed, the image or notion of consensus is built into the very language of the media: they contrast 'compromise' with 'dogmatism', 'order' with 'chaos', 'realism' with 'ideology', 'responsibility' with 'irresponsibility' and so on.[30]

The cumulative effect of the 'up-market bias' and the consequent conformity which seeps downwards, is to orient the press towards one section of the community (the wealthy and comfortable middle classes) and away from another (women, blacks, the poor, etc.). The media, concentrated in London, then reproduce a specific view of the country and its ills – a view well rehearsed in the prosperous South but somewhat unreal in the less prosperous North. The result is an absence of diversity – a key requirement for a truly representative press and one suited for political democracy.

A more sustained attack on the impact of advertising on the press can be found in James Curran's writings. Curran has argued that advertising pressures have 'helped to ensure that it (the Left press) has developed in a depoliticised, deradicalised and disabled form':[31] advertising patronage curtails the radical tendencies of the left press. These conclusions are based on a study of the demise of the *Daily Herald* and the 'depoliticization' of the *Daily Mirror*.

However, one major weakness of the study is that by concentrating on advertising as the major culprit, it overlooks the structural changes which media necessarily go through – or do not go through – which themselves place them at risk. The demise of a medium may, therefore, be the final outcome of a combination of factors rather than the result of one specific one. This is certainly a very plausible *alternative* explanation for the demise of the *Daily Herald*.

The *Daily Herald* was an extremely popular Labour daily. Its daily circulation in the 1960s stood at well over 1.3 million copies. But it was the 'wrong' sort of readership. Unlike the *Daily Mirror* (see below), it was unable to break away from its predominantly old, male, working class, Labour supporter readership and expand in other areas. These factors alone would have been sufficient to convince advertisers that it was not the medium for the affluent 'never-had-it-so-good' Macmillan era. However, there was another factor, often omitted or underplayed, which made the demise of the *Herald* even more of a certainty. In 1947 it had an average daily circulation of 2,134,000 copies but in 1961 it only sold 1,394,000 copies. In a period when all other popular newspapers *gained* substantial readers, the *Herald* lost over 700,000 copies in sales.[32] A decline of such proportions, probably due to a variety of factors, is a clear indication of a severe crisis and would itself justify either a re-launch or closure.

A substantial injection of advertising revenue, or an increase in its cover price, might have saved the *Herald*, albeit as a temporary solution. In a competitive commercial environment, neither option is really open: advertisers would soon lose clients and newspapers would lose readers if their competitors were cheaper. The solution to this problem is the one the *Mirror* adopted in the 1940s and after, that is, of broadening its appeal to other groups of readers. Whereas most of the *Herald*'s readers were Labour supporters, only two-thirds of the *Mirror*'s were. The *Mirror*'s readers were also young.[33]

Does this solution lead to 'deradicalization' and 'depoliticization' as Curran claims? Curran is convinced that it produced a 'muted radicalism' but it would be equally justified to claim that the *Mirror* had to change because it could not portray the 1950s and 1960s in the language or imagery of the 1940s. Periods of change produce changes in those professions which reflect them; it is the medium that does not change with its audience that is likely to suffer.

Newspapers are continually undergoing changes. They respond to external forces, to a variety of other pressures and to the changing requirements of their readers; they evolve and adapt to changing circumstances. In the late 20th century, the newspaper is an important means of communication but it sits alongside the broadcast media. It has had to accommodate with changes brought about by television and radio: television and radio deliver news instantly and usually with sound and/or visual images. In consequence, newspapers have to adopt other roles; they can become more entertaining and popular, or provide in-depth information to a select few. Such options merely indicate the manner of their evolution.

To argue, therefore, that changes in newspapers – in their content, style, readership, etc. – may be undesirable (e.g. 'deradicalization', 'depoliticization') is to confuse that which one may desire (and which may be socially desirable) with the actual and real choices which individuals and groups make in the market-place. Such choices may be exploited, and fed, by commercial considerations but they ultimately reflect an actual desire for a specific type of medium. *Sun* readers will not become *Times* readers simply because the latter is somehow 'superior'; they are *Sun* readers because it 'serves' them better in a complex social and psychological way.

3. THE DEPOLITICIZATION OF THE PRESS: EVOLUTIONARY CHANGE OR STATISTICAL ARTIFACT?

The 'depoliticization' of the popular press, according to Curran and Seaton, can be seen in the reduction of space allocated to 'political affairs', namely, political, social and economic news, over a period of decades. This conclusion is based on their content analysis of newspapers in the years 1936, 1946 and 1976. 'The editorial content of the popular press', they write, 'has shrunk during the last forty years. There has consequently been *a marked reduction in the amount of public affairs news and analysis* published in all popular papers.'[34]

Though their conclusions are clear, the precise nature, and meaning, of the process of 'depoliticization' is much less so. For example, they write that the 'depoliticization of the popular press merely reflects a *reversion* to the pattern of the inter-war years. . .The make-up of most popular papers in 1976 is *similar* to that in 1936'.[35] In which case, 'depoliticization' took place during some *earlier* – unidentified – period. The attempt to identify the process of 'depoliticization' – perhaps for specific ideological reasons – is not matched by either careful empirical analysis or sufficient historical insight. For if we are to follow through the themes outlined in Chapter 3, then the process which is identified as 'depoliticization' is nothing more than the gradual erosion of the supremacy of explicit political content in the press and it is not germane to any specific period. One can hardly expect newspapers *not* to change over four decades!

A more detailed analysis of 'depoliticization' can be found in Curran *et al.*'s critique of the 'human interest' story.[36] Specifically, 'common-denominator' content spread across the tabloids

> at the expense of public-affairs coverage. The *Daily Mail* and *Daily Mirror*. . .reduced coverage of political, social and economic affairs during the inter-war period. Most strikingly, the *Daily Mirror* almost halved its public-affairs coverage as a proportion of space in 1937 compared with 1927.
>
> There was no change in the content of *The Times* comparable to that in the *Daily Mail* and the *Daily Mirror* between 1927 and 1937.[37]

A quick reading of the above statements – and of their other similar statements – produces the desired effect: concern over the declining fortunes of the press, the reduction in 'public-affairs' – an élitist concern? – coverage, and the intrusion of the human interest story in unbounded proportions. *Yet the full analysis of the data does not support this view.*

To understand why this should be so, it is necessary to examine two specific weaknesses in Curran *et al.*'s work: the first concerns the years chosen for the analysis; the second, the analysis of the figures themselves.

The years in question

Curran *et al.*'s statements are based on an analysis of figures for the years 1927 and 1937. (These can be found in the report of the 1947 Royal Commission on the Press.) But there are four reasons why these years should not be used as anything more than points on a continuum.

First, 1927 is the first year for which a full set of figures is available. But 1927 is only some thirty years away from the beginnings of the mass circulation press in Britain and so can hardly be justified as a bench mark. It is a point in time.

Second, this period represents the height of the circulation wars and the figures may therefore be a product of this period. Again, it may not be possible, therefore, to use them, and those relating to 1937 in particular, as guidelines.

Third, this period represents the 'flowering' of radio. Though there is much evidence to indicate its increasing popularity *as a news medium*,[38] radio's impact on the popular press has yet to be taken into account when examining this period.

Fourth, it may not be appropriate to use the *Daily Mirror* as a guide. It was originally launched at the turn of the century as a woman's paper and was re-launched in the period 1935–7 in its more working class, non-Conservative mould.

Facts, figures and percentages

Curran *et al.*'s observations emphasize the following:

(i) the *Daily Mail* and the *Daily Mirror.* . . reduced their coverage of political, social and economic affairs during the inter-war period;

Table 4.4 The printed area of the *Daily Mirror* in 1927, 1937 and (for comparison) 1975 changed as follows:[39] (All figures in square inches.)

	Total printed area	
1927	*1937*	*1975*
3170	4240	3952

	Editorial space in 1927, 1937 and 1975	
2124	3138	2490

Editorial space increased by 48% between 1927 and 1937 and subsequently fell between 1937 and 1975 by 21%

The number of square inches taken up by '*news*' in those years were:

634	1145	1107

of which only

101	92	199
(or 16%)	(or 8%)	(or 18%)

was devoted to political, social, and economic news.

(ii)   the *Daily Mirror* almost halved its public affairs coverage as a proportion of space in 1937 compared with 1927;

(iii) other newspapers, that is, *The Times*, fared better.

The data are as shown in Table 4.4 Thus, whereas total editorial space between 1927 and 1937 increased by 48% (from 2124 to 3138 square inches) and the 'news' content of the paper increased by 81% (from 634 to 1145 square inches), the amount of space devoted to public affairs 'news' declined by 9% (from 101 to 92 square inches). Had public affairs 'news' expanded space, it should have taken up 149.5 square inches as against the 92 square inches which it actually took up. It is this sort of calculation which leads Curran *et al.* to conclude that the *Mirror's* coverage was 'halved'.

Two points arise at this stage:

- should the newspaper have changed in arithmetical proportions? A similar analysis for *The Times* belies the nature of the changes implied by Curran *et al.* Whilst its coverage of public affairs 'news' was not comparable to the *Daily Mirror* – the amount of space devoted to such news declined between 1927 and 1937 by 59 square inches or 5% – that decline is one of 19% if one assumes that that content should have expanded in line with the expansion of total editorial space. Admittedly, this decline is not 'comparable to' that in the *Mirror*, but given that *The Times* was 'a newspaper of record' whilst the *Mirror* was a popular newspaper, one can argue that the decline in *The Times'* coverage was more serious.

- Curran *et al.*'s conclusions make much of the *percentage* decreases. In practice, and using square inches as measures, the area of space devoted to public affairs 'news' decreased by some 9 square inches only. The *Mirror* grew in size but the physical space devoted to public affairs news between 1927 and 1937 decreased by very little! Curran *et al.* admit as much in a note to their text to the effect that: 'There was not, however, a corresponding reduction in the space devoted to public affairs due to the *Daily Mirror's* increased size.'[40]

The above discussion focuses on public affairs 'news' and excludes 'features'. 'Features' took up more and more space in daily newspapers as this century progressed. In the case of the *Mirror* the amount of space devoted to 'features' as a proportion of total space increased by some 78% between 1927 and 1937. In 1927 features amounted to some 380 sq. in, in 1937 some 678 sq. ins. (For *The Times*, the increase was a mere 19%.) But the space given over to public affairs features also showed an increase (see Table 4.5).

Table 4.5 Public affairs features as % of total features

1927	1937	1975
3% (or 11.4 sq. in)	4% (or 27 sq. in)	16% (or 126 sq. in)

If one takes news and public affairs features together, then the physical space devoted to them is as follows:

1927	1937	1975
News		
101 sq. in	92 sq. in	199 sq. in
Public affairs features		
11.4 sq. in	27 sq. in	126 sq. in
Total		
112.4 sq. in	119 sq. in	325 sq. in

That is, there is an *actual* increase of some 7 sq. in devoted to news and public affairs features between 1927 and 1937 and a *percentage* increase of 6%! In the case of *The Times*, there is a decrease in total space devoted to public affairs news and features – 1184 sq. in to 1164 sq. in – even though its features space increased enormously by 67%.

From these figures, it is possible to arrive at a number of quite different versions of what changes took place in the years in question. Clearly, changes in the content of newspapers did take place but that is in itself not surprising. Newspapers that do not change are likely to be the exception rather than the rule. Furthermore, there are no logical grounds on which to argue that some changes are more inimical than other changes. In fact, one can plausibly argue that the 1937 *Mirror* reader had just as much public affairs news as was available in 1927. In absolute figures, he/she had more. If one were to include other categories of 'news', such as 'Law, police and accidents' – a category *excluded* from the public affairs one – then the reader would have had access to substantial amounts of information about the outside world.

The actual data are obviously open to continuous analysis. It cannot resolve the problem one way or another because the nature of the problem is itself ill defined. In many respects, impressions of change may be more important than actual data.

Despite the ambiguity of the statistical debate, it is clear that advertisers do play a part in the lives of our media. To suggest, however, that it is the determining role is to ignore the role that the audience itself plays. Without readers, no newspaper can survive; with sufficient readers, and willing advertisers, the chances of survival are greater but the medium still has to prove itself. Unless it does so, it is likely to lose both readers and advertisers. It is this complex environment that decides the fortunes of the media.

4. THE DEMISE OF FLEET STREET: NEW TECHNOLOGY, EDDIE SHAH AND WAPPING

The ownership of newspapers has rarely been seen as either an easy or a sure way of acquiring fortunes. Newspapers have traditionally moved from profitability to loss and vice versa at regular intervals as their costs and revenues – always delicately balanced – have come under attack from a variety of quarters.

Increases in the price of newsprint, increases in wages, a slump in advertising, a decline in classified ads as the rate of unemployment increased, all impact on the newspaper's balance sheets. More significantly, it is not always possible to transfer these increased costs onto the consumers, the newspaper-buying public: newspapers are competitive products and one newspaper's increase in costs can often lead to another newspaper putting on circulation as readers switch titles.

These difficulties have long dogged the newspaper industry. Newspapers are peculiar products in as much as their first copy costs – the cost of producing the issue irrespective of the size of the print run – are so high. Moreover, they have no shelf life.

Consequently, delays in production, printing and distribution cost dearly. But the newspaper industry has also suffered from mismanagement. Managers suffered from a 'congenital disability to understand what its [the newspaper's] purpose *is*..'. Was Fleet St an industry striving for profit only or was it dedicated 'to the public service at the expense of profit'?[41]

One area where mismanagement was legendary was in the production rooms. Traditional methods of newspaper production involved a number of key processes (see Fig. 4.4). A story would be typed by a journalist and then cast into metal, usually lead, by compositors. After correction, the newspaper page would eventually be cast in metal by printers and made ready for the presses to roll. This was a lengthy and labour-intensive (and therefore costly) process. Two other properties of this process caused concern for newspaper organizations. First, the printing unions controlled the process; their powers included the hiring of staff and deciding the level of manning in print rooms. Second, over many decades not only did those print rooms become overmanned but wages were enormously high.

For the unions, the prospect of modernization using the 'new technology' was anathema. The 'new technology' – a term used to describe the computerization of the printing industry using word processors and computer-designed pages as well as the direct input of copy by the journalist into the computer (Fig. 4.4) – would gravely affect employment in the industry as it did away with compositors and printers. For the employers, however, the 'new technology' was a means of re-establishing control over the industry and of driving it into profit. The employers' position had, in fact, long been favoured by analysts. As the 1976 Royal Commission noted, 'the only route to at least temporary salvation [was] the dramatic savings in labour costs that can be achieved with the rational introduction of new technology. . .'.[42] The transformation of the industry would undoubtedly be both costly and painful but it was the only means by which it could ensure a future for itself.

But the enthusiasm so often expressed in favour of change produced little movement within the industry. The unions were always able to exert their control over the industry by, say, threatening to stop production, and the proprietors were never brave enough to withstand significant financial losses. This

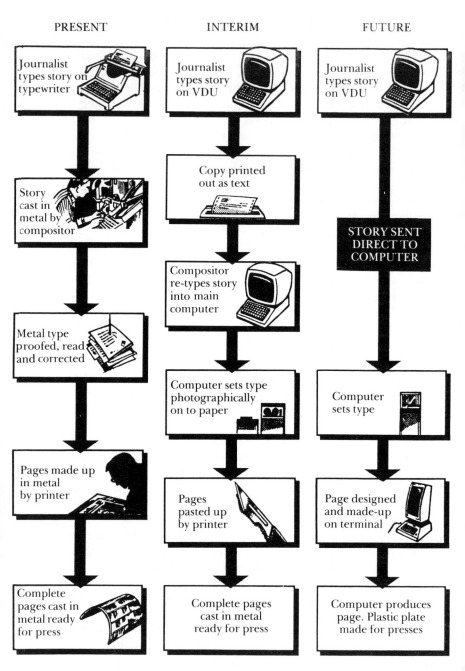

PRESENT	INTERIM	FUTURE
Journalist types story on typewriter	Journalist types story on VDU	Journalist types story on VDU
Story cast in metal by compositor	Copy printed out as text	STORY SENT DIRECT TO COMPUTER
Metal type proofed, read and corrected	Compositor re-types story into main computer	
Pages made up in metal by printer	Computer sets type photographically on to paper	Computer sets type
Complete pages cast in metal ready for press	Pages pasted up by printer	Page designed and made-up on terminal
	Complete pages cast in metal ready for press	Computer produces page. Plastic plate made for presses

Figure 4.4 Saving time and money: how new technology cuts out the middle man. (Reproduced by kind permission of SOGAT 82)

90

impasse was to last until a number of dramatic events changed the face of the industry and markedly reduced the power of the trade unions. The key event was the dispute surrounding the Eddie Shah group of free newspapers and it was resolved with the help of two pieces of trade union legislation introduced in the early 1980s which henceforth placed the trade union movement on the defensive.[43]

Eddie Shah owned a series of local free newspapers in the North. After acquiring a new printing plant on an industrial estate in Warrington, he refused, in effect, to recognize the NGA(the printer's union)'s closed shop and preferred instead to introduce more flexible working arrangements within his organization. What was a local dispute soon became a national concern. The print unions saw this as a direct attack on their members and their traditional working rights; for Shah, it was a matter of being able to print and manage his own organization. The scene was set for confrontation and as these confrontations continued without an end in sight, it became clear that the usual tactics of the unions were not going to work. They could not rely on support from all of their members and the TUC nor could they call out the membership so as to hit other newspapers and so bring indirect pressure to bear on Shah. Both were traditional tactics but now neither could be used because of the Conservative Government's trade union legislation.

Two pieces of legislation were of particular significance: the 1980 and 1982 Employment Acts. According to Goodhart and Wintour, they were drafted with the print unions in mind. Their purpose was to weaken the closed shop and to outlaw secondary picketing. The effect of the Acts 'was to remove legal immunity from almost all forms of industrial action that were not aimed at the worker's immediate employer or related conditions of work'.[44] Also, 'for the first time since 1906 union funds were exposed to the threat of damages claims if official support was given to action which was no longer immune'.[45]

Shah made use of both pieces of legislation to great effect. The NGA was, at one point, fined £150,000; some time later it was fined £375,000 and it had its entire assets of £11m seized. The TUC was never able to offer its full support for fear of challenging the law and a lawfully elected government. Without that support and with mounting costs, the NGA called off a proposed one-day strike. It bowed down to the inevitable defeat and Shah emerged the victor in the 5½-month dispute. The trade union movement as a whole would, in the future, face similar challenges to its powers in other industries.

Shah's victory opened the door to a brave new world in which the proprietors could, once more, manage the industry and bring about the sorts of changes which they had long desired. The more moderate print unions now counselled compromise. After a brief visit to the United States in 1985 to examine the uses of the new technology, SOGAT concluded that

> Opposing technological change is not an option for trade unions in printing – it is simply a rapid road to deunionisation. As a result of new technology there has been a 50% job loss in the US.[46]

As the consequences of the change in union power sank in, the introduction of new processes in the industry became a reality. Shah next embarked on a new project of launching a national daily, *Today*, which would eschew traditional printing practices. Not only was it not based in Fleet Street, but it had a completely computerized process and the paper was being contract printed in satellite centres. Other newspaper organizations sought to follow suit in the hope of modernizing their operation and reducing their labour costs.

But the initial simple desire for change soon took on a more sinister hue when Rupert Murdoch completely switched his printing operation from Fleet Street to Wapping in the East End of London. Murdoch had long planned to move part of his operation to Wapping so as to increase his printing capacity. This had led to a lengthy series of negotiations over the sort of contracts which should bind printers in his new plant.[47] Unknown to the print unions, Murdoch had also embarked on recruiting electricians to work in his plant instead of the traditional printers. The electricians appeared to accept the kind of binding agreements which he had vainly sought from the print unions. In an operation which continues to be a major point of argument, Murdoch sacked his 6,000-plus workers in Fleet Street and re-opened his operation – for legal reasons, under a different organizational name – in Wapping.

The precise details of the methods used by Murdoch to reform Fleet Street are not directly relevant here although they illustrate the bitterness and enmity that pervades the industry. Rather, it is the consequences of these changes that are of significance. These are easily illustrated. After decades when little change had taken place, most – if not all – the newspaper groups have introduced plans to modernize their plants by introducing new technology, reducing manning levels and moving out of central London to the East End.

The effects of the transformation have taken many forms. At one extreme, Murdoch employs a small fraction of the 6,000 production workers he had in Fleet Street. This reduction has forced others to move in a similar direction. The chairman of the *Guardian* and *Manchester Evening News* announced in his 1986 annual report that '*The Times* now has a cost structure much lower than our own. . . we must get our own costs down to their level as soon as possible'.[48] The group has since announced a reduction in staff of one-fifth and it has moved over completely to computer setting and direct input by journalists. The *Telegraph* group, a group in direct competition with both *The Times* and the *Guardian*, has also announced a modernization programme as well as a 50% cut in staff in the composing section. The same story can be repeated for the *FT*, *Observer*, *Mirror* group, *Express* newspapers and the *Mail* group of newspapers.

These reductions in the labour power required to produce newspapers inevitably impact on the cost structures of the media groups concerned. The 1977 Royal Commission on the Press found that for a quality newspaper, production costs accounted for 31% of total costs; the next largest group of costs were attributed to newsprint and ink. Editorial costs were a mere 17% of the total. A popular paper differed from this in that its large circulation ensured that newsprint and ink was its major cost category (36%), followed by production costs (30%) and editorial costs (13%).[49] Whilst it was clearly not possible for news organizations to make many savings in editorial costs since they employ relatively few full-time journalists, they necessarily turned to the production areas. Whether the costs savings are very considerable is hard to say but there have undoubtedly been some savings; what is clear, however, is that costs have been whittled down and that this has had a widespread effect on the production of newspapers in Britain.

What the 'new technology' and the restructuring of Fleet Street have patently not yet done is introduce the variety that had once been optimistically promised. Newspapers remain expensive propositions and the cost of running them until they turn in a profit is immense. Few can afford those sorts of funds: Maxwell was finally forced to close down the *London Daily News* in 1987 in the face of mounting costs. Eddie Shah's *Today*, in many ways the model that inspired many aspirants, illustrated that even a fully computerized newspaper did not guarantee success.

The *Independent*, another new title founded in 1986, also employs comparatively few full-time journalists (200; *Guardian* 170, *Daily Telegraph* 300) and, significantly, it too contracts out its printing. Although its circulation is about 350,000, it appears to be more successful in finding the gap in the market which will ensure its continued survival.

Despite the 'new technology', the organization and ownership of the newspaper industry is little different from what it was in previous decades. Some change has inevitably taken place but it has been less significant than many would have predicted. Nevertheless, it is now clear that newspaper proprietors have successfully exploited the *perception* that there would be an abundance of new titles as a direct outcome of the 'new technology' whilst confidently bringing enormous structural changes to the industry.

In the process, they have also ensured that newspapers continue to remain unregulated yet firmly in the grip of private capital.

Chapter Five

BROADCASTING IN BRITAIN

Contemporary discussions about British broadcasting have, almost inevitably, taken as their starting point the threats the new media pose to a well established public service broadcasting tradition. The new media offer, as it were, a prism through which we are better able to understand the existing structures of broadcasting: the threat makes it easier to appreciate what will vanish as well as what will come about. The often mentioned 'crisis' in British broadcasting – 'crisis', in Gouldner's phrase, being that the system 'may, relatively soon, become something quite different than it has been'[1] – thus acts as a backdrop for numerous contemporary analyses of broadcasting.

It is unfortunate, however, that the 'crisis' is so often seen in negative terms. A changed environment also offers new opportunities. Yet discussions of the threat to public service broadcasting have ignored not only the potential for change but also the deficiencies of the existing system which would make us question its benefits and its claim to permanence. It is as if all plans for radical reform (and it must be remembered that the new media bring about substantial structural reforms to broadcasting) cannot be contemplated; although, in fact, what *is* missing is a coherent argument *for* the preservation of the existing system. As we shall see later in this chapter, the case for the status quo is perhaps too general and too romantic in its assessment of the value of the existing structures.

One cannot deny that there are real threats to British broadcasting but, at the same time, it would be a mistake to label all threats as a 'crisis'. The main argument running through this chapter and the next is that there have always been, and will always be, threats to broadcasting organizations and, more generally, broadcasting structures. Technological developments and social, political, and economic changes inevitably force the broadcasting organizations to adapt to new and continually changing circumstances. Few would now see the introduction of commercial television in 1955 as the threat envisaged by, say, Lord Reith. Similarly, in twenty years' time, the threat of the new media may prove to be no more than a means for liberating the viewer from the duopoly's straightjacket. It is difficult, therefore, to be dogmatic about the prospects for change; one can only set out the patterns or trends which may come about.

A discussion of these trends will form the basis of the final section in this chapter (and Chapter 10). Section 1 will explore the essential features of the British broadcasting structures and the ways in which these are organized and regulated; Section 2 deals with the concept of public service broadcasting; Section 3 explores the financial problems of the BBC as a way of introducing the current proposals for changing the structure of British broadcasting and the final section; the final section, Section 4, looks at these proposals in the context of the development and organization of Channel Four. The next chapter, Chapter 6, returns to the subject of British broadcasting and outlines, in detail, the historical relationship between broadcasting and politics and the nature, and extent, of political control over broadcasting.

1. THE DEVELOPMENT OF BRITISH BROADCASTING

The decision of the Post Office to set up the British Broadcasting Company in 1922 as a co-operative of radio set manufacturers was an attempt to overcome a series of essentially technical and organizational problems: the need to satisfy set manufacturers by ensuring that all participated in the birth and development of broadcasting, the need to avoid chaos on the airwaves on the American scale, and the need to guarantee an efficient and satisfactory service to all listeners. It was only later that the company came to acquire a social and political direction; in its inception it was an 'expedient solution to a technical problem'.[2]

One distinctive element in this particular solution was the decision to finance the service out of a licence fee payable by all those in possession of radio sets rather than some form of advertising revenue. In this way, the company was guaranteed a yearly income and it could thus pursue a programme policy that was developed with little regard for the wishes of the audience.

This approach to the role of broadcasting in British society was more than matched by authoritative official interpretations of its duties. Radio, many argued, was a scarce national resource and should therefore be developed, and regulated, in the interests of the nation. As the Crawford Committee recommended in 1926, 'the broadcasting service should be conducted by a public corporation acting as Trustee for the national interest and its status and duties should correspond with those of a public service'.[3] It is here that one can trace the foundations of public service broadcasting with its emphasis on public duty, on providing for all and on informing, educating, and not simply entertaining. John Reith's part, both in his capacity as the company's managing director and as the director general of the corporation, in the creation of this ideal model of public service broadcasting, has been amply documented and he was undoubtedly able to exploit such thinking in a way not equalled elsewhere or since.

For the politicians, and for those in charge of broadcasting, the problem was how to reconcile the need for accountability on the part of the broadcasters with their need for a maximum degree of autonomy so as to be able to carry out their work without undue political or other constraints. The 'solution' was to delegate power to a broadcasting authority to run the service along the lines decreed by Parliament. This would ensure that the broadcasting institution was ultimately accountable to Parliament but at the same time would free it from direct government control in its day-to-day affairs. The authority, 'a body of people acting as trustees for the public interest',[4] does not however exercise executive control over broadcasting. In theory, and to some extent in practice, it does act as a means of distancing broadcasting from government. This arrangement was used for the BBC (the corporation) in 1927 when it was set up under Royal Charter, and for the commercial broadcasting sector from 1954 onwards.

Thus, the governors of the BBC – who are constitutionally the BBC – have to ensure that it is run in the public interest; they also have to review its work. In the past, this has involved both reprimanding the broadcasters and offering them support, particularly when under attack from outsiders. This dual role, which is also part of the Independent Broadcasting Authority (IBA)'s work, contains glaring contradictions. Since both bodies are appointed by, or on the advice of, government they have come to be seen by some as a buffer between the state and the broadcasters but by others as an indirect mechanism by which the state can exert control over broadcasting. The membership and strengths or weaknesses of these two authorities, as well as their working relationships with those in executive control of broadcasting, have obvious and significant repercussions for broadcasters and their autonomy. The regulatory structure of British broadcasting is set out in Fig. 5.1.

The state's ultimate authority over broadcasting exemplifies one of the deficiencies of public service broadcasting, though, paradoxically, John Reith, the BBC's first managing director/director general, would not have been able to develop the BBC as he did had he not had the full support of the state. His vision of broadcasting was based on four major principles:

1. assured sources of funding
2. the brute force of monopoly
3. the public service motive
4. a sense of moral obligation

These principles enabled him to develop the BBC as an instrument for the achievement of excellence and for the delivery of the 'best of everything'. As the BBC's funding was 'assured', it could pursue quality in programming without concerning itself with the needs of the public for, say, popular entertainment. Furthermore, the monopoly guaranteed the success of that particular policy of providing education, information and entertainment: the BBC had total control over broadcasting output in Britain.

But none of these principles could have been exploited or pursued in the ways in which they were had there not been tacit approval and support on the part of the state. When faced with threats to its broadcasting monopoly or to its programme policy from, say, either wireless exchanges (the precursors of today's cable systems) or overseas commercial radio stations, it was only natural that Reith would turn to the state to guarantee the monopoly.[5]

This dependence on the state was well appreciated by Reith. Though it created problems in times of political crisis, it was the price one had to pay for pursuing high ideals. With domestic

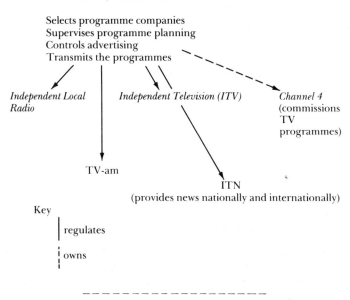

Independent Broadcasting Authority

Members:
Chairman, Deputy, 10 members (appointed by Home Secretary)

Functions of the IBA

Selects programme companies
Supervises programme planning
Controls advertising
Transmits the programmes

Independent Local Radio

Independent Television (ITV)

Channel 4 (commissions TV programmes)

TV-am

ITN
(provides news nationally and internationally)

Key

| regulates

┊ owns

British Broadcasting Corporation

Board of Governors:

Chairman, Vice-Chair and 12 (max) Members (appointed by Home Sec.)

Board of Management:

Director-General, Deputy Director General, Managing Directors – Network Radio, Network Television, Regional Broadcasting, External Services; Directors – Engineering, Personnel, Finance, Corporate Affairs.

Figure 5.1 Regulating terrestrial broadcasting in Britain

competition effectively prohibited, the BBC became the main national instrument of broadcasting in Britain. According to Tom Burns, Reith developed it into:

A kind of domestic diplomatic service, representing the British – or what he saw as the best of the British – to the British. BBC culture, like BBC standard English, was not peculiar to itself but an intellectual ambience composed out of the values, standards and beliefs of the professional middle class, especially that part educated at Oxford and Cambridge.[6]

The principles of public service broadcasting were also incorporated into the development of the BBC's television service after the Second World War. It took root, and remained intact, despite considerable public and commercial dissatisfaction with the monopoly in broadcasting. Attempts to introduce alternatives in broadcasting had always, for one reason or another, met with failure but the election of a Conservative Government in 1951 saw the start of a concerted campaign in favour of commercial television.[7] After considerable lobbying, the Television Act was passed in 1954 and this set up the Independent Television Authority (ITA) to supervise a federal structure of commercially funded television companies, each serving a different region or market. To offset the allegedly harmful effects of relying on major advertisers or of sponsors dictating programme content, a system of spot advertising was introduced. This intervention was seen as a way of minimizing the harmful and the more undesirable side-effects of commercially funded media.

Funding ITV as an advertising supported channel had one other important advantage: it brought into existence an institution which was not in direct competition with the BBC for revenue. Each had their separate sources of funding and, as a result, would not necessarily have to chase the largest audience nor produce lowest common denominator programmes so as to please as many as possible. Direct competition for funding was, after all, the major weakness of the competitive American broadcasting system and the British solution overcame it. Each broadcasting organization could henceforth pursue its programme policies without fear of a direct challenge to its sources of revenue. The competition would be in terms of programming and not straightforward commercial terms.

It soon became obvious, however, that the introduction of

commercial television indirectly threatened the position and security of the BBC. The immediate popularity and novelty of ITV's programmes forced the BBC to review its output and made it aware of the need to survive in an increasingly competitive environment. While the BBC had remained a monopoly, television viewers had no programme choices nor, for that matter, could there be any argument as to which institution ought to be allocated the revenue obtained from the licence fee. Independent Television undermined the BBC's historical sense of privilege and security: with less than 30% of the national audience – it went down to 27% in the 1950s – the BBC's position as the main instrument of broadcasting was clearly threatened, as were its claims to the full licence fee. The competitive threat led the BBC to reassess its broadcasting strategy and it began to respond more positively to the requirements of the audience. Since the early 1960s, the BBC has therefore aimed to reach a 50% share of the total audience as a means of supporting its claim to the licence fee and of ensuring its continued survival.

With the two institutions in competition for the audience, their policies converged towards the demands of the audience. The process of competition has, to some extent, eroded the differences between the commercial and the publicly funded television services. One consequence of this has been that further additions to the existing radio and television services would become deeply contested as efforts were made to detach them from the duopoly. As the case study of Channel Four (see below) amply demonstrates, concerned groups and individuals attempted to keep these services out of the competitive struggle between the two giants of broadcasting in the hope that they would be better able to serve previously excluded minority groups in society.

Though some of the effects of competition, particularly on the BBC, were beneficial, others were not. The process of competition stretched the finite resources of the BBC and was to highlight one of the major differences between the two organizations. Whilst commercial television could meet its costs out of a pool of advertising revenue that was continually growing, the BBC had to meet its costs out of a licence fee that was, at best, inadequate. Prior to 1988, the BBC's licence fee was set every three years at a level that was mid-way between what the BBC wanted and what politicians thought was electorally acceptable. Because that level was set by the government, the licence fee was too often seen as a political issue and a source of political pressure. Following a recommendation of the Peacock Inquiry[8] (see below, pp. 107–11) the Thatcher Government agreed that from 1988 the licence fee would be increased annually in line with the rate of inflation. This would not only reduce its political significance but it would allow for yearly increases (though broadcasters have been quick to point out that the general rate of inflation is below the industry's rate and so an increase would still leave a shortfall which can only be made up by savings). So, although there have been moves to improve the BBC's financial plight the essential character of the inequalities inherent in the broadcasting system remains.

From the 1960s onwards, the British broadcasting system began to change. At first that change was gradual but it soon accelerated. In 1963, the BBC was allocated a second TV channel (BBC 2) and by the end of the decade there were also a large number of local, commercial, and non-commercial, radio stations. In addition to these structural changes – and they were to continue in the 1970s and 1980s with Channel Four and TV-am, to say nothing of cable systems and satelite broadcasting – the underlying philosophy of broadcasting was being increasingly and powerfully challenged.

It is possible to identify three processes at work during this period of transition from a minimal system of broadcasting to a more expansive one. First, the structural changes identified above were acknowledgements of the heterogenous nature of the national audience and, in themselves, transformed the broadcasting institutions into vehicles to serve and exploit different sections of it. BBC 2 was, for example, a 'highbrow' service; Community Radio is aimed at distinct ethnic groups, and pop music radio stations at the burgeoning youth market. Second, technological advances have made it possible to provide many more, and different, broadcasting facilities. Finally, under the Thatcher Government, there has been a sustained ideological and political attack on the pillars of public service broadcasting. Not only has there been a serious questioning of the principle of the licence fee,[9] but there has also been a reassessment of the idea of scarcity in the airwaves, the idea of equality of service to all, and of the need for regulations.[10] The idea of a national public service paid for by the community is under attack from those who favour the concept of 'consumer sovereignty' and subscription ('pay-per-view') television. The combination of these influences has encouraged the opening up of the airwaves to competition.

Each of these three processes has contributed something to the changing broadcasting scene. Just as the first two processes have led to the gradual expansion of the broadcasting scene, the last, and most critical, process is aimed at a complete reappraisal of the role of broadcasting, and the broadcasting organizations, in British society. The effects of this can be seen both in the current major reviews of BBC funding and in discussions over the future of Channel Four.

2. 'PUBLIC SERVICE BROADCASTING' AND THE DUTIES OF THE BROADCASTERS

The difficulties inherent in creating a successful broadcasting structure are immense. For although one might be able to construct an elaborate system of control and accountability, there is never any guarantee that such a system would produce programmes of a high quality. Regulatory frameworks and obligations do not in themselves translate into good programming. Yet, Britain has been fortunate in benefiting from a healthy, successful and much envied system of broadcasting. What explains the successful evolution of this system?

A key consideration here is undoubtedly Reith's direction. The four pillars of broadcasting − assured finance, brute force of monopoly, sense of moral obligation, and public service motive − combined to direct broadcasting to reach the highest of ideals.

In due course, attempts were made to specify more precisely what made British broadcasting unique. One could point to facets of the system and to the ideal of public service broadcasting, but somehow the whole defied adequate description. The Pilkington Committee[11] was reduced to observing that 'good broadcasting is a practice, not a prescription' and even the Peacock Committee felt confident in stating that 'there was no simple dictionary definition of [public service broadcasting]'. It too was reduced to quoting the Pilkington Committee's view that 'though standards exist and are recognisable, broadcasting is more nearly an art than an exact science. It deals in tastes and values and is not precisely definable'.[12]

Given the lack of precision, it would not be too far fetched to claim that there is an element of post hoc rationalization in some of the definitions of the public service broadcasting notion. What is clear, however, is that the ideal of public service broadcasting has combined with the imposed statutory obligations on the broadcasters to produce a system of broadcasting which has proved itself over many decades.

These obligations are derived from the relevant statutory instruments which established the broadcasting organizations: the IBA Act for Independent Television and the Royal Charter for the BBC.

In practice, the authorities responsible for broadcasting – the governors of the BBC and the members of the IBA – oversee their respective organizations and ensure that certain statutory obligations are met. The most often quoted obligations deal with the nature of the service and the need to ensure that content is impartial.

> Each Authority has a duty to provide its respective radio and television services as public services for the dissemination of information, education and entertainment, and to ensure that its programmes maintain a high general standard, in particular as respects their quality and content, and a proper balance and wide range of subject matter. . . .[13]

> The BBC must ensure that. . .due impartiality is preserved in news programmes. . .[14]

> The IBA must ensure that a sufficient amount of time in the programmes is given to news and news features and that all news given in the programmes . . . is presented with due accuracy and impartiality.[15]

Other regulations deal with such things as questions of public taste and decency, the proportion of foreign programmes permitted on air and the extent of permissible foreign ownership in British commercial television (and radio) companies. (Many of these 'public service' obligations do not apply to the new media (see Chapter 10). In that sense, the new media present a fundamental departure from the practices, as well as the spirit, of public service broadcasting.)

Although the authorities are directly in charge of broadcasting, governments are not without considerable powers over broadcasting. Ultimately, the broadcasting services operate within the broad regulatory and structural decisions made by governments. Such decisions would include how many channels exist, how they will be funded, who will run them, what sort of cable systems will be built, what radio structures will exist and so on. Other contemporary 'strategic' decisions include the Green Paper on Radio (1986/7), the proposed White Paper on broadcasting (1988) and, from 1987, the Conservative Government's intention to raise the percentage of independent productions broadcast by the existing organizations to 25%.

Governments have it within their powers 'to exercise some general control in the national interest over the total financial resources available for broadcasting'[16] though these powers do not extend to regulating expenditure on programmes. Until the very recent past governments would also set the level of the licence fee. Although this will now be index-linked to the rate of inflation, it was the government which finally decided the base figure (£65). Governments can also direct the IBA on establishing and managing reserve funds, set the 'levy' paid by ITV companies, and request annual reports from the broadcasting authorities.

To these powers, one must add the power to appoint governors (BBC) and members (IBA) of the authorities, and in the context of programmes, the government's power of veto over programmes. Governments are also often drawn into disputes about matters of public taste and decency.

The combination of these legislative acts, governmental powers, and regulatory oversight makes British broadcasting a heavily regulated system of broadcasting. But within this regulatory system, one also finds the basis of the idea of public service broadcasting. It is as if the legislative and regulatory shell has protected and encouraged the growth of a complex philosophy of broadcasting. According to the Broadcasting Research Unit, there are eight principles of 'public service broadcasting'. These are:

- geographic universality – everyone should have access to the same services;
- catering for all interests and tastes;
- catering for minorities;
- catering for 'national identity and community';
- detachment from vested interests and government;
- one broadcasting system to be funded directly from the corpus of users;

- competition in good programming rather than for numbers; and
- guidelines to liberate programme makers and not to restrict them.[17]

This list represents a normative, desirable combination of all the good things which one would like broadcasting organizations to do. But it is not clear from the list, or indeed the document itself, whether it relates to some real organization, namely the BBC, or to some underlying philosophy which such an organization is identified with. For if it relates to the BBC *per se* then it conveniently overlooks its seedier and more questionable aspects, whilst if it relates to some imaginary institution it ignores the real pressures on institutions which make them somehow less ideal than one would desire.

That there is a real disjunction between what the ideal institution ought to do and what it does can be seen in yet another attempt to describe the BBC as the ideal typical 'public service' institution. In a volume titled, perhaps significantly, *The BBC and Public Service Broadcasting*, Krishnan Kumar emphasized its duty to create and extend a 'national broadcasting culture'. Public service broadcasting ought to provide a 'daily service that is continuously and throughout infused with a sense of its public function'. That is, 'serving the public as a living audience with potential for growth and development'. Such a conception should embrace a whole range of programmes and contents from Shakespeare to *Minder*, for 'without such breadth public service broadcasting can become élitist and authoritarian'.[18]

Paradoxically, his subsequent statements do, in fact, make his conception élitist and authoritarian: Shakespeare and *Minder* are to be applauded but *Dallas*, *Dynasty* and quiz shows are to be decried because they 'show a contempt for the audience, not simply as it is but also as it might be..'.[19] Yet there is no cultural measure which allows one to distinguish between these types of programmes; similar criticisms can be levelled against both *Minder* and *Dallas* and this makes it difficult to accept Kumar's position in its entirety. His argument is further weakened when he seeks to defend the very institution that does bring us *Dynasty*, *Dallas* and *Blankety Blank*! His conception of the ideal institution is clearly at variance with the real competitive environment in which the BBC exists and from which it draws its sustenance.

These contradictions reflect the impossibility of condensing a series of traditional practices and guidelines based on a wealth of cultural history into a set of universally meaningful statements. Britain has been particularly fortunate in acquiring the sorts of institutions which she did acquire. There are obviously many reasons for the conjunction of forces which produced its institutions and these must include the Reithian spirit (described above), a political system secure enough to grant broadcasting a relatively free hand and the absence (or the negation!) of deep social divisions.

Finally, and this returns us to Kumar's statements, it is unlikely that with the elimination of the scarcity of resources – and this made cultural direction incredibly simple – and the internationalization of media productions a nation can ever maintain its defensive walls unbreached. But a breach in the wall *à la* ITV or even *Dallas* does not in itself destroy the fundamental nature of the existing system; it may contain within it forces which threaten it but a well established and respected institution such as the BBC ought to be able to adapt to change. Its ability to adapt is, however, inextricably bound up with its financial underpinnings and, as the next section points out, these do not provide very secure foundations for facing the future.

3. THE FINANCIAL PLIGHT OF THE BBC

The evolution of British broadcasting has demonstrated an ingenious method by which to avoid direct competition *for revenue* between organizations. The ITV companies rely on advertising revenue for their funds, while the BBC is funded out of the licence fee which must be paid by all those who possess a television receiver. In this way, neither institution seeks to undermine its rival since there are no financial incentives to do so; it is not a competitive market-place. Similarly, although there is competition for the viewer this does not usually impact on the financial fortunes of either organization. Clearly, if there were substantial losses of audiences, advertisers and licence payers would object since this would indicate that neither institution was properly serving the audience. However, by and large, the audience split between the commercial and non-commercial sectors has been in the 40:60 ratio (or vice versa) and, therefore, within acceptable limits.

For the commercial sector, advertising revenue has represented an ever-growing pool of funds. Unfortunately, this cannot be said of the licence fee. Whilst the BBC was a monopoly organization, the licence fee was an adequate source of revenue. The BBC could plan ahead and not concern itself with chasing large audiences since its funds were guaranteed. When the monochrome television licence fee was supplemented by the transition to the more expensive colour television licence fee in the 1970s, the BBC's funds remained buoyant. In more recent times, however, this has ceased to be the case. The real value of the licence fee has grown at a relatively slow pace and has never quite caught up with the rate of inflation. Thus, with a rate of inflation averaging 4% in the 1980s, the £58 licence fee set in 1985 would have had to increase by £7 by 1988 if it were to keep up with the increase in the general price level only.[20] But broadcasting costs are more volatile than other costs and also rise at a faster rate so that even a licence fee increase which keeps up with general costs is an actual real decrease in its total value.

The financial difficulties of the BBC can also be observed in the following data. (NB In practice, these figures are adjusted and are estimates of revenues.) In the year ending March 1985, the revenue of the BBC was £723m, of which £555m went towards television and the rest (£220m) to radio. ITV's revenue in the year ending January 1986 was £1056.9m. Of this, some £934.8m was spent on programme services (£709.3m) and Channel Four subscriptions (£168m). In effect, ITV's expenditure on its television services easily exceeds the BBC's expenditure on its television services. In the early 1970s, the differences in expenditure were insignificant but by the mid-1980s, ITV was spending over one-and-a-half times more on its television services than the BBC.[21]

Nevertheless, and despite these perennial financial difficulties, the BBC – and countless others – have continued to argue in favour of the licence fee. However, the continuing and, to some, insoluble, problem of the licence fee and the advent of new means of television distribution – satellite television, cable television – and different ways of paying for those services – subscription, sponsorship, advertising or pay-per-view – significantly alter the parameters of British broadcasting. There is now room for a radical rethink of the foundations of British broadcasting.

For economic libertarians, the starting point for such a reform is the licence fee itself which they have long regarded as an outdated imposition on the public and a regressive tax to boot.[22] (See also pp. 00–00.) Others, most notably the members of the Peacock Committee on Financing the BBC (1986), have seen the question of the licence fee as a small, but key, part of the much needed review of British broadcasting. As the Peacock Committee observed,

> practices widely accepted during one decade may become quite inappropriate in the next, in which different social conditions may prevail and different technological considerations apply. No political decision. . .can be right for all time. It must be reviewed in the light of changing circumstances.[23]

> Given the current technical framework and the likely developments in the future, how can British broadcasting be financed in such a way as to bring the greatest enjoyment and pleasure to as many viewers and listeners as possible while at the same time fulfilling the public service obligation?[24]

This broad philosophical sweep led the Committee to consider the following areas:

- to assess the effects of the introduction of advertising or sponsorship on the BBC
- to identify a range of options for the introduction of advertising or sponsorship
- to consider proposals for securing income from the consumer other than through the licence fee.

In short, to explore ways by which the BBC could pull itself out of the on-going financial crisis but, at the same time, to maintain the quality of the product.

The Peacock Committee was convinced that it was no longer possible to recommend 'no change' to either the licence fee system or the funding structure of broadcasting as a whole; the differences between the two sources of revenue would create recurring crises for the BBC and put it at a competitive disadvantage compared to the ITV structure. The effects of new systems of signal delivery on British broadcasting could also not be ignored.

Although the Committee recommended that the BBC should not

accept advertising on its television channels on the grounds that it would not be a satisfactory long-term solution to the impending restructuring of broadcasting, it made a number of significant proposals which would have the effect of recreating broadcasting as a market of consumers and producers. Viewers would pay for what they watched. Such a system of financing broadcasting would ensure that the public exercised a choice over what it watched and expressed its preferences through direct payments. No longer would a viewer pay for what he/she did not watch or for a service which he/she did not use.

The philosophical underpinnings of Peacock's thinking are discussed elsewhere; suffice it to say in this present context that such a method of financing broadcasting would completely change the face of British broadcasting by redefining the nature and duties of the broadcasting organizations. The 'public service' ideal would no longer apply across the whole of each service though the public would be 'better' served by exercising real economic choices.

For Peacock, then, the problem with the licence fee is only part of the difficulty which broadcasters will experience in the future. A temporary solution is not a satisfactory one since it does not confront the broader pattern of changes which the new media bring in their wake. What is required, and what Peacock presented, was a thorough review of all the possible changes *including changes to the commercial television sector* which could be introduced in the future without having an *a priori* commitment to the status quo.

Peacock's recommendations have not been extensively supported. Critics of the Peacock Committee have been happier to work within a framework of change that is more limited than that envisaged by the Committee. In other words, they view the future as involving little radical change; in this latter scenario it is possible to foresee a situation in which the existing broadcasting organizations continue to operate effectively and efficiently, albeit with some modifications.

At the time of writing, moves towards the greater 'liberalization' of broadcasting are in fact gaining governmental support. The Government's Green Paper on the development of radio proposes the creation of national commercial competition for the BBC and also the creation of a new regulatory body to supervise these developments in commercial and community radio. Like the Cable Authority, this new radio body will exercise a 'light regulatory touch'. It will thus undermine much of the valuable work done by the IBA (and the BBC) to ensure that radio is in tune with public needs.

The Government is pursuing a similar line of developments in television. With proposals for a fifth terrestrial channel currently being studied and a variety of plans to introduce pay-TV under consideration, the Government is clearly embarking on a policy of opening up the airwaves. Not only will the BBC be under 'attack', but the ITV network is no longer immune from the competitive urge which the Government wishes upon us all. Its proposed White Paper on television will likely herald a new era in British broadcasting.

Despite the conflicting views about the nature and speed of future change, the concept of 'public service broadcasting' will continue to haunt its supporters and advocates. For those in charge of the BBC and the ITV companies, the real (and ideal) meaning of the concept will continue to be tempered by the competitive environment in which their organizations seek to survive. In practice, Shakespeare will sit alongside *Dallas*, and *Minder* alongside *Blankety Blank*, as different audiences make choices from a standard menu of 'information, education and entertainment'. However, the danger is that in a newly created, lightly regulated, competitive environment it will become increasingly difficult to justify the mixed menu currently available. Not only will the specialist interest programme go but so too will the minority programmes so carefully nurtured by organizations seeking to satisfy a broad spectrum of interests and groups.

Channel Four: 'better by design'

It is impossible to understand the significance of Channel Four if one has no comprehension of the context in which it developed. Similarly, it is not easy to appreciate its uniqueness without some knowledge of its structure. Without doubt, it is probably the most novel and most different television service in the world. How did it come about and what does the future hold for it?

Discussions about the allocation of the 'fourth channel' – the last available national off-air broadcasting channel for Britain – began in the early 1970s. That this 'fourth channel' was the last available national channel transformed it into a very valuable national resource and, consequently, there has always been some concern lest one make a terrible 'mistake' in allocating it to some unworthy body or organization. If these fears were likely to prolong the discussions over its future, the socio-political context of its development made the whole affair even more complex. One aspect of this broader context was the perception that British society had undergone momentous change during the 1960s and 1970s and that, as a result, the 'fourth channel' ought to be able to reflect, and comment, upon those changes. As the Annan Committee on the Future of Broadcasting put it,

> the new vision of life (from the 1960s onwards) reflected divisions within society, divisions between classes, the generations and the sexes, between north and south, between the provinces and London, between pragmatists and ideologues. . . .[25]

This catalogue of divisions, the 'erosion of cohesion and unity'[26] and the questioning of society which it gave rise to were now important features of the British scene. The 'ideals of middle class culture'[27] which had informed British broadcasting in the past seemed at odds with a divided Britain.

Other commentators also remarked on these changes. Asa Briggs, the historian of British broadcasting, has noted how changes in society – and trends such as professionalization and unionization in the BBC – have made 'governing the BBC'[28] more difficult in the 1970s than at any other period. This view was echoed by a BBC director general, Alasdair Milne, who remarked that the prescriptions for broadcasting set out in previous eras – even only a matter of a decade or so ago – were of little value in a rapidly changing social and political environment.[29]

In this new climate, 'balance', 'impartiality', and 'objectivity' were rather inadequate practices. They failed to reflect the political spectrum in its entirety and they tended to exclude or denigrate all those who strayed outside the centre of the political stage. They were also too crude to cope with the complexity of contemporary life in Britain. The notion of balance, for example, was too narrow to explore divergent opinions and subtleties: it necessarily divided and exaggerated differences for the sake of political television.

The changes – as well as the perception of change – in the socio-political environment, together with the criticisms of broadcasting practices, highlighted the rather difficult positions which the broadcasting organizations had come to occupy. They remained in control over the means of mass communications but those whose work or views they had long ignored were now clamouring for access. The artist resented the duopoly and its restricted, middle-of-the-road media fare; the politician objected to the continued emphasis on a vanished consensus; the moral entrepreneur objected to its irreverence and irresponsibility, and the political activist resented the narrowness of its political outlook. But the institutions of the 1970s were too rigidly set within the competing duopoly (BBC1 + BBC2 = ITV) to be able to meet fully the demands made upon them. Nor were they able to serve new needs in radically different ways. Television was still too scarce a resource – and politically and commercially too important – to be granted the freedom to exploit the richness and diversity of contemporary life.

To create new vehicles of communication in this context meant creating a system of broadcasting which could survive outside the duopoly yet one which would not fundamentally damage the ecology of the system. It is this development which made Channel Four so special and which continues to demonstrate the possibility of encouraging differences through imaginative regulatory and funding mechanisms.

During the ten or so years leading up to the inauguration of Channel Four in 1982 many proposals were considered but there seemed to be a degree of agreement amongst those favouring a novel form of organization that allocating the 'fourth channel' to the commercial sector would only

> complete the symmetrical straitjacket of broadcasting in Britain and continue it forever: two public institutions would each supervise two channels and they would compete, two by two, for parallel audiences in perpetuity.[30]

By and large, these criticisms were widely accepted and so efforts were directed to making this channel one which would allow for diversity, for new ideas and for experimentation. In the event, the 1980 Broadcasting Act allocated the fourth channel to the IBA in preference to creating a new authority specifically to run this channel.

However, the IBA would not run Channel Four as a franchise in the same way as it ran the other regional companies, but would instead own it. Furthermore, it had to regulate it in such a way as to ensure that it would 'contain a suitable proportion of matter calculated to appeal to tastes and interests not generally catered for by Service 1 (i.e. ITV 1)'.[31] Unlike ITV, Channel Four would not seek to serve the vast audience but would have to satisfy parts of the audience at various times during the week. Another difference from the ITV companies was that Channel Four would not itself make programmes but would commission them from other sources. Its output would come from independent producers, regional ITV companies, ITN, and foreign sources.

Channel Four's funding structure was, perhaps, the most radical feature of the service. It was funded by the existing television companies through a system of subscriptions. In return, the commercial television companies would sell the advertising time on Channel Four in their own regions and retain the revenue. This method of funding insulates Channel Four from direct pressures from advertisers in search of large audiences and it protects the ITV companies from a direct assault on their own sources of revenue.

On paper then, the structure of Channel Four is both intricate and ingenious. In practice, one problem has persisted: can a national television service aimed at minorities – the 'tastes and interests not generally catered for' – exist in the commercial sector? Since the size of the audience is critical for a commercial medium, would there be sufficient viewers and enough advertising revenue to justify the channel both culturally and financially?

After five years in operation, Channel Four has proved itself on both counts. It has reached the viewers and, perhaps more importantly, its success has guaranteed its subscribers, the ITV companies, more than enough revenue to match their subscriptions to the service.

Despite, or perhaps because of, these successes Channel Four is also under scrutiny from the ideologues and reformers. During the review of broadcasting which began with the Peacock Committee, one proposal for Channel Four has been under constant discussion. That proposal has a number of different themes to it; briefly, Channel Four would be floated off from the IBA and would then be franchised as any other ITV company. In this new form, it would be independent of the ITV companies and it would sell its own advertising air-time for its revenue. This change would also break the ITV companies' monopoly over advertising revenue (a change much favoured by the Peacock Committee and advertisers, amongst others).

The one major drawback with this proposal to 'give Channel Four its freedom' is that it would make it compete with the existing ITV companies. Whether it would be able to survive in the new, more competitive, environment and obtain as much advertising revenue as it does now is far from clear. Opinion is divided over whether it would benefit financially from such an arrangement. Equally important is the effect of this 'flotation' on Channel Four's original remit to serve minorities. Could that remain intact as the channel strives to keep advertisers happy?[32]

As with all other proposed changes for broadcasting, the details of the Thatcher Government's reforming zeal are as yet unknown. The White Paper will clarify many of these issues and will give a good idea as to how the viewer will fare in the next decade. What is certain is that the 'no change' option will not be high on the list.

SUMMARY

The strongest theme in the above discussion is that of constant change. In recent years that change has clearly accelerated; indeed, the technological threat has made it even more important to plan ahead and to plan for radical change. But technological change alone cannot explain the many strategies for reform which the Thatcher Government has inspired. Although the threats to the BBC may have been ideologically motivated, a different sort of explanation is required for the current review of the commercial television sector. One possible explanation for the interest in reforming the commercial sector may be the Thatcher Government's desire to break the trade unions' 'hold' on the industry. By forcing the companies to reform their practices and structures, the Government is also forcing them to deal directly with the role of the unions in the ITV sector. The parallels with developments in the print industry (see pp. 91–3) are clear for all to see.

Whether the outcome of all these changes will be a 'better' broadcasting system is impossible to tell. Public service broadcasting probably cannot survive in the market-place and it therefore needs financial, political, and cultural support. If those no longer exist, its own future is at risk. In which case, the British public may look back on the era of scarcity as a golden age of broadcasting.

Chapter Six

THE POLITICS OF BROADCASTING: 'LIBERTY ON PAROLE'

Television is now probably the single most important medium for the communication of political information. For many, it is the crucial source of information about the outside world. But its importance also derives from its role in industrial societies. Unlike many other institutions, television is implicated in processes of change: it is both the creator and the product of change in society. In the field of politics, its treatment and coverage of conflict, elections, or nuclear energy has had enormous consequences for political organization and behaviour. Similarly its treatment of social issues has provoked many questions about its role in creating, and not merely reflecting, a changing society.

The growing awareness of the nature of the television medium and its far-reaching, if unquantifiable, effects has contributed to a major reassessment of its work and location within the political system. Television's output has ceased to be a 'mirror' of society; a subtler view sees it as a

> heavily selected interpretation of events, one which structures reality for us, which shapes and frames a world for us to inhabit and accept as real and legitimated, one which sets the agenda within which. . . we are led to discuss the terms of our lives.[1]

By raising these issues, it has become possible to see television as one of the core political and ideological institutions in any society. It has also opened the way to a fuller analysis of its work: an analysis of its agenda-setting function, its part in re-enforcing cultural norms and, most crucially, its work in relation 'to those who rule dominant institutions. . .'.[2] But if the broadcast media are not reflecting some already achieved consensus, or given 'reality', but tend to select and reproduce those definitions of 'reality' which favour and legitimate existing structures in society, then their work is part of a wider process of legitimation and consensus formation.

This major reconceptualization of the role of television has made its political output, that is, mainly news and current affairs programmes, a highly controversial and contested area. It has raised questions about television's capacity and willingness accurately to reflect the wide range of views present in contemporary Britain; instead, it has highlighted its prior commitment, and allegiance, to a specific political perspective and its treatment of all political issues from *within* the ideological framework of a liberal democratic policy.

One effect of this analysis has been to shift attention away from specific fields of enquiry and to a closer examination of the location of the broadcasting institutions in the political system. A central issue here is the relationship of the broadcasting institutions to the state and the ways in which this sets real limits to the work and autonomy of the broadcasters. As was argued in Chapter 5, the institutions of broadcasting are in a position of dependence on the state. The institutions of the state, after all, created the structures of broadcasting and governments retain powers which could radically change those structures. Moreover, broadcasters have often seen their role as adjuncts to the political system. For if the broadcast media have 'a responsibility to [the] political process and political environment, not merely to serve it but to sustain it. . .',[3] then the broadcasters' freedom of action and interpretation are circumscribed. There are certain limits and constraints which are set by the terms of the relationship between the institutions of the state and the broadcast media and by the articulation of professional practices within that political system.

In exploring these broader issues in the relationship between broadcasting and politics, it becomes necessary to abandon the simpler views of the location of broadcasting in British society. Concepts such as 'pressure and resistance' and even autonomy are inadequate as explanations of the work of these institutions. As Stuart Hall has argued,

The question of 'external influence' (on broadcasting) is a thoroughly inadequate way of framing the problem. It is predicated on a model of broadcasting which takes at face value its formal and editorial autonomy: external influences are then seen as illegitimately encroaching upon this area of freedom. . . the real relationship between broadcasting, power and ideology is thoroughly mystified by such a model.[4]

Yet the much criticized model has had widespread currency in Britain because of a combination of deficient alternative conceptual frameworks and much anecdotal evidence which continually breathes life into it. Thus, the many instances when the broadcasting institutions have stood their ground in the face of 'illegitimate encroachment' lend support to the cruder forms of analysis. The conflict surrounding the BBC's treatment of the 1956 Suez Crisis and such programmes as *Yesterday's Men* (1971), *The Question of Ulster* (1972), and to a lesser extent *Real Lives: At The Edge of The Union (1985)*, all contribute to the 'pressure and resistance' model by demonstrating its ability to withstand pressure from governments. Similarly, because the Home Secretary's power of veto over television programmes – a power contained in the BBC Charter and ITV Act – has never been used in relation to specific programmes, it is still possible to claim, if disingenuously, that it is 'a reserve power and the Corporation (i.e. the BBC) has enjoyed, and enjoys, complete freedom in the handling of its programme activities'.[5] In this way, the daily compromises which are in the nature of all political institutions are obscured by the claims of autonomy and the exceptional examples of resistance.

But as studies of the relationship between broadcasting and the institutions of the state demonstrate, it has never been necessary to exercise the power of veto because the broadcasting organizations themselves are well aware of the practical limits to their theoretically wide freedom. As one student of the BBC has written, 'the kind of arrangement arrived at between the government and the BBC at the time of the General Strike (in 1926) provided the mould for the kind of compromise solution and understanding which has prevailed since then'.[6]

During the General Strike of 1926, the fledgling BBC – it had been in existence for a mere four years and had not yet even acquired its own news organization but was dependent on the news agencies – was under enormous pressure from 'legitimate' political authority to deal with the strike as a potentially destabilizing influence on social order. Although Reith, as managing director, did not approve of the Government's directions to him to refuse access to broadcasting facilities to such people as Ramsay MacDonald, he complied because he knew that the BBC was not, in his own words, 'entirely a free agent'.[7]

The BBC, and Reith more specifically, sought continual guidance and clearance from J.C.C. Davidson – parliamentary secretary to the Admiralty and vice president of the Emergency Committee – the Cabinet, and the Prime Minister. Though it was clearly not a free agent it was not fully under the complete direction of the Government. Reith was aware of these inconsistencies and the ways in which they bound the BBC to a limited and partial role during 1926. As he noted in his diaries, '[T]hey will not say we are to a considerable extent controlled, and they make me take the onus of turning people down'.[8]

These inconsistencies troubled Reith and he subsequently put a great deal of effort into obtaining a clarification of the BBC's constitutional position so as to avoid a repetition of the General Strike episode. But these inconsistencies remain: at times of political 'crisis' – and the General Strike was such a time – can the broadcasting organization behave impartially when the social order which underpins it is itself under attack? More specifically, should broadcasting organizations ignore requests from government concerning programme contents, be it on the grounds of 'national security', danger to life, or matters of law and order?

The case studies examined here suggest that the broadcasting organizations do not, and cannot, ignore the possible consequences of their actions and that such considerations restrict autonomy. By appealing to the possible 'undesirable' consequences of the broadcasting organizations' actions, governments, their representatives as well as individuals, can often constrain the broadcasters. Recent examples where such considerations applied include: *Real Lives* (1985, see below), 'The Zircon Affair' (1986/7), *Death of a Princess* (1980, see below), the 'Carrickmore Incident' (1979/80), *The War Game*[9] (1965) and *A Question of Ulster* (1972). In all these instances, the alleged after-effects of the programmes in question – glorifying hatred and violence, damaging national security, damaging diplomatic relations, glorifying terrorists, causing national panic, and so on – ensured that broadcasters would have second thoughts about the content and possible transmission of those programmes. Such appeals to the conscience of the broadcasters are particularly effective if those who express concern are members of governments.

In the face of such pressures broadcasting practices become, inevitably, cautious. Can broadcasters disbelieve those in authority when they claim that national and state, as opposed to governmental, interests are at stake? What authority do broadcasters possess which would allow them to ignore such pleas and what knowledge do they possess which would permit them to question such statements? Inevitably, then, broadcasting organizations take heed of 'authoritative' advice and concede to its superior nature. The outcome is well summed up, if scathingly, by Burns when he notes that

> the BBC fell an easy victim to. . .the calculated imprecision of its relationship with the State. . ., an imprecision which the BBC has been lulled, or gulled, into believing allows it all the liberty, independence, autonomy that can be hoped for, but which has proved, time and again, to be liberty on parole – the terms of which can be altered, without notice, by the Government.[10]

Political interventions are made easy by the fact that the broadcasting institutions have always defined their position as being within the liberal democratic (capitalist) political system. They, therefore, implicitly endorse its main principles. Despite having to acknowledge and reproduce alternative and radical viewpoints in order to ensure that most views are, to an extent, represented, the broadcasting institutions recognize that they are 'part of the nation, and the constitutional creation of Parliament'. The BBC (and this would also apply to the IBA) could not, for example, 'pretend to be impartial between the maintenance and dissolution of the nation. Nor could it be impartial about those things which Parliament had decided were unacceptable by making them illegal'.[11] Thus, although claiming to be 'impartial' and 'autonomous', the BBC would nonetheless see itself as 'an institution within the constitution' – the phrase used by Reith in 1926 to explain his actions during the General Strike. Claims to detachment and disinterestedness in the context of highly charged political issues therefore rest uneasily next to an inevitable and systemic commitment to the existing social and political order.

Broadcasting institutions have also accepted Parliament as a natural pole and have interpreted their task as one of reproducing 'a picture of political discourse dominated by Parliament. [Broadcasting] is. . .not part of a "fourth estate". . . but rather operates impartial brokerage within a prevailing political system'.[12] And, despite numerous lapses, it has attempted to apply an even hand mainly in relation to the major protagonists in the political system. The resultant practices of balancing opposites, perhaps the only satisfactory way of handling governments and their opposition in Parliament, has come to be seen as an operational solution to the need for 'due impartiality' in *all* matters of political broadcasting.

Such practices are linked, in turn, to certain rules and agreements which govern political broadcasting. These include the need to ensure due impartiality and due accuracy in relation to matters of public policy, rules which regulate coverage during elections (see Chapter 9), and rules which govern political broadcasting by Ministers of State. Many of these rules and agreements were set out in the late 1940s in a BBC *Aide Mémoire* in order to define the terms of the relationship between politicians and the broadcast media, and they remain relevant today. Their significance lies in the fact that they were accepted by the television services and that they have become key practices and points of reference in all broadcasting matters.

As political television developed, the practice of preserving an overall political balance between the major parties took on an added significance.[13] It produced, in effect, a continuing circus which could not function unless all the respective partners were present. The broadcasting institutions could not, therefore, be bounced into producing a programme which was not balanced. A similar example relates to ministerial broadcasts. Ministers have the right to request the broadcasting institutions to carry a ministerial address to the nation, but unless that address deals with an uncontroversial issue – and that is itself a matter for argument – shadow ministers have an automatic right of reply. This practice had enormous implications during the Suez crisis and continues to have implications since it forces political parties to acknowledge the existence of oppositions and their access to the medium.

The key to understanding all these practices and similar rules or agreements is that they reflect, particularly in the case of the BBC, what it has imposed on itself in the past and its continued acceptance of their importance in the present. The Charter of the BBC and the Television Acts contain little that relates directly to programme policies apart from several general injunctions to ensure due impartiality, balance and fairness. Their translation into actual practices was undertaken by specific institutions in specific political contexts. These mirror the self-definition of a broadcasting institution within a certain political system and the repeated use of particular practices tends to reinforce this self-definition.

Broadcasters are aware of their location within the political system and are sensitive to the views of those who wield power. The comments of a prominent politician cannot easily be ignored. This sensitivity can produce a timidity which will result in submissions in the face of threats. The last decade has witnessed numerous instances when broadcasters have readily (or with protests) responded to calls, mainly from politicians, to alter, delete, or suspend programmes.[14]

One of the root causes of conflict in the relationship described above is that the broadcasting institutions do not – and perhaps cannot – passively reproduce the agendas and definitions of 'reality' favoured by those in power to the exclusion of other perspectives. For broadcasters, the avoidance of conflict with those who rule amounts to an abdication of their responsibilities and professional duties as journalists. Furthermore, their work is to a large extent premised on such professional imperatives as 'news values' and these cannot be ignored without a loss of credibility. This helps to explain the existence of many programmes or programme items which create problems for the broadcasting institutions. Whether it concerns nuclear power, Northern Ireland, or the Falklands, those who dissent from the actions of the state may need to be represented. This is, after all, one of the three elements of impartiality – 'the expression of the widest range of views and opinions' – considered by the Annan Committee.[15] When the form of that dissent is dramatic, e.g. demonstrations, it is even more newsworthy and so more likely to obtain media coverage. The result of this is that the broadcasters and 'those who rule' are imprisoned in an unequal relationship which inevitably produces tensions.

CASE STUDIES IN THE POLITICS OF BROADCASTING

Introduction

Studies of the relationship between 'politics and broadcasting' usually illustrate their main themes through examples of events which have traumatized the BBC: 'the General Strike', *Yesterday's Men*, 'the Suez Crisis', the BBC in the inter-War years, *Real Lives*, and so on. There are no extensively documented case studies which examine those very same processes of intervention within commercial television. Yet ITV has not been without its problems. Why then is the BBC so central to all these studies?

One possible reason is that the BBC is 'the national instrument of broadcasting'. It has a long history and its place in British culture and politics is unique. Despite ITV's successes, the BBC remains the *British* Broadcasting Corporation: what it does is, almost by definition, of cultural and political significance. Commercial television, on the other hand, does not have either that status or that degree of importance. It is perceived, rightly or wrongly, merely as a commercial enterprise devoid of cultural or political direction. Consequently it does not occupy those in authority and politics in quite the same way. For example, MI5 worked within the BBC *and not ITV* to vet employees applying for certain posts[16] and Norman Tebbit, when Conservative Central Office chairman, chose to attack the BBC's reporting of the American air raid on Libya even though ITN also had a case to answer.[17] In fact, the Conservative Party's obsession with the alleged excesses of the BBC are legendary; abhorrence of the BBC appears to be a litmus test for the Conservative-ness of MPs.[18]

Whatever the reasons for the political obsession with the BBC, it has masked the difficulties which the commercial television companies have experienced. Although some of these difficulties were the result of government advice against the transmission of programmes, many others are the outcome of the Independent Broadcasting Authority's regulatory decisions.

The IBA has to ensure that programmes do not contravene the Television Act either by not being 'impartial' or by taking an editorial line. This duty has brought it into conflict with programme companies and programme makers on many occasions. Many of its decisions have involved programmes on the Irish issue. Of the 44 television programmes or programme items 'on the North of Ireland' which Curtis lists as having been 'banned, censored or delayed' between 1970 and 1983, 21 involved a commercial television company.[19]

Other programmes have suffered similar fates. A programme on the Tottenham riots was pulled from the schedules when the IBA asked the producers of the programme to make several cuts.[20] A more public affair was the IBA's objection to the John Pilger film on nuclear armaments, *The Truth Game* (1982), which was delayed until the IBA could 'find a programme which will reflect other equally valid arguments on this crucial subject..'.[21] The same fate befell the Channel Four programme, *Greece: the Hidden War* (1986). As the programme became embroiled in a raging dispute about the nature of historical truth, the IBA was forced to request that 'other views' on Greek history be aired.[22]

In asking for these changes the IBA was clearly fulfilling its duties as a regulatory body which has to ensure that 'balance' and 'due impartiality' are observed in all matters of controversy. Yet such interventions in editorial matters have come under attack for being both extreme and restrictive. The Annan Committee felt that the IBA's interventions sometimes 'went too far' and beyond the IBA's role as 'protector' of the public interest. Moreover, it was usurping the editorial duties and responsibilities of the individual programme companies. Sometimes, according to Annan, the IBA was unnecessarily involved in the production process; for example, 'in a period of nine months the IBA intervened ten times over programmes produced by Thames' *This Week* team';[23] in the case of a John Pilger programme on Bangladesh, IBA officers examined the text 'almost line by line'.[24]

Such interventions tie the hands of the producers and stifle public discussion. Critics of the IBA have argued that the requirements of 'balance' and 'impartiality' and its insistence that all views be given equal prominence or be dealt with fairly gave rise to 'neutered' programmes and not to 'neutral' programmes.[25] The continuous need to balance weakened strong arguments and powerful programmes.

Appeals against IBA decisions were not usually received with much sympathy. In response to one such appeal, it claimed that it, the IBA, was the ultimate watchdog,

> . .whether a programme was duly impartial by virtue of its reasonable presentation of available facts and arguments *was, under the terms of the Act (and programme contract), a matter for the Authority's opinion alone*.[26]

Because these interventions initially only involve the IBA and an individual company, they result in a muted, often private, outcry.

Rarely is the IBA involved in an action which produces the public outrage that usually accompanies attacks on the BBC. One programme which did trouble the ITV companies in the 1980s, and pushed them and the IBA onto the international stage, was *Death of a Princess*, made in the late 1970s and shown in April 1980.

The programme, a drama-documentary on the execution of a Saudi Arabian princess for alleged adultery, caused a diplomatic row between Britain and the Saudi Royal Family. After Saudi requests that the film not be shown were turned down on the grounds that the broadcasting institutions were independent of the state, the Saudis expelled British diplomats and they also threatened economic sanctions against Britain.

Though the film was transmitted as planned, British ministers lost no time in criticizing both the IBA and the ITV companies for their lack of 'tact'. What appeared to concern them most was the damage done to Saudi-British economic and political relations by a programme which did not

> seem to be a serious attempt to understand Saudi society. It exploited the atmosphere of mystery and rumour. . . to compile a salacious detective story fallaciously presented as fact.[27]

The mixing of genres – the drama-documentary or the detective story as fact – is open to criticism because it mixes forms and, in the public's and authorities' view, facts and fiction. Ministers were also alarmed that this weakness in the programme directly affected a powerful economic and political friend. These two objections to the programme were undoubtedly intertwined since one could not imagine less powerful nations having the same impact on British ministers and politicians.

Like all the other incidents in the history of broadcasting, the affair was short-lived. However, the implications of the affair are not lost on future programme makers.

The Suez crisis and the Falklands conflict

In the summer of 1956, President Nasser of Egypt nationalized the (then British owned) Suez Canal. His action was condemned internationally and British opinion quickly turned against him. During the early part of the summer – and immediately after the nationalization of the canal – there was unanimous condemnation but as the impasse wore on, divisions began to appear. These divisions took on a party political character. Whilst Anthony Eden's Conservative Government was making preparations for military action against Nasser in order to reclaim the canal, the Opposition (Labour) Party increased its objections to any military adventure, preferring instead to negotiate.

The nature of these divisions – deep-rooted and strongly held – impacted on broadcasting and on Fleet Street. The national press reproduced these divisions with bold headlines and stark statements. Such words as 'appeasement' and 'sabre-rattling' began to appear in the Fleet Street vocabulary and they expressed the chasm that had appeared between the two major political parties.[28] Inevitably, because the news media are all part of the same process of news making and agenda setting, television and radio became involved in the struggle to dominate the headlines and to control news output. But there was a unique element in this affair. As Ian Jacob, the BBC's then director-general, was to write,

> the procedures which govern political broadcasting were designed for domestic controversy of the kind that normally accompanies political life; *a national emergency when Government action was not nationally supported presented a new problem.*[29]

For the BBC the problem had several aspects. It ran an internal radio and television operation but it also ran the external services which could be heard in Egypt, the 'enemy'. As far as Eden was concerned, at times of (foreign) conflict, opposition and dissenting views ought not to be broadcast. Such broadcasts would give 'comfort to the enemy by reporting domestic divisions, thus weakening the credibility of our threats'.[30] The duty of the external broadcasting services was to present a united front to the outside world.

However, the BBC did not feel that it was possible to distinguish between internal and external needs. It could not abandon its consistency between its internal and external programmes: if there were major divisions of opinion in the nation then they ought to be broadcast to both the domestic and the international audiences. This view created two specific difficulties for the BBC. When Eden requested a television ministerial in November 1956, the BBC felt obliged to comply with the rules which cover ministerial broadcasts, namely, that if the matter is considered to be a controversial one and the opposition party requests the right of reply, then such a reply ought to be conceded. In due course, Hugh Gaitskell did broadcast on behalf of the Labour Party. His words, considered by some to be inflammatory, occasioned an informal request from Downing Street for a toned-down transmission lest those who heard it overseas should take comfort from the divisions that Britain was experiencing. The BBC did not comply with this request.

This event took place alongside more serious problems for the BBC. The external services of the BBC, which are funded by the Foreign Office, came under immense pressure to play down the extent of opposition in Britain. In the daily summary of the British press, the external services of the BBC accurately reflected both sides of the argument. Despite representations from the Foreign Office, the BBC refused to tailor its foreign output to suit the desires of government. Not only did it feel that it would have been unjustified editorially but it also felt that it would have given rise to an inconsistency between internal and external reportage. The BBC was to suffer for its actions: the Foreign Office immediately cut its budget to the external services.[31]

Needless to say, the BBC's actions exposed it to considerable pressure. Nevertheless, the contrast with the BBC's débâcle in 1926 when the government of the day exercised direct editorial control over its radio output is very striking. Eden did not attempt to take over the BBC. Though there are accounts to the effect that he had produced 'innumerable schemes to discipline the BBC' there is little hard evidence to support such statements.[32] Instead, he 'appealed' to the BBC (much as Leon Brittan did nearly thirty years later in the context of the *Real Lives* controversy). He wrote to the Chairman of the Board of Governors (Cadogan), that

> Of course, the Government have no intention of interfering with the freedom of the BBC. . . . But I hope that the Governors will bear in mind the very heavy responsibility which rests on the BBC at this crucial time. . .
> This is not a Prime Minister's representation but a personal comment which I thought you should have in view of our [telephone] talk last night.[33]

There is a danger of exaggerating the importance of the Suez crisis as an instance when broadcasting asserted its formal independence from government. Though the BBC did resist considerable pressure it is important to take into account those circumstances which enabled it to retain a degree of formal independence. Perhaps the most important factor here was the violent disagreement that the Government's policy over Suez generated. This disagreement spilled over into the Fleet Street newspapers which, in turn, eagerly contributed to it. Even ITN, which was still in its infancy, reproduced the political divisions which were daily being aired in Parliament.[34] In that sort of 'hot house' atmosphere, not reporting disagreement would have been a dereliction of journalistic duty.

Similarly, there appeared to be no single solution to the crisis and hence no single definition of the 'national interest'. With an opposition party offering an alternative view of, and solution to, the crisis it would have been difficult not to grant it access to the media. Indeed, the BBC's rules of political broadcasting were designed to ensure that such opposition could not be ignored or overlooked.

The BBC's handling of the Suez crisis, then, was in line with its own practices; practices it had helped to formulate many decades earlier. Clearly, had there been no political party in opposition to the Government's actions, or widespread disquiet nationally and in the press, the BBC would have found it much more difficult to pursue an impartial line. The reproduction of the Parliamentary struggle, though it does expose broadcasting organizations to numerous threats, does not ultimately place it in mortal danger since it is only balancing competing and legitimated parliamentary views. So long as it employs those general principles which had been established in order to govern the relationship between broadcasters and the political parties in Britain, its independence is secured.

In this respect, there are some interesting comparisons to be made between the Suez crisis and the Falklands conflict nearly three decades later in 1982. In both instances, Britain was reacting to an act by a 'dictator' against her interests and people; both acts took place far away from Britain; both involved Conservative Governments afraid to repeat the lessons of appeasement, and both incidents involved sending a task force to foreign lands. Unlike Suez, however, there was little Parliamentary opposition to the Thatcher Government's decision to send a task force to the South Atlantic. The Labour Party under Michael Foot was in broad agreement with the Government's actions and it was left to a small group of MPs to voice criticisms of those actions. Similarly, Fleet Street appeared to reflect agreement and unity, not disagreement and deeply felt opposition. In the absence of widespread disagreement, both within and also outside Parliament, the BBC or any other broadcasting organization could not legitimately provide a different – and more 'oppositional' – coverage.

Under those circumstances, any attempt to question the wisdom of British policy would prove immensely difficult. Two BBC programmes came in for major criticism: the first was the late-night BBC2 news programme, *Newsnight*; this was soon followed by criticism of the current affairs programme *Panorama*.[35]

Newsnight came under attack for maintaining an air of 'objectivity' and 'impartiality' by using, to the chagrin of the Government, such phrases as 'British troops' and 'the British' rather than 'our troops' and 'we'. *Panorama*, shown just over a week later, devoted nearly the whole programme to a critical appraisal of the Government's policy. Both programmes, the BBC's critics maintained, gave equal credence to the Argentinian case as to the British one.

This was the central issue – should the BBC treat the Argentinian case as if it was merely one side of a two-sided argument or should it, and many would have preferred this, assume that the Argentinians were obviously 'in the wrong' and had no argument whatsoever? A jingoistic Fleet Street had no doubts over this matter; neither did many MPs in Parliament. They felt that the primary duty of the BBC was to support the Government and the troops; for its part, the Government was also concerned lest support for the venture and morale should decline.

These fears were clearly in evidence in Thatcher's comments about the BBC *Newsnight* programme in the Commons on 6 May 1982:

> Many people are very concerned indeed that the case for our British forces is not being put over fully and effectively. I understand that there are times when it seems that we and the Argentinians are being treated almost as equals and almost on a neutral basis.[36]

The following week's *Panorama* programme did nothing to endear the BBC to its critics. The populist press and members of the Conservative Party continued to express their doubts about the 'British-ness' of the British Broadcasting Corporation and its commitment and support for 'our' troops.

The most curious aspect of the Falklands conflict episode was that the BBC overwhelmingly accepted the British Government's case. Leaked confidential minutes of the BBC news and current affairs team certainly support this claim.[37] Even Mrs Thatcher's comments in the Commons about the *Panorama* programme make reference to the fact that the Chairman of the Governors 'has assured us, and has said in vigorous terms, that the BBC is not neutral on this point'.[38]

What the BBC lacked in 1982, but had in 1956, was a vigorous national press with which to highlight criticisms of government policy. When Parliament and the press are both at one, the BBC lacks any external point of reference with which to present alternative views on particular situations. As with news practices, it merely reacts to, and reports, events.

These two examples also demonstrate the general reluctance to tamper explicitly and publicly with the freedoms that the broadcasting institutions allegedly enjoy. This does not disguise, however, the readiness with which those in authority express their displeasure and this, of itself, can act as a brake against future indiscretions. Calls to broadcasters 'to put their houses in order' – the phrase used by Mrs Thatcher after the BBC filmed (though never showed!) the IRA in Carrickmore, Northern Ireland – fulfil a number of immediate and future functions.

They question the wisdom of existing practices, define the limits of freedom, warn of future consequences and usually have direct effects on programme practices and supervisory mechanisms. In these ways, traditional and established practices are maintained and reinforced and those that are likely to cause difficulties, discouraged. This (sometimes) subtle, informal and indirect process of control retains and lends support to the public image of autonomous broadcasting institutions. As Reith wrote in his diary during the General Strike, the Cabinet 'want to be able to say that they did not commandeer us, but they know that they can trust us not to be really impartial'.[39]

'Real Lives. At The Edge of The Union'

In the Spring of 1985, the producers of the BBC's documentary series *Real Lives* embarked on a programme which focused on the lives, and views, of two politicians in Northern Ireland. One aim of the programme was to profile two elected representatives from across the opposite ends of the political divide: Martin McGuinness, leader of Sinn Fein, and Gregory Campbell of the Democratic Ulster Unionists.

The programme was originally scheduled for August 1985 but it was pulled out of the schedules, amidst accusations of government censorship, when it became the centre of a controversy and the cause of much turmoil within broadcasting and journalism generally. This programme, and the surrounding controversy, highlight the many influences that come into play when 'pressure' is applied to broadcasting organizations. It also illustrates the way in which broadcasting organizations form part of a larger socio-political complex which itself has a bearing on its programmes. In order to gain a better insight into the nature of control over broadcasting, it is first necessary to deal with the programme's background.

Background

The programme was part of a series produced by the BBC's documentary features department. The department's actions in profiling 'Ulster extremists', albeit elected ones, fell foul of some well-known rules concerning the conduct of interviews in Northern Ireland. These rules note that, in effect, permission must be sought *prior* to the making of any programmes about terrorist organizations and the interviewing of any individuals closely associated with terrorist organizations. In addition to being required to seek prior permission for the making of the programme, prior permission must also be sought for its transmission. This two-stage referral system ensures that a tight control is kept on all coverage.

These rules are part of the every-day practices of the news and current affairs departments and it is possible that they may have been less familiar to other departments. In the event, whether the proper authorities within the BBC had or had not been properly informed about the intentions of the programme makers also became an issue. This matter was further complicated by the fact that the two men profiled in the programme were democratically elected representatives in Ulster and had been interviewed on several previous occasions by the BBC. Did they, therefore, fall into the categories set out in the News and Current Affairs Index? As elected representatives, they could not be kept off air and, since neither were members of proscribed organizations, the producers of the programme felt that they were on fairly safe ground. Furthermore, the programme was finely 'balanced', with each contributor being given the same amount of air-time.

Despite these qualifications, the programme ran into trouble as soon as its transmission date was publicly announced. And the event which triggered the affair was an unusual one!

For some weeks prior to its original date of transmission on 7 August, the world's attention had been focused on the hijack of an American TWA jet in Beirut and particularly on the American television news organizations' apparent willingness to allow themselves to be used by the 'terrorists'. At times, it seemed as if the 'terrorists' controlled the news from Beirut. These practices gave rise to much concern and in a speech to the American Bar Association Mrs Thatcher, the Prime Minister, suggested that the news media ought to get together to 'consider whether those who, like terrorists, used freedom should have so much publicity for their work'.[40]

These sentiments were repeated during a scheduled press conference in Washington on 28 July 1985 when Mrs Thatcher was asked by a *Sunday Times* reporter how she would react if the British media had made such a programme. As she had no knowledge of the film nor of its contents, it was a 'hypothetical' question which deserved a reply in general terms. She replied to the effect that she would 'utterly condemn' such a broadcast. She then made reference to her speech to the Bar Association and to her belief that terrorism 'thrives on the oxygen of publicity'. These remarks were sufficient to produce an immediate response from the Home Secretary and the minister responsible for broadcasting affairs, Leon Brittan.

By the next day, Monday 29 July, it was abundantly clear that the BBC had entered a political storm and that, once the story had broken, its Governors and Managers had to act. Despite the mounting pressure, the Board of Management, at its regular Monday morning meeting, decided to go ahead with the transmission of the programme. The Board of Management – the executives in charge of the BBC's day-to-day work – thus reaffirmed their confidence in the work of their colleagues.

But neither this decision, nor the status of the decision makers, appeared to influence the Home Office. Leon Brittan – who was asked by Mrs Thatcher to keep her informed of developments – then decided to appeal directly to the Governors on the grounds that the programme was not in the national interest and that Martin McGuinness was 'a prominent member for the IRA'. Following a meeting between Home Office and BBC officials at which the former repeated the Government's fears about the programme, Brittan wrote formally to the Chairman of the Board of Governors, Stuart Young. That letter, quoted at some length below, outlines the degree of 'imprecision' which continues to haunt the relationship between Westminster and the broadcasting organizations. After a brief opening statement, the letter continues

May I first make it quite clear that I unhesitatingly accept that the decision to broadcast or to refrain from broadcasting this programme must rest exclusively with the corporation.

It is no part of my task as the minister responsible for broadcasting policy generally to attempt to impose an act of censorship on what should be broadcast in particular programmes. To do so would rightly be inconsistent with the constitutional independence of the BBC, which is a crucial part of our broadcasting arrangements.

I do, on the other hand, also have a ministerial responsibility for the fight against the ever-present threat of terrorism, and I would be failing in my duty if I did not let you and your colleagues have my considered views on the impact of this programme in that context.

The BBC would be giving an immensely valuable platform to those who have evinced an ability to murder indiscriminately its own viewers.. . .

[Showing the film] would also in my considered judgement materially assist the terrorist cause.. . .

It must be damaging to security and therefore wholly contrary to the public interest to provide a boost to the morale of the terrorists and their apologists in this way. I cannot believe the BBC would wish to give succour to terrorist organisations.[41]

On the Tuesday morning, the Board of Governors and representatives of the Board of Management met to discuss the programme. In the absence of the director-general, who was away on holiday, the management team was led by Michael Checkland, deputy director-general. The Board of Management argued that the film should be transmitted as planned. It had been dealt with properly within the organization and should therefore not be treated in an exceptional way.

The Board of Governors, on the other hand, felt that they could not usefully contribute to the discussion nor could they make a decision about the film without first seeing it. The Governors' request to see the programme was itself very unusual and departs from BBC practice which implicitly acknowledges that if a programme is cleared internally, the Governors should support the broadcasters in the public interest. Such a departure from practice has happened only once before and that was also during the controversial period of the *Yesterday's Men* episode.[42]

Having viewed the film, the Chairman of the Board of Governors replied to the Home Secretary's letter. His letter confirmed that the programme would not be transmitted 'in its present form: the programme's intentions would continue to be misread and misinterpreted'. This view was repeated a week later when the Chairman insisted that the programme had been banned because it was flawed, 'was not balanced [and] showed terrorist organizations in a favourable light'.[43] Or, as one Governor is reported to have said during the *Real Lives* controversy,

> Once we'd seen the film, there was no doubt that the vote (on whether to show it or not) would go against it. The opponents' argument was that TV is a great image-maker. Once you show a terrorist as a nice guy with a baby on his knee, it becomes difficult to shake that image.[44]

The Governors' action occasioned a 24-hour strike by BBC journalists which did incalculable damage to the BBC's internal and international journalistic reputation. In the event, the *Real Lives* programme, with the addition of several seconds of material, was shown the following autumn. The controversy guaranteed that its audience was at least three times the normal audience for a documentary of its kind!

One other point is of interest here. Although the programme was stopped, video technology ensured that copies would be available for showing across the country. As with the 'Zircon Affair',[45] the availability of VCRs suggests that copies of 'banned' programmes can make the rounds very rapidly. Stopping a programme is no longer a guarantee that it will not be seen.

RESUME

One of the most insoluble problems which the *Real Lives* programme generated is whether broadcasters can ever comment on issues of such a controversial nature without bringing protests from all quarters. The reporting of the Irish question is one such area but it is conceivable that reporting other internal or external conflicts or struggles will create similar difficulties. Problems of this nature are part of the general 'problem' of the 'management of broadcasting in a democratic society'.[46] How much freedom should broadcasters have, given that they have an almost monopolistic control over the means of mass communication? How 'responsible' are they? To whom are they 'responsible' for their charge of the enormous power of the medium? And, in areas where the nature of 'truth' is itself contested, can broadcasters turn a blind eye to the clamours for more 'responsibility', more 'fairness', more 'openness'?

An audio-visual medium attempting to represent 'reality' fairly and 'impartially' also faces other difficulties. Not only are such concepts very tricky to deal with under normal circumstances but they become points of controversy when the subject matter is itself steeped in controversy. As the leader in *The Times* on the *Real Lives* affair put it, the notion of 'balance' is ' "objectionable" if it is meant to imply a moral equivalence between the crimes copiously committed' by the organizations represented by the two main characters in the programme.[47]

The *Real Lives* controversy neatly encapsulates all of these problems. Broadcasters clearly cannot ignore the political and social 'realities' which are the eternal backdrops to their work. Indeed, one criticism of the BBC during the whole affair was that it had not been properly attuned to the signs of an impending storm; that it had failed to make a connection between the Beirut hijacking and its own work; that it was still reeling too much from the debate over the licence fee and the prospect of advertising on the BBC to take note of the *Real Lives* programme and its possible impact on a society well acquainted with some of the consequences of terrorism.

The *Real Lives* programme probably slipped through a rather complex system of control. The management's response to this temporary breakdown in the system was to create a post of 'controller of editorial policy' in July 1987. One of the controller's duties will be to act as an early warning system so as to circumvent the sorts of difficulties that the *Real Lives* programme brought to the fore.[48]

It is important to stress three final points which reveal the nature of the relationship that underpins politics and broadcasting. First, Leon Brittan did not order the BBC to stop the *Real Lives* programme, even though he had the power to do so. As his letter clearly stated, the BBC is constitutionally independent and acts independently. In this way, the 'constitutional fiction' remains alive and well. Second, Brittan's actions illustrate his own inadequate grasp of the intricacies of the exercise of power. This was underlined during the Westland Affair when his actions – once again involving the writing of letters – finally led to his resignation. During the *Real Lives* controversy, many commentators pointed out that a more skilful and experienced minister would probably have used the informal mechanisms of pressure – phone calls, luncheon engagements, and the like – to arrive at a speedy and relatively peaceful conclusion of this affair. By writing formal letters in a blaze of publicity, Brittan merely ensured that the affair would occupy the nation's front pages for many weeks and that it would follow a course of its own.

Finally, the *Real Lives* controversy brought to light the Thatcher Government's practice of appointing Governors who are broadly sympathetic to it. This action over a period of many years probably helped it in this matter and also in the course of controversies over the reporting of the security services. The inherent danger in the overt politicization of the Governors is that the BBC will lose its credibility as an impartial medium of communication. It would then become a 'political football' and 'part of the spoil of electoral victory', a condition which terminally afflicted the French and Italian broadcasting systems in the recent past.[49]

Chapter Seven

NEWS AND THE PRODUCTION OF NEWS

Every newspaper when it reaches the reader is the result of a whole series of selections as to what items shall be printed, in what position they shall be printed, how much space each shall occupy, what emphasis each shall have. There are no objective standards here. There are conventions.[1]

INTRODUCTION

The study of news focuses attention on one of the most critical issues in media studies: namely, how is media content produced and what are the factors which play a part in its production? Does news content serve the interests of proprietors or is news a reflection of 'reality'? Are journalists mere 'relay systems' of proprietors or do they exercise some degree of independence in their choice, and interpretation, of stories?

A detailed analysis of news must also take into account the social context of news production. The production of news takes place in large, hierarchically organized, technically complex and (except for the BBC) profit-making organizations. Journalists are part of such organizations and their work will reflect, and sustain, the needs of the 'profession' as well as those of their respective organizations. Indeed, the economic and political 'needs' of media organizations – the need to survive, to maximize profit, to increase sales, to increase advertising revenue, to maintain a political line, to placate politicians – form an important backdrop to the study of the production of all media content.

News organizations, like all other organizations, also have finite resources and this has enormous consequences for their ability to carry out their work adequately. It determines not only how many journalists are employed but also, as we shall see below, where those journalists are placed and what news material is collected. Furthermore, the production of news takes place with the interest of the audience uppermost in the minds of the journalist, sub-editor, editor, circulation manager, advertiser and proprietor. Without sales, newspapers cannot survive and without audiences television news broadcasts cannot exist indefinitely.

All these considerations feed into the study of news production and they make it difficult to answer such questions as 'what is news?', 'who controls the news?' or 'who makes the news?' in a simple way. Explanations of the news production process usually turn to complex accounts of the competing and interacting factors noted above. One such explanation, offered by Herbert Gans, makes this point well. News, he writes, is information

> which is transmitted from sources to audiences, with journalists
> – who are both employees of bureaucratic commercial organiz-
> ations and members of a profession – summarizing, refining, and
> altering what becomes available to them from sources in order to
> make the information suitable for their audiences.[2]

An equally complex approach to the study of news can be found in Golding and Middleton's study of images of welfare. Finding both the 'biographical' approach – namely, individuals determine the nature of news – and the 'organizational' approach – namely, journalists are constrained by organizational and proprietorial interventions – somewhat deficient as explanations of the news-making process, they develop the 'ideological' approach. This approach incorporates elements from the first two but goes beyond them in seeing these as only contributing to 'the complicated machinery by which the dominant values of British society are given form and authority by the news media'.[3]

By drawing attention to the wider social context of news production and to the dominant values in society, Golding and Middleton emphasize the ways in which ideological considerations and commonly accepted views and assumptions about the nature and workings of British society also feed into the news-making process. As they point out, writers of social security news have 'a populist-pluralist mix of strong commitments to self-help, individualism, anti-bureaucracy and the work ethic'[4] and these values act as filters of all news about social security. It is in such ways that 'the dominant values of British society' refract all news content.

A related point is that for journalists the 'process of making an event intelligible' embodies certain assumptions about society and how it works. On a very basic level, for example, the process of communication assumes a common language. At the more complex level of mass communication, media professionals assume or need to assume that the public as a whole 'inhabits to some degree the same classifications of social reality, [otherwise] we could not make sense of the world together'. Thus, one assumption media professionals make is that society is *consensual*. This assumption colours much of what they write: 'the process of *signification* - giving social meanings to events – *both assumes and helps to construct society as a "consensus"*.'[5] Whether this 'crucial background assumption' is still valid at a time of rapid social change is a debate of major significance but it does not detract from the more general point that media professionals make certain assumptions about their audiences for the purposes of communication. It is therefore not surprising to find Stuart Hall describing news values as 'based on inferred knowledge about the audience, inferred assumptions about society and a professional code or ideology'.[6]

WHAT IS NEWS?

An infinite number of events take place every minute of every day. The news media make a selection from this infinite number of events and present that selection as news. Without a routine method of dealing with this abundance of events and information, no news organization could function properly. The requirements of, say, regular broadcast news bulletins are so extreme as to create the need for a routine with which to manage the continuous flow of information.

But if the need for a regular production cycle accounts for the existence of routines, what factors explain the selection of items? Why are some events more 'significant', newsworthy, or more 'important' than others? What is news?

Walter Lippmann observed that 'the news is not a mirror of social conditions, but the report of an aspect that has obtruded itself'.[7] Because it only deals with overt, and usually recent or immediate, signals – a strike, a murder, a disaster – it necessarily overlooks processes which are, almost by definition, complex and ambiguous. News is about the planting of a seed, its germination and its flowering, but not about the intervening period the struggle for food and light and the general processes of growth.

The processes of selection and inclusion, and, by implication, of exclusion, contradict the view that the news media give a full and comprehensive account of 'world events'. They offer only a selection of world events. This has major implications for the 'news' and its claims to 'truth'. As Lippmann also argued, 'news' and 'truth' are not the same. The 'function of news is to signalize an event, the function of truth is to bring to light the hidden facts, to set them in relation with each other, and make a picture of reality on which men can act'.[8]

In an attempt to identify which events were likely to be signalled or selected by the news media, Galtung and Ruge analysed the coverage of three foreign crises in Norwegian newspapers.[9] Their analysis led them to focus on eight major factors and four cultural ones as key influences on the choices of news items for inclusion in newspapers. These were:

1. Frequency – 'the more similar the frequency of the event is to the frequency of the news medium, the more probable that it will be recorded as news by that news medium.'
2. Amplitude – a certain level of, say, violence must be reached before an event will be considered newsworthy.
3. Ambiguity – the less ambiguous, the more likely that it will be noticed.
4. Meaningful – culturally relevant or culturally proximate events are more likely to make news. The event must also be 'relevant'.
5. Consonance – the more expected the event, that is the more the event is predicted and wanted, the more likely that it will become news. ' "[n]ews" are actually "olds", because they correspond to what one expects to happen..'
6. As a 'corrective' to the above two, an event must not only be meaningful and consonant, but unexpected – an event has to be unexpected and rare to become news.
7. Once an event is defined as news, it will continue to be news even though its amplitude may be less.

8. Composition – news is composed to give a balance across stories.

In addition to these eight factors, there are four culturally relevant ones. The more an event concerns (9) élite nations and (10) élite people the more likely it is to become news. Similarly, the more (11) personalized and the more (12) negative the event, the greater its potential to become news. Generally speaking, the more an event scores on these 12 points, the more likely it is that it will become news (the additivity hypothesis) but if it scores low on many of these criteria, it can still become news if it scores very highly on some, e.g. massive earthquake in non-élite nation.[10]

Despite some criticisms of this study[11] and, in particular, its focus on foreign crisis reporting which is itself based largely on news agency material, it represents an important analysis of news. More recent studies have paid greater attention to those selection criteria which are specific to the medium of television. For example, television news also requires that events be visually dramatic, attractive and entertaining.[12] These criteria are in addition to those identified by Galtung and Ruge – importance or significance, size or amplitude, proximity, élites, negativity, recency, and so on. As Golding and Elliott point out,

it is hard to imagine broadcast journalists anywhere seeking news which dealt with small events, the long-term, dull, distant, visually boring, unimportant people, and so on. Yet many of these labels describe events and processes which may well have significance for news audiences, but which are not news. *The application of news values is part of the process by which this labelling occurs.*[13]

That visual considerations are absent from the selection criteria of newspaper journalists is hardly surprising. In his own account of factors which are likely to influence news selection, Alastair Hetherington, a former editor of the *Guardian*, placed the social, political, economic and human 'significance' of events at the top of his list of criteria. His other criteria were:
- Drama – excitement, action, etc. in the event;
- Surprise – the unexpected, the fresh;
- Personalities – royalty, showbusiness, political actors, etc.;
- Sex – scandal, crime, etc.;
- Numbers – numbers affected, etc.[14]

The editor of a tabloid newspaper would probably change the order somewhat and place greater emphasis on 'scandal', 'sex', and 'personalities'.

Hetherington's understanding of 'significance' is particularly interesting because it locates news values firmly within the middle ground of British political life. 'Significance' is, first, an interest in news items which affect world peace and the prosperity and well-being of the public at home or abroad. Second, he believes that a journalist's 'foremost unstated assumption' is that we live in a liberal democracy whose continuity and harmony we wish to preserve as far as possible. Threatening or disruptive events are therefore significant: they are 'important but unwelcome news'. These two criteria combined lead journalists (and journalism) to support the status quo 'regardless of whether or not it will be beneficial to the community as a whole'.[15]

Such views about the 'significance' of events are undoubtedly ideological: events are perceived from particular points of view. More importantly, these measures of 'significance' are also commonly understood by all journalists – hence the interchange-ability of journalists and the common agenda across the media. In this way a common world view is presented in all news media.

This critique of 'news as ideology' is developed at some length in Golding and Elliott's work on broadcast news. They argue that news is ideology because 'it provides an integrated picture of reality' and 'a world view. . . supportive of the interests of powerful social groupings'.[16] Broadcast news

(a) fails to deal with social processes. News is about today's events; a succession of 'incomprehensible' and 'interchange-able events' succeed each other with little recourse to historical, economic or political analysis;

(b) fails to deal with power in society. News, as described above, is about actions and individuals. 'Power is absent from news by virtue of [the] severance of politics from economics. . .'[17]

These deficiencies in the content of news not only produce a partial account of events but also provide us with a particular explanation of the world and world events. It 'precludes' views which would question the status quo and the existing distribution of power in a capitalist society. Furthermore, the organizational setting of news production, routine processes and the practices of day-to-day journalism ensure that a particular world view dominates. Or, as Gans put it,

> Access (to the media) is differentially distributed. . .the economically and politically powerful can obtain easy access. . .those who lack power are harder to reach and are not sought out. . . access reflects the social structure outside the newsroom.[18]

THE ORGANIZATIONAL SETTING
AND ROUTINE PRACTICES

The analysis of news makes it difficult to maintain the view that news is simply 'random reactions to random events'.[19] Some events – a nuclear meltdown, a massive earthquake, the assassination of a major world leader – are, undoubtedly, random and unpredictable and so momentous as to demand widespread and universal coverage. But such events are not common and, in an important sense, it is their rarity which makes them news. It is more usual, in fact, for the news media to select from a number of less spectacular occurrences. Yet, as research shows, not all occurrences have an equal chance of becoming news. Some obtain more media attention than others, whilst still others are completely ignored. This suggests, therefore, that it is not the quality of the event itself which makes it news but rather that the event is recognized as newsworthy because it conforms to certain criteria of newsworthiness. One common illustration of this is the way royalty consistently makes 'news'.

One other weakness of the 'news is random reactions to random events' approach to the study of news is that it ignores the organizational setting of news production. News production is continuous and has to be so if newspapers are to be produced every twenty-four hours and if broadcast news bulletins are to be transmitted at regular times. The process must be organized, routinized and freed from a haphazard supply of news so that the news vehicles appear professionally produced and at set regular intervals. News organizations are, after all, only part of much larger enterprises which also take in the needs of the advertisers, the requirements of the printing/production centres (in the case of the press) or an entertainment business and a television schedule (in the case of television). All these separate and different interests must be satisfied. The news organization cannot treat them cavalierly by only producing newspapers, say, when there is 'news'. Production must be tailored to meet strict deadlines so that the consumption of the product can take place at appropriate intervals.

The news organization must then have a method by which to filter and select from a vast array of items just the right quantity of material to fit into the news spaces available: in the case of newspapers, it is the space available after the adverts have been slotted in and in the case of television it is a set amount of time. These spaces are fixed and are only varied if a major news story – a major disaster, death of royalty or political leader – occurs.

A final criticism of the 'random reactions to random events' approach is that it overlooks the way in which news organizations can determine the newsworthiness of items and create news areas. News organizations exercise a great deal of power in deciding which areas they want to cover. Thus, they can decide to cover, or ignore, say, the environment and lead pollution (see Chapter 8). Similarly, they can create a new specialist area of journalism. In recent years, for example, all the quality papers have created 'media' specialists and this then makes the 'media' a newsworthy area.

The importance of organizational considerations can be seen in the following four aspects in the production of news:[20]

1. News organizations are hierarchically and bureaucratically organized so as to manage the flow of news. Both newspaper and television news organizations have an elaborate system to control, process and routinize the production of news. This ensures that a regular flow of usable news items are processed and accepted (or rejected) by workers who have a common, and tested, 'nose for news'. It also ensures that the 'right' amount of news is selected.
2. To regularize the flow of news and to use the news organization's labour power efficiently, journalists are placed in institutions (Parliament, the Courts, police stations) which guarantee a regular supply of news. This has the effect of making news fairly predictable – there will be political news, news from the courts, from police sources – even though one attribute of news is its unpredictability!

A related practice which also makes news predictable is the

reliance of news organizations on set events and 'the diary'. The category of set events includes 'pseudo-events': events which have no real existence in themselves. Such events are not 'spontaneous' but are 'planned, planted, or incited' and their 'occurrence is arranged for the convenience of the reporting. . . media'.[21] 'Stunts', sponsored events, and gala openings are examples of such pseudo-events.

Many of these events are usually included in the newsroom 'diary'. This is a record of forthcoming events – political conferences, speeches by prominent people, press conferences – compiled for the purpose of easing the collection of information. Though it can stifle initiative and produce bland news, its advantages for television in particular are immense. The technical requirements of television put it at a disadvantage as against the press; television journalists are not as flexible in their working patterns and the need for visual material imposes its own requirements on the process of news gathering. The 'diary' is, therefore, a great aid of television news. According to Schlesinger, some seventy per cent of BBC news bulletins were stories originating from the 'diary'.[22]

3.   This relates to an important feature of contemporary journalism: its passivity. 'News production becomes increasingly passive as it grows in scope and technical complexity.'[23] The handout, the press release, the journal, the mail, and the use of the telephone, now tend to replace to some extent the newsgathering activity that used to take place outside the newsroom. That, and the availability of the ubiquitous round-the-clock agency tapes in all newsrooms further reduces the need to venture out from the newsroom to seek news and perhaps even to be critical. The result is a passive form of journalism which, in the context of news about the welfare state, also leads to a readiness to accept the 'prevailing definition of what social policy is about'.[24]

4.   The creation of 'specialisms' and 'specialist' correspondents[25] also ensures a regular supply of material. Specialists cover specific areas – education, technology, social services – and this brings them into direct and regular contact with their sources of news, usually government departments. Specialist correspondents, particularly in the fields of politics (lobby, diplomatic, foreign affairs), have a high status and this propels much of their work onto the front pages of newspapers.

145

But if this is an organizationally convenient and cost-effective method of gathering news material, it is not without its flaws. Officials with assured access to eager journalists can often exploit their source status for their own personal or organizational needs. They, and their public relations departments, will often attempt to 'manage the news' so as to influence public debate. Although this practice has been extensively documented in relation to briefings for political (lobby) correspondents,[26] it is by no means exclusive to them. Golding and Middleton have described a similar process in their study of correspondents working in the field of social security/social affairs and conclude that 'social security news, like other species of journalism, is highly dependent on its sources'.[27] Not only does it 'take the writer too close to the sources, creating an unhealthy symbiosis that rapidly chokes journalistic independence', but it also creates a 'narrow dependence on a limited circle of authoritative sources' for social security news – namely the government, 'the relevant professional establishment and, for reaction, to the more active pressure and interest groups'.[28]

That such a dependence can expose correspondents to the full panoply of news management techniques and also have an effect on the nature of public debate can be seen in the following example. In 1983, the Thatcher Government was considering a series of changes in the duties of, and the charges made by, opticians. But, by excluding 'health correspondents from (lobby) briefings to "reform" the optician's service',[29] it ensured that those with knowledge about the opticians' service would not be there to ask awkward questions and, perhaps more significantly, that the following day's news would be less technical and critical than it might otherwise have been.

Not surprisingly, many journalists have disagreed with this interpretation of their work routines. Some have argued that collaboration with sources allows reporters to pay close attention to the views of those in power and that this is of the greatest interest to the public[30] and that, in any case, collaboration does not amount to domination. Tunstall's study of specialist correspondents throws some light on this matter. His data, culled from interviews and questionnaires, suggests that some caution ought to be exercised when discussing source–journalist relationships. He points out that 'although news sources may maintain substantial control in one area such as Motoring . . . it does not follow that news sources can control, for instance, Foreign correspondents; [Foreign correspondents] appear to be largely free of news-source control'. [31] This suggests that there are differences between specialisms and specialist correspondents which cannot be reduced to some single notion of 'domination', 'source-control' or even 'journalistic independence'.

These points notwithstanding, one still has to bear in mind the central issue that underlies the discussion about 'source domination', namely, that although sources may not determine the news, they may still be able to influence the perspective from which it is viewed.[32] Some media critics have argued that the media's routinized organizational dependence on 'legitimate' sources of information such as the courts, the police, and politicians, ensures that they *reproduce the definitions of the powerful*, without being, in a simple sense, in their pay'. Herein lies the distinction between the '*primary* and *secondary definers* of social events'; the former 'define' the problem and the latter, the media, by the sheer act of repetition, concur. One consequence of this is that

> the institutional definers ... establish the initial definition or *primary interpretation* of the topic in question [which] then "commands the field". Arguments *against* [it] are forced to insert themselves into *its* definition of "what is at issue"[33]

Another related 'danger' for specialists is that, even if they are not 'dominated' by a source, they may still gradually absorb source values and perspectives until source and reporter become 'virtual allies'.[34] As Gans observes in relation to the coverage of the Watergate scandal, the story was discovered not by the regular political correspondents but by general reporters.[35] The outsiders were not compromised by the close relationships which had been established between the regular political reporters and their political sources.

General reporters are under greater editorial direction in their newsgathering activity than specialist correspondents. They can be assigned to a variety of news/events, often work simultaneously on stories from different subject areas, and are sometimes required to assist specialist correspondents. They develop their own, though less frequent, sources according to their given assignments. But even this temporary source–reporter relationship is not entirely free of the danger of source control. While it is true that compared to the specialist the general reporter has fewer restraints upon his/her freedom to ask probing questions, lack of familiarity with the source or subject can result in a situation where the source can exploit the reporter's inexperience and so 'manage' the news. Unfamiliarity with a subject can also lead to inaccurate reporting since 'reporters may cover one side of a story without ever knowing there are other sides'.[36]

The media as 'secondary definers': are they orchestrating public opinion?

The analysis of source-journalist domination and collaboration contains within it a suggestion that public opinion is orchestrated by the powerful for political and social purposes. It is here that one can make use of Hall *et al.*'s distinction between 'primary and secondary' definers: an incident is defined as a threat, authoritative persons pronounce on it (the 'primary definers') and the media (the 'secondary definers') exaggerate and amplify the threat. The courts and the police then act to eliminate the threat. Thus, the 'moral panic'[37] over muggings in the early 1970s was a specific response to a more generalized crisis in society and a means by which the state could re-establish its domination. In this respect, Hall *et al.* see such panics more as 'an index of the disintegration of the social order. . .'[38] than as exaggerated and amplified responses to 'threats to societal values and interests' which are themselves the products of social dislocation rather than crisis.

These different perspectives are related to the extent to which one sees deliberate intent in the media's exaggeration and amplification of 'moral panics'. Are 'primary definers' politically motivated and deliberately manipulating public anxieties for a higher purpose? Or is the process, though ideologically biased, without intent? Does the model of 'primary/secondary definers' describe a process of deliberate *manipulation* rather than a less conspiratorial *orchestration* of public opinion?

Studies which employ the concept of 'moral panic' leave one in no doubt that the media do *reproduce* the opinions of the powerful; but do the media also *reflect* public concerns? Is it possible to suggest, in other words, that whilst they unjustifiably exaggerate and accentuate news stories, the mass media at the same time are resonating unarticulated public concerns? (A related issue is the

148

extent to which the 'powerful' may be said to *represent* public opinion.)

One can explore these issues in both Hall *et al.*'s *Policing the Crisis* and Golding and Middleton's *Images of Welfare*. One of the main themes of *Policing the Crisis* is that a 'moral panic' was created over the crime of 'mugging' in the 1970s. As the authors point out, there was no statistical evidence to suggest that the crime of 'mugging' – which they see as a very traditional form of crime – had either increased or become so commonplace as to represent a dramatic rise in violent crime in British society. 'Mugging', they claim, 'provoked an organized response' that 'was out of all proportion to any level of actual threat which could be reconstructed through the unreliable statistics'.[39] One could only explain the creation of the 'panic' by referring to the 'crisis' in Britain.

Whilst their conclusions, based as they are on a reading and analysis of the statistical data, may be valid, the book makes the erroneous assumption that the media mirrors, or ought to mirror, a statistical reality. In fact, the media do not do so. They reproduce in a selective, distorted, and exaggerated fashion aspects of the world which stand out. Indeed, one of the interesting features of the 'mugging' stories examined in *Policing the Crisis* is the apparent 'senselessness' of the crimes, that is, robbery with violence for very small sums of money. It was these features of the crimes which the media reflected.

Thus, whether or not these crimes were variants of an older form of crime and whether or not the police and the courts acted as 'primary definers' are important, but secondary, issues. To argue, as Hall *et al.* do, that statistically there was no real evidence for an increase in the incidence of the crime, is to conflate two issues: a debate about method and a concern about crime. It was the latter 'reality' which the media conveyed.

It could be argued, then, that in conveying this 'reality' as well as commenting upon it, the media were voicing concern – shared by the public – at the occurrence of such crimes and the defenceless status of the victim. The media may have therefore been articulating and feeding on public concerns rather than creating them. There is a danger that in a model of mass communication which consists of 'primary and secondary definers', public anxiety and public opinion will be seen as a product of the mass media and perhaps even a cynical construction by the powerful. Public concern – which is not readily or easily manifested and which may or may not exist – is thus too easily dismissed. In these studies, and with a sleight of hand, the public is doubly disenfranchized: once by the primary definers and the media, and once by the media critic. Yet the relationship between the media, public opinion, and attitudes and 'primary definers' is too complex to allow for such simplistic treatment.

The complexity of that relationship can be seen in *Images of Welfare*. Although the authors retain the 'primary and secondary definers' distinction, they are careful not to dismiss public concerns and attitudes which may have non-media origins. As they point out, the media's 'moral panic' over 'scroungerphobia' was an assault on the welfare state, but it was successful because it exploited *existing* ways of thinking.

> Contradictory attitudes in working class thought were thus *orchestrated* . . . though the role of the media was to *interpret and organise rather than to create attitudes and myths.*[40]

Public attitudes are immensely complex condensations of contradictory ways of thinking: materialism, hedonism, decency, individualism, ambition, impatience with bureaucrats and so on. These produce a 'potent brew' which contains within it the seeds of scepticism about the welfare state. And one major reason why it fell such an easy prey, according to the authors, was 'that the so-called "welfare consensus" has never taken deep root'[41] and so

> 'Thatcherism' has been able to draw on a critique of the welfare state already clearly argued within the party and immediately recognisable in popular prejudice and mythology.[42]

Despite crude and extreme distortions, media stories may also sometimes 'resonate'[43] with public anxieties.

THE QUESTION OF BIAS IN TELEVISION NEWS

Although there is widespread agreement with the view that news is unavoidably influenced, and therefore 'biased', by organizational routines, production constraints and journalistic values, contention still surrounds the problem of identifying the causes of bias. Some bias is unavoidable: journalists, like everybody else, carry ideological baggage and so cannot report events in some pure and universally truthful way.

But such influences and biases are 'the inevitable but unintended consequences of organization'[44] rather than deliberate acts of bias. The Langs first drew attention to this form of bias in their study of 'television's unique perspective'[45] (see Chapter 1, pp. 9–10). They were describing a process by which the television images of the MacArthur day celebrations somehow 'distorted' the nature of the 'reality' which it was supposed to mirror: the television pictures focused on a small part of the whole, the commentators played up the excitement of the event, the sound amplified the cheers and the whole affair was personalized around the character of General MacArthur. Those who experienced the event at first hand had quite different perceptions of 'what really happened'.

It was the difference between the participants' reports and the perceptions of the event as seen on television which led them to develop their views on the origin of this form of bias. Such bias was not intended but it derived from television's own audio-visual requirements for entertainment and spectacle. It was an 'unwitting' or 'unintended' form of bias.

One obvious major weakness of this study is that it assumes that one can obtain a commonly agreed view of 'what really happened'. It is more likely in fact that each individual's perception and interpretation of an event will differ; it may vary according to physical factors, such as where they stand, but also according to social and cultural factors such as social class, education, and so on. This makes it even more difficult to *identify* and *justify* claims that content is 'biased' since individuals will vary in their interpretations and perceptions of any one event or report.

The inability to capture events in their totality is compounded by another difficulty. The media rely on language and images for the purpose of communication. A newspaper report is mainly based on the written word (language), whilst the television news report is a combination of images and spoken text. Yet neither language nor images are without some degree of ideological refraction; as the Glasgow University Media Group put it, television news is

a sequence of socially manufactured messages, which carry many of the culturally dominant assumptions of our society. *From the* *accents of the newscasters to the vocabulary of camera angles. . .*the news is a highly mediated product.[46]

This perspective on news emphasizes the extent to which all content is mediated and it does, therefore, suggest that the attainment of objectivity is well nigh impossible. The process of mediation – choice of camera angles, choice of words, choice of images, etc. – necessarily refracts the 'reality' it is meant to capture. It was this critique which led the group to question the ability of television to fulfil its regulatory requirements of 'objectivity', 'fairness', and 'due impartiality' in all matters of controversy. It also revived concern over 'bias' in television news.

The reasons for this concern were succinctly put by Colin Sparks in a review of a study of the coverage of the miners' strike in 1984–5.

> The critical school of media studies (e.g. Glasgow Univ. Media Group) has held, as a central tenet of its position, the view that the products of the mass media are *systematically organized so that they represent a picture of the world which is such as to assist in the reproduction of the relations of domination existing in society.*[47]

But what procedures does one adopt to determine the validity of this, or similar, 'hypotheses' to the effect that the media do aid the 'reproduction of the relations of domination'?

Evidence for the existence of bias is generally obtained from the results of content analysis, a method which, although useful and informative, is unable to reveal anything about news producers' intentions concerning content or the actual or intended audience effect. As the GUMG found out, even appealing to scientific methodology inherent in content analysis is no escape from the task of demonstrating bias. One of their examples illustrates an aspect of the problem.

On 3 January 1975, the then Prime Minister Harold Wilson delivered a speech in a Labour club in his Huyton constituency. This speech got wide coverage in the media. In his speech, Wilson covered a range of subjects including the state of the motor industry and the role of the state in funding loss-making industries. As the GUMG point out, television news focused on the section of the speech in which Wilson made a reference to 'manifestly avoidable stoppages of production' in the car industry. This reference, according to them, was interpreted by TV news in such a way that it presented strikes as the main problem facing the car industry. A related criticism is that though the speech was critical of unions *and* management, television news only singled out the unions. 'The speech . . is defined as being directed solely at workers and the reference in his speech to the problems of private capital has been cut.'[48]

But what did Wilson 'actually say' and what did he 'mean'? Wilson did make a reference to 'management' in his speech but was that reference more than a passing one, a throwaway comment of little note? More pertinently, how does one interpret what a two-page speech 'is all about'? Given the context in which the speech was made – a Labour club, an impending strike by car workers, an industry clamouring for government funding – what interpretations can one make of the speech? As Harrison notes, in

> politics, where delicate problems are being aired, formal and political meanings may diverge. In assessing the speech one must not only see it as text but note his [Wilson's] choice of venue. . .and his known attitudes on wage claims and strikes . . . .[49]

A close reading of the speech (which can be found in Harrison's, but not the GUMG's, book) raises many doubts about the GUMG's interpretation and analysis of the text; in fact, it would be hard to justify their claims that television deleted critical parts of the speech. A different, and perhaps more valid, interpretation of the speech would be that it focused primarily on the unwelcome action of certain trade unions.

This example, of itself, does not deny the value of the group's other work though it does identify the complexity of justifying accusations of 'bias', irrespective of how sophisticated the analysis on which they are based is. Certainly, the criticism of television news *vis-à-vis* the Wilson speech begs more questions than it answers and it employs a very naïve view of the determination of 'what really happened'.

A similar set of problems can be found in the recent controversy over the coverage of the miners' strike. The authors of the study *Television and the Miners' Strike*[50] have been accused of playing down the extent to which 'the news is a selective interpretation of events: i.e. that it is biased'[51] and, by extension, of playing down the extent of bias in the reporting of the miners' strike.

The content analysis of the coverage of the strike does show television's selectivity: the largest single category of issues was 'talks and negotiations' followed by 'picketing and picket violence'. The category of 'pit closures' and 'economics' was, by comparison, barely covered. Cumberbatch *et al.* explain television's preference for exploring the 'conduct of the strike rather than its causes' by referring to the 'event driven' nature of news (rather than to any form of bias). To emphasize this, they point out that the issues which received little attention in news programmes were well covered in documentaries and current affairs programmes.[52]

But television is not completely exonerated. Their survey respondents continue to point to television's bias: although the majority of their sample (58%) thought that television was unbiased, those who thought that television was biased against the miners heavily outnumbered those who thought it favoured the miners (by 3:1 in the case of BBC and ITN). Respondents also believed that Arthur Scargill, the president of the NUM, was interviewed far more critically than Ian McGregor, chairman of the NCB. This finding was also confirmed in the content analysis of the coverage.[53]

In defending their work, the authors[54] point out that their critics use the term bias in a very general way and so do not distinguish between deliberate and unintentional bias. As the discussion above emphasized, the processes of selection do inevitably bias accounts but this hardly substantiates Sparks' 'hypothesis' concerning the media's role in assisting in the 'reproduction of the relations of domination'. The authors of *The Miners' Strike* add another pertinent comment. They tried, they explain, to explore complex issues rather than compare television and reality since there are no means by which one can obtain a version of reality that is 'reliable, comprehensive and independent of the media'.[55] The issues which they examined were those which were presented in the news broadcasts, not those which *one would have liked* to see presented.

Although these examples point to difficulties inherent in actual studies they also highlight real theoretical problems about the meaning of bias. What is it? Can it be satisfactorily defined? What is an un-biased story? How does bias relate to objectivity, impartiality or even 'due impartiality'?

In this highly contentious area there are, not surprisingly, major differences of opinion. For Herbert Gans, the idea of bias is a valid, but a relational, one. News can be judged as biased but only in relation to a standard of non-bias. Such standards are, however, not absolute because they involve some reality judgement concerning the nature of external reality, knowledge and truth. 'Identifying distorted news and proposing a standard for undistorted news is a political act, and while the act itself is desirable, the actor ultimately must take sides.'[56] His solution to this problem of news bias would be to create vehicles for news from different political perspectives; biases would then cancel each other out. Though apparently reasonable, this solution ignores some fundamental attributes of news. For, as McQuail reminds us,

> the idea of news is that it is beyond a "plurality of viewpoints". . . without an attribution of credibility by the audience, news could not be distinguished from entertainment and propaganda.[57]

A very different approach to the subject of bias, impartiality, and objectivity can be found in Golding and Elliott's study of broadcast news. They define 'impartiality' as

> a disinterested approach to news, lacking in motivation to shape or select material according to a particular view or opinion. Objectivity. . . [demands] . . a complete and unrefracted capture of the world.[58]

Their definition of impartiality accords to an extent with the view of the broadcasters. For the BBC, '*due* impartiality' does involve an attempt to avoid taking sides in any controversy and consequently balancing different accounts of each issue, but it also acknowledges 'the weights of the opinions which hold those views'.[59] This can be achieved in a number of ways. Professional journalists could, for example, seek out the 'facts' and ensure their accuracy and relevance and they could give 'all sides of the story'. Such mechanisms are common and enable journalists to claim that their reports are presented professionally, accurately and without bias. These procedures for handling stories – procedures which include balancing opposites, presenting supporting evidence, accessing opposites, using quotation marks in written reports, and so on – are 'strategies' or 'rituals'[60] of newswork and so protect the journalist from outside interference and attack.

But for some academics this 'impartiality' is merely an illusion.

To ask whether a particular story is 'impartial' or not, 'biased' or not, is to miss the point; in the 'long-term and routine, unreflective practices of journalism' which, for instance, deny the existence of power relations and social processes in news stories, there *is* bias, there *is* an ideology. 'News does not enable us to fully comprehend or grasp the significance of events in society, rather it mystifies them.'[61]

Changing the forms, structures or content of news broadcasts – for example, longer news bulletins or more in-depth reporting – is therefore of little value. One has to completely restructure broadcasting as a whole so as to make more room for 'the extended presentation of abstraction and complexity'.[62] However, is there only *one* way in which one can 'comprehend or grasp the significance of events'? For if there are more ways than one, then it may be that acknowledging and allowing for divergent views is in fact not only a more practicable solution but also truer to the divergences of opinions in our complex society.

Finally, and contrary to the view that changing forms produces little benefit, evidence from the study of the reporting of the miners' strike shows that the longer news programmes (*Channel Four News, Newsnight, Weekend World*) are perceived as better vehicles for informing the public. The longer broadcast, the in-depth analysis, and the avoidance of the 'facts, faces, and events' approach all work in their favour.[63] As Channel Four News is produced within ITN and by many ex-*News at Ten* or BBC journalists and cameramen, it also suggests that the same journalists, using similar news values, can produce a different sort of product if the structure and format of the news programme is changed. It is therefore the form and the context of the programme and the slight *modification* of news values that results in some significant shifts in public perceptions of bias and fairness. Could the solution to the problem of news – assuming that it is identified by the public as a problem – then lie, not in the wholesale restructuring of broadcasting but in some mildly radical changes to the existing forms?

NEWS MANAGEMENT AND SPECIALIST REPORTERS: THE CASE OF THE LOBBY CORRESPONDENTS

The coverage of the conflict in the South Atlantic over the Falklands brought to light practices of news management, that is, the deliberate feeding of (sometimes inaccurate) information to journalists in the hope of confusing or duping the enemy (or the readers).[64] Such practices are not new but they illustrate the ability of those in power to manipulate others by selectively releasing information to journalists who, for whatever reason, often use that information. Another form of news management is the co-ordinated release of information at appropriate times, for example, 'bad' news on Fridays and in time for the Saturday papers, or 'good' news to swamp the 'bad' news. In recent years, the Conservative Government has also taken a great interest in the handling of information. The release of information is now carefully controlled through the Prime Minister's press office not only as a means of co-ordinating information – all ministers, say, making a similar set of points in their speeches – but also as a way of ensuring that a stream of good news stories do find their way into the media.

The success of news management techniques obviously depends on the degree to which journalists reproduce the released information. It also depends on the closeness and secrecy of the relationship between source and journalist. If attempts at news management are visible and crude, it is not likely that they will succeed. One area of journalism which has all the makings of an ideal setting for news management practices is that of the lobby correspondent.

The lobby system has long fascinated outsiders because of its curious mix of mystery, ritual and ordinary news-gathering techniques. Yet, because the lobby correspondents are at the centre of political news-gathering and news-making, the whole question of the lobby has often been seen as not only an issue of propriety in journalism but 'an issue *in* British politics' itself.[65] Are they too close to government? Is the journalist-source relationship too cosy for the good of journalism and open government? Are lobby correspondents too easily managed by government sources? Have they become a tool of political decision-making?

Although this unease about the proper role and efficiency of the lobby is not particularly new, it took on a greater significance when two national dailies, the *Independent* and the *Guardian*, finally withdrew from a system of news-gathering which had long been under scrutiny and attack. This rupture with a 100-year-old system occasioned a debate among lobby journalists about their own future and the future of the system itself. That it has so far survived this momentary crisis suggests that its practices are found satisfactory by many of its members. What then accounts for its longevity and, simultaneously, its unpopularity?

The 'lobby system' is a short-hand term used to describe the system of political journalism in Britain. Lobby correspondents, sometimes referred to as Political Correspondents, have privileged access to the lobby of the House of Commons. Unlike specialist correspondents in, say, education or industrial affairs, the lobby correspondents' specialism is geographical in origin. Their access to the lobby – a privilege granted in 1884 – and other areas of the Commons means, in effect, that they share a common area with ministers, MPs and officials. This 'access to the troughs and watering holes frequented by our elected legislators'[66] places them in a unique position from which to observe and report upon the heart of the British political system.

Lobby correspondents have other important privileges which enable them to carry out their tasks more easily: they have access to documents prior to their official publication and they also have a right to attend lobby briefings which are held in Downing Street and in the Commons. It is in these various ways that they are able to collect information on, and to report, the gossip and the ebbs and flows of the political and Parliamentary system.

The lobby correspondents are, therefore, the key mechanism through which a considerable amount of political information from government (and opposition) finds its way into the public domain. Indeed, their stories are very often the front page leads of the national dailies and they are also very prominent in broadcasting news. Though other reporters may also gain access to politicians or the House of Commons, it is only the lobby correspondent who is placed within the system itself.

Unfortunately, their privileges are part of a complex trade-off: their access to the heart of the political system is conditional on their reports being unattributable to any particular source of information. Their work is carried out 'on lobby terms', that is, they never report the source of their information. Even the daily briefings arranged for the lobby are usually on a 'not for attribution' basis. For many lobby correspondents, this practice of non-attribution is one of the strengths of the lobby system. It is part of the paradox that 'upon secrecy, rests openness'.[67] If sources of information were to be named, so the argument goes, they would soon refuse to divulge information; by not naming sources, one is then better able to gather information from the 'deep throats' of Westminster.

One immediate consequence of the non-attribution rule is that lobby correspondents use tortuous phrases to disguise their sources of information. Phrases such as 'Ministers are. . .', 'Sources close to the Prime Minister. . .', 'MPs in the House of Commons. . .' intentionally disguise the real source of information but it leaves the lobby correspondents and their practices open to numerous criticisms. As the reports are usually written in an opaque fashion, the reader of those reports may find it difficult to know who to believe, particularly as many of these reports can often subsequently be denied by politicians. Another criticism is that by using these well known phrases, the correspondents may be magnifying the importance of their source and/or presenting guesswork as fact. In all these cases, it is not possible to check on the veracity or the accuracy of the report since it has no named source.

A closely related criticism of the lobby system is that it misrepresents both the real source of power in Britain and the real nature of the news-gathering operation in the Commons. First, lobby correspondents portray Westminster as the centre of the political and legislative universe; in the process the Whitehall side of the political equation is overlooked. Second, the idyll picture of the lobby system at work conjures up images of individual journalists buttonholing ministers and MPs and doggedly pursuing leads and investigations at the very heart of the political establishment. But, in reality, the system is very different. Lobby correspondents are generalists and so not always able to deal with the range of subjects on which they are briefed. Consequently, they may be easily 'guided' in ways which would not work for the specialist correspondent (see example on p. 146 above). Moreover, at present there are some 100 to 150 accredited lobby correspondents and this large number imposes its own constraints upon the ability of individuals to gather information. In effect, as the number of correspondents has increased so too has the tendency to rely on collective news-gathering arrangements; 'it is the *collective* activities of the lobby which modern critics abhor as a cosy cartel between Government and press.'[68]

The image of the 'cartel' is apt for the mutually advantageous trade-offs that take place between the two parties in this very cosy arrangement. The lobby correspondent is given easy and ready access to information, gossip and leads, and, in return, they protect their sources. For critics, this system has all the makings of a comfortable existence and so can lead to lazy and 'pack' journalism, that is, the collective reproduction of ready made political statements disguised as fact. But this criticism has a far more serious side to it which also takes for granted the dangerous qualities of the non-attribution system: does it leave the lobby system open to abuse by those willing and able to manage it?

A good example of these dangers was given by Ian Aitken in the *Guardian*. He described an off-the-record briefing to the lobby in which an 'unidentifiable spokesman from the Prime Minister's press office slagged off Neil Kinnock' for his comments on the government's prosecution of Peter Wright in Australia. According to Aitken, the

> entire episode ... provides a classic example of what is wrong with non-attribution in such circumstance. ... the rule, when applied to the principal source of day-to-day information about government policy, *enabled the Government to evade responsibility for their own questionable statements whenever it suited them.* That has been the increasingly frequent practice of Downing Street spokesmen under Thatcher, though the target has more often been her own ministers than Opposition party leaders.[69]

His more specific point is that the episode presented lobby correspondents with a grave problem. If they reported the comments they would be giving 'readers a certain amount of authority for a statement whose only real authority stemmed from the fact that the Prime Minister' was associated with it.

Such a use of the lobby for political purposes and for scoring political points is neither of recent origin nor unusual. Past Prime Ministers have also employed similar techniques to attack their enemies both within and outside their own political parties and they are able to do so because lobby practices allow them to avoid responsibility for their own statements.

Such 'positive deception or the manipulation of news as an instrument of policy'[70] is the reason why the system should be opened up. But those who support it argue that news management of this sort takes place in all walks of life and in all branches of journalism. No press secretary or public relations person of any merit would *not* seek to release/'leak' material in such a way and at such a time and place as to suit their particular needs. Media practices – routines, deadlines, laziness, lack of inquisitiveness – make the exploitation of the media an easy affair.

These discussions about the lobby are far from new and one can draw on examples from many periods of British history to illustrate the process of 'guidance' which so infects this particular system. And just as the criticisms are not new, neither are the present debates about reforming the lobby. Yet, and despite murmurings about reform, the lobby system has persisted. The break with tradition came with the decision of the *Independent* not to take part in the lobby system. Although it had its share of political correspondents, they would not attend the off-the-record lobby briefings. The *Guardian* followed suit but with a less radical plan: where possible, it would name the source of information. No longer would 'Downing Street' suffice as a description of the source. Its ultimate aim was to name Bernard Ingham, Thatcher's press secretary, as the true source of its political information in lobby briefings. Both newspapers gained support for their actions from the leaders of the opposition parties who promised to do away with off-the-record briefings.

These decisions by two quality papers led to a debate within the lobby about its own future. A motion to change the rules of non-attribution – a fundamental criticism of the system – was, however, defeated by 67 votes to 55 votes. An inquiry by lobby members into the lobby system not only replayed the divisions of opinion about its status that had long dogged its life but it also hinted at the reasons for its longevity. As the inquiry report observed, two themes emerged:

> that the system of unattributable lobby briefings should be ended in the interests of more open government, and that the lobby system, for all its faults, is the 'least objectionable' . . . way of ensuring the flow of information from the Government to the public and that to discontinue it would be to inhibit the flow.[71]

It would seem that many lobby correspondents do still feel that the present system does allow much sensitive information to flow out of government. It is worth noting in this respect that though the *Independent* does not take part in the system it has access to information that derives from those who do. Similarly, many correspondents do feel very strongly that their privileged access to individual MPs and ministers does often produce important insights into the workings of government. Few would contemplate giving up the direct access to all the members of Parliament which is their prized possession. Their obvious fear is that opening up the system would drive away information and informants who want to remain anonymous.

The lobby correspondents work in an endemically secretive system and so reforming this part of it would be of minor consequence though it would have a symbolic value. Moves to openness would not only require legislative reform but a change in the 'nanny state' philosophy that runs like a binding thread through most of Britain's administrative machinery.[72] It would also require that much greater attention be paid to Whitehall rather than Westminster. It might also require a review of the effect of ownership on the work of the lobby: a more politically varied press might not be so easily manipulated.

Chapter Eight

'M IS FOR MEDIA': THE POLITICS OF MEDIA PRESSURE

Increased awareness of the central importance of media coverage has convinced many pressure groups that they need to seek the aid of the media in order to achieve their aims. By obtaining favourable media coverage, such groups are very often and speedily propelled onto the political stage. Their work and their aims, as a result, acquire an invaluable public dimension; paradoxically, the public dimension also appears to confirm to the groups their own perceptions of their importance and significance.

Of greater importance, however, is the realization that groups that successfully use the media also usually acquire a political status. Some groups will become the focus of opposition to government policy (e.g. Friends of the Earth), others will become legitimate sources of information (e.g. Amnesty), still others will be accepted as commentators on social legislation or policy (e.g. Shelter, Child Poverty Action Group). Many of these groups cease to be purely private, 'behind-the-scenes', affairs; their public political dimension moves them out of the administrative decision-making process and into the political arena. Such groups, therefore, no longer simply seek influence within the 'corridors of power', their aim is to mould public (and private) opinion and so transform 'what had previously been a humdrum administrative matter into a sensitive political issue'.[1]

Not all pressure or lobby groups seek such notoriety. Furthermore, not all groups are able to obtain the publicity which they desire. Nevertheless, there now exist numerous groups whose priority is to win the battle for column centimetres. The belief that one ought to capture the media as a prerequisite to shaping perceptions and definitions of problems so as to win an argument has now filtered down from politicians to trade unionists[2] to pressure and lobby groups.

Some groups have in fact been extremely successful in their liaison with the media. Shelter, National Viewers and Listeners Association, Child Poverty Action Group, the Campaign for Lead-free Air, and groups within the environmental lobby generally are particularly good examples. Others have clearly been much less successful. Yet, and irrespective of their degrees of media success, all groups work on the assumption that media attention is a prerequisite for success. In Des Wilson's *Pressure: The A to Z of Campaigning in Britain*,[3] M for Media occupies by far the largest section; admittedly, it covers a whole range of media and illustrates the author's ability to use the media, but it also highlights the view that '[t]o have media sympathetic to the campaign or cause of a lobby group is a powerful asset'.[4]

There are many instances which lend support to this view. In 1978, Greenpeace intervened in a proposed seal cull in Orkney. Media coverage of the event – resplendent with pictures of defenceless, dewy eyed, baby seals – forced the Secretary of State for Scotland to call the cull off.[5] Another example usually cited to illustrate the importance and effectiveness of the media is the Conservation Society's revelations in 1971 of the extent of illegal dumping of toxic waste. These revelations forced the Government to act in a very short space of time even though it had had proposals for controlling such dumping under consideration for over two years. The publicity created a situation which necessitated a speedy resolution of the problem.

It is likely, however, that specific circumstances surround these examples of success and that these may have more to do with the nature of the concern – usually environmental – than with the use of the media *per se*. The environment provides a fertile ground for many stories. As few members of the public are likely to welcome *more* pollution and *more* destruction of the environment, such environmental stories normally attract much attention. They offer

a strong emotive and moralistic appeal which can be presented as a simple conflict of good versus evil, hence the standard formula for many news items of:

the people		the bulldozers
the community	threatened by	the planners
a rare species		speculators[6]

Environmental stories also benefit because the environment is not defined as a political area in editorial terms and this allows journalists a greater degree of freedom and even an opportunity to conduct campaigns against environmental threats.

Non-environmental groups often struggle for media attention. Unlike the environmental lobby, they may also be perceived as political and, worst of all, *party* political. The CPAG or Shelter, for example, lobby on behalf of the poor and the homeless; in so doing they question both governmental and administrative policies and decisions. This pushes them into an overtly political role; a role (and a set of issues) which the media find more difficult to deal with than the overtly 'apolitical' issue of environmental destruction.

The media, then, do not treat everyone equally and fairly. Stories do not get published or broadcast on the basis of their merit alone nor, sometimes, on the basis of their 'newsworthiness'. As the case study of the Campaign for Lead-free Air demonstrates, the media can exercise an enormous degree of freedom in its choice and treatment of stories. Media attention has to be *sought* and *fought for* – a process which emphasizes the need to capture the media with 'interesting' 'stories' and 'events'. Des Wilson insists that

> On the whole, the media will help you (the campaigner) if there's something in it for them. That 'something' is 'a good story', whether it be a news item or feature, and, of course, the best story is a good story that is also exclusive.[7]

But is the assumption that media success brings with it political trophies a valid one? Is there evidence to show that media attention translates into policy successes?

THE INFLUENCE OF THE MEDIA: THE REPORTING OF 'DISASTERS'

Media coverage does bring issues to public attention and public prominence. The category of events that proves the point is that of 'disasters'. 'Disasters', as a category, takes in natural disasters such as earthquakes and famines but also man-made disasters such as nuclear accidents and chemical spills – the ferry disaster at Zeebrugge in 1987, the nuclear accident at Chernobyl, the chemical accident at Bhopal, the famine in Ethiopia in 1984–5, and so on. Generally speaking, it is usual for the mass media to give considerable coverage to such events albeit for a short period only. More importantly, this coverage usually does have a measurable impact: aid is mobilized, money is raised, charities make appeals and politicians are forced to act.

Cases from the recent past also illustrate the idiosyncratic nature of the media's 'disaster' reporting. Often serious 'disasters' are not covered because reporting teams are not present, or on the grounds that they are not sufficiently 'newsworthy' or that there has been a 'glut' of 'disaster' stories. The media's shortcomings in attempting to fulfil their 'surveillance' role has always been well known and they were further confirmed during the Ethiopian famine of 1983/4/5.

It is now difficult to conceive of that 'story' not appearing on the world's television screens but, in fact, it did take many months for it to become 'news'. Reports, and even photographs, of the famine failed to interest news organizations as far back as 1983.[8] Later, when interest in the famine began to develop, it was still not clear whether it would run as a story. One account of the media's treatment of recent 'disasters' noted that television 'did not have an easy task in reporting Ethiopia. American TV did not readily accept the story, it was not a clear-cut case of immediate interest. . .'.[9] The media were also eclectic and cynical in their work: for example, both the Eurovision news exchange and American television executives had to be persuaded to use the Visnews/BBC/Amin/Buerk film of the famine in Ethiopia. Once used, the film generated international concern and the public responded in a variety of ways.

The central concern here, though, is not the issue of increased public awareness of events nor of the public's response to such events but whether these instances are typical of the way the mass media work and of their 'impact'. Are 'disasters' unusual in the reactions they bring forth? Does the public react in a similar fashion to all 'disasters'?

Experience suggests that each 'disaster' is a unique phenomenon and that reactions to media coverage differ enormously. On a scale of concern, few would generate the level of involvement that the Ethiopian famine did; the more usual response, in addition to a greater awareness, is a heightened concern which does not usually produce any behavioural change. Thus, while the Ethiopian famine led to the creation of the Band Aid phenomenon, few other disasters have led to responses of a similar magnitude. In a different fashion, although pictures of slaughtered baby seals, of dirty rivers and polluted air, do raise the level of concern they rarely, if ever, lead to a mass mobilization for change.

The reasons for these different responses are undoubtedly complex and must relate to the public's perception of their ability to create change. Donating money has a visible and direct impact on the situation whilst the pursuit of political and social change – say, establishing more adequate pollution control mechanisms – requires a different strategy altogether: a strategy that is long-term, politically informed and based around organizational, rather than individual, action.

If the above argument is correct, are attempts by groups and organizations to capture the media based on a simplistic understanding of the media's impact? Is the pursuit of media attention as a prerequisite to bringing about change a waste of effort? Is the belief that media coverage is a causal factor in bringing about change, say, in policy, unfounded?

THE PROBLEM OF CONCEPTUALIZING THE INFLUENCE OF THE MEDIA

To suggest that the news media play a role in a policy or decision-making process is to presume a certain linkage between media content and the policies or decisions emanating from these processes. The premise is, then, that one can detect the news media acting upon policy-makers – a broad term which covers politicians, civil servants and those whose decisions have public consequences – in such a way that the media's intervention has altered, sometimes significantly, the situation, be it at the point where decisions are made or the information on which decisions are based. In practice, then, a pressure or lobby group would seek media attention in the belief that media coverage will not only garner support behind it but that it will have an impact on those who make decisions.

However, this conceptualization of the relationship between the media and policy-makers in general has a number of weaknesses.

In the first place, it fails to distinguish between the different sources of information available to political actors, as well as differences in the behaviour of different groups of actors. Although there is no recent research on the media habits of policy-makers, it is highly probable that they would read the quality newspapers as well as a whole range of specialist journals. These sorts of assumptions about policy-makers' media preferences skews a pressure group's effort in very significant ways and forces them to ignore large sections of the more 'mass' media.

Second, it treats the mass media as if they were external agencies acting upon the political process rather than as part of the process itself. In Chapter One, it was argued that the mass media contribute, and give meaning, to the relationships between the different levels of the political system. News values, for example, are predicated on some implicit understanding of the importance of certain elements in, and for, the political context; that context cannot be seen as external to the mass media since they play a part in its determination by setting the agenda, amongst other things.

As the media are implicated both in setting the agenda and in giving meaning to events, *but do not do so singlehandedly*, it is enormously difficult to analyse their part in the policy-making process. A substantial amount of published 'news' needs to be seen as *information in the form of 'news'* which emanates from particular sources pursuing particular goals and using the media to achieve these. 'Leaks' are a good example of this form of 'news' but they also illustrate a complexity which is often overlooked. To the untutored mass public, 'leaks' are 'ordinary' news stories though they undoubtedly also succeed in their purpose of moulding public opinion; but those who are knowledgeable about the ways of the media – and this category will include politicians and administrators – will view 'leaks' differently. Their judgement on the status of the news story will be mitigated by their knowledge of the process that has made it 'news'. Consequently, they will view it in a different light. There is a particularly good example of this in Barbara Castle's diaries on the Wilson and Callaghan era. Commenting on a political story in the press, she wryly noted that

> The papers are full of the 'dressing down' Harold [Wilson] is supposed to have given Jim [Callaghan] on Thursday. Harold has clearly compensated to the lobby for what he failed to do in Cabinet.[10]

Her verdict on the stories in the press was coloured, in other words, by her knowledge of the circumstances of the making of those stories.

Rather than assume that the policy-makers – who are the targets of all the hard sought media publicity – are susceptible to media influence, one ought to take into account the possibility that they also may be suspicious of the media and news stories for the sorts of reasons which are implicit in Castle's comments. They might 'discount' a particularly horrendous story about pollution on the grounds that the journalist is keen on environmental issues and only an extension of the environmental lobby.

Furthermore, since policy-makers have access to a wide range of media outputs, a single story in one newspaper is unlikely to prove a determining factor. Other media may have decided to ignore the story or may have presented it in a quite different way; unless there is concerted action in the press, the occasional missive is likely to be of limited use. Moreover, with the current availability of databases, policy-makers have easy access to all media output and can judge for themselves the nature of press opinion.

Third, is the influence of the media more powerful than all the individual or combined pressures and influences that bear on policy-makers and the policy-making process? Pressure groups work within an already established context of policy and economic constraints, competing demands for favours, departmental interests, and the need for policy continuity, and this must severely limit the impact of even the most favourable media coverage.

These qualifications suggest that there are, as it were, two sides to any analysis of media influence on policy-makers: a visible and accessible one and an invisible or private one. These correspond to two areas of research, namely

- how much coverage do particular groups obtain? Are the mass media acting independently of such groups or are they acting in complicity with, and on behalf of, such groups?
- are mass media accounts accepted unquestioningly by policy-makers/élites and acted upon?

In their analysis of the reporting of the Welfare State, Golding and Middleton illustrate the difficulty of determining whether the mass media are of primary significance or merely one of many, and lesser, influences on policy-makers. On the one hand, they write that the media shape the political climate. . . so that ultimately legislation and the overall allocation of resources are influenced by mass mediated versions of priorities and necessities [and] they influence the cultural context . . . by setting the tone for public discussion and providing the imagery and rhetoric . . . [for] administrators[11]

Yet, on the other hand, they concede that 'legislation, of course, emerges as a response to a variety of pressures of which media agenda setting is but one'.[12]

One must not assume then that media coverage of itself has an influence or effect; it is necessary to examine the influence of the mass media on policy-makers themselves. Unfortunately, this research area remains largely uncharted and we still know little about the place of the mass media in the decision-making process.

THE MEDIA AND THE POLITICAL ELITE

Like the *New York Times* and the *Washington Post*, the British quality press could be described as constituting 'one network in the central nervous system of the. . .government'.[13] But because professional news practices and the need for news tend to 'bias' the press towards 'authority', it can often be easily manipulated. According to one analysis of American politics, officials use the press 'to change relationships or to attempt to alter policy by changing or feeding information to those who make decisions so influencing the information on which decisions are premised' so as to 'affect policy outcomes'.[14] Politicians, as a general rule, seek to influence by shaping the perceptions of events or by defining the nature of 'reality'.

But is the proposition that the press is instrumental in affecting policy based on anything more than assertions? The press does invariably contribute *something* to all negotiations: it informs the main protagonists of oppositional views and it disseminates information to those not directly involved and to the public. However, the quality of that contribution very much depends on the quality of the journalists and their sources and whether private/confidential information is ever released.

Furthermore, daily press comment is too episodic and decontextualized to be of much use and it usually follows, rather than precedes, the event. One American correspondent admitted that the failing of the press lies *'in not breaking into the policy process before issues are already decided'*.[15] According to this account, decisions are made, but made elsewhere, and the press merely responds to this or, at best, feeds information into the process. The press may be the instrument by which 'policy positions are advanced and defended'[16] rather than the stuff of which policies are made. Being 'news' and 'in the news' may have, therefore, little to do with *influencing* or *altering* policies or *participating* in a process of decision-making.

With so many political, ideological, and economic factors contributing to policies, it is unlikely that the press will in fact be decisive. It rarely indicates the range of organizational and ideological factors that need to be considered before decisions are made. Press copy necessarily simplifies and distorts the essential multifaceted nature of events and proposals. The concept of 'news' also militates against the sorts of discussions and lengthy pieces in the press which would be necessary if the press were to make a meaningful contribution to a decision-making process. The deficiencies of the popular press and of television – the 20th century's mass medium – are greater still.

The campaign examined here – the Campaign for Lead-free Air (CLEAR) – sought to change government policies and public opinion, and it used the mass media to do both.

The politics of pressure: CLEAR, the Campaign for Lead-Free Air

The Campaign was officially launched on 25 January 1982 at a press conference held in London. Des Wilson, the Director of CLEAR, was exploiting a well known fact about the British media, namely, that '[W]ith the British media so highly concentrated in London, even a small group based there can aspire to a national role through effective public relations'.[17] And he was rewarded for his efforts in the following days' press. *The Times, Guardian, Financial Times, Evening Standard* and *Morning Star* all gave the campaign favourable coverage. Although the tabloids gave it little or no coverage, the occasional short piece under a headline such as the *Star*'s 'Children in Peril of Petrol' was sufficient to indicate both the cause of concern and the solution to the problem.

Wilson was to repeat his success with the media the following month with the publication of the 'Yellowlees Letter' (see below) and he made sure that throughout the following two years, CLEAR would appear in the papers at regular intervals. Even a cursory glance at CLEAR's extensive clippings file would confirm the organization's success in media terms. From front page leads in *The Times* and the *Observer* to smaller pieces in a host of local newspapers, CLEAR was never far away from a newspaper story. But how does one assess its success in other terms and in relation to its main objective of the setting of a date for the elimination of lead from petrol? How does one examine its media coverage alongside its other activities?

Air pollution has always been an issue of great public concern. Such concern about a deteriorating environment does indeed 'provide an important outlet for campaigning and investigative journalism..they allow for expressions of editorial "outrage" or concern without the danger of giving political offence to readers. . .'[18]

Although the issue of lead in petrol is more specific, and more complex, than the general one of air pollution, it nevertheless gained a great deal from the general societal concern about air pollution. Those who cared about the environment could not help extend their concern to the issue of lead in petrol; in fact, the issue of lead in petrol had an altogether more dangerous and undesirable quality than simply dirtying the atmosphere. According to CLEAR, it damaged children and stunted their development.

Lead has traditionally been added to petrol in order to boost the Octane rating and so ensure the smooth running of car engines. One subsequent, and key, aspect of the debate was whether car engines could be redesigned to run on unleaded petrol and whether this would adversely affect motoring and the motorists. There were other complex issues. Lead is non-degradable and with each passing year it continues to accumulate in the environment. Although lead emissions from motor cars account for much of this, lead pollutants also derive from the addition of lead in paint, in solder, and in piping. Were lead emissions from motor cars the main culprit of environmental air pollution?

Lead is also a well known neurotoxin and can, and does, cause damage to the brain. Were lead emissions from motor cars the main cause of high lead blood levels in children and adults? Were lead emissions of greater significance than the lead which would derive from paint, solder or piping? Finally, did raised blood lead levels actually result in brain damage as measured by IQ scores?

All these questions were crucial for determining the precise relationship between lead in petrol and the alleged *effects* of lead in petrol. That relationship was never properly explored in the media. The media preferred to dwell on the simple 'black and white' quality of the story with an obvious culprit and an even clearer solution. Lead in petrol was accused of 'poisoning children's brains', of lowering their IQ, and of damaging children generally. To prevent any further damage to children, one simply had to remove lead from petrol. The financial and industrial difficulties of attaining such an objective, e.g. the cost to the motor industry of converting engines to run on lead-free petrol, were rarely aired.

The campaigners were in no doubt that the addition of lead to petrol resulted in damage to children. High concentration of petrol fumes, and consequently of lead particles, was the main cause of damage. Their opponents – the oil refiners, the motor manufacturers and the associated companies – cast doubt on these claims. They maintained that lead in petrol was a possible contributor rather than the sole contributor to the problem. Lead could also be ingested from food and could be derived from the extensive network of lead water pipes which are still in existence. They would also observe that the scientific evidence was by no means conclusive; the evidence was ambiguous.

Notwithstanding the important scientific questions that were raised in the course of the campaign, the issue proved a winner with the media. Sections of the press were only too happy to give it substantial coverage and Des Wilson cleverly managed and manipulated it. His coup was, without doubt, the leaking of the 'Yellowlees Letter' to *The Times*.

The Yellowlees Letter

Before the launch of the campaign, Wilson had obtained a copy of a letter written by Sir Henry Yellowlees, Chief Medical Officer at the DHSS, to his Whitehall colleagues. The long letter made a number of significant points which were, according to Wilson, 'dynamite'. Yellowlees, in effect, appeared to contradict a government report by the Lawther Committee and subsequent government statements which made much of the (scientific) *uncertainty* over the danger of lead to children and of the risks of lead in the environment. Not only did Yellowlees point to further evidence which supported the view that lead in petrol contributed to raised levels of lead in the blood, but he also admitted that there was 'a strong likelihood that lead in petrol is permanently reducing the IQ of many of our children'.[19]

Although he also set out in the letter the policy options that were available to the government – total or partial elimination of lead from petrol – he went on to recommend that 'action be taken to reduce markedly the lead content of petrol . . .'.[20]

Wilson did not use the letter at the campaign's launch. He held it back for some weeks and planned to use it once the initial impact of the launch had died down. The letter would re-establish the momentum of the campaign. As he points out, 'as a leak it was an extremely good story. As an "exclusive" to one newspaper, it clearly was a real scoop'.[21]

Following a meeting with Harold Evans at *The Times*, itself an indication of Wilson's status, Wilson agreed that *The Times* should carry the 'exclusive' provided certain terms were met. The story had to be on the front page and Wilson would be given an opportunity to put the issue and the campaign in context. Finally, Wilson would choose the date of publication so as to enable him to present MPs with facsimile copies of the report on the morning of publication.

Evans agreed. He fully appreciated the significance of a Chief Medical Officer writing to Whitehall colleagues expressing concern and doubts about the government's position and its decisions. He also accepted Wilson's argument that had the letter emerged during the discussions in Whitehall the previous March about government policy, the outcome would have been in favour of moving to lead-free petrol instead of simply pursuing a reduction in the amount of lead in petrol.[22]

Wilson got his front page story on 8 February 1982. The full text of the letter was printed on page 2 and his article was printed on page 8. To add to his trophies, *The Times* published a leader calling for the elimination of lead from petrol on the following day. The *Guardian* and the *Morning Star* also gave the letter extensive coverage on the 9th.

Other set pieces marked the progress of CLEAR. A report by city analysts, a public opinion survey, and a specially convened symposium all confirmed the high profile status of the campaign. Each guaranteed Wilson more coverage. But that coverage was never evenly spread. Different newspapers pursued different news values, sometimes ignoring what would, to an outsider, appear newsworthy. The *Telegraph*, for example, did not mention the launch of the campaign. Even *The Times* was never wholly taken by the campaign. Although it carried the campaign's material eagerly, this was largely due to Harold Evans' editorial leadership. After his removal from the editorial chair, *The Times* took a much cooler attitude to the campaign.

The campaign highlighted other journalistic dilemmas with implications for any analysis of news values. This emerged in an editorial conference at *The Times*. ' "Is this [CLEAR] a campaign?" asked. . .the news editor. "What do you mean, a campaign?" said Douglas-Home in the chair. . ."I mean", replied [the news editor], "do we go beyond normal news values?" '[23]

Of equal concern is whether the press should have given equal treatment to those who opposed CLEAR. When Yellowlees wrote to *The Times* to the effect that his views as set out in the leaked letter had been 'misrepresented', it did not produce any supporting articles. Little wonder then that those who doubted the validity of CLEAR's case described the press as unwilling to give equal opportunities for the presentation of all views, and of acting as censors.[24]

Wilson's campaign continued to pile on the pressure as story followed story. However, the media campaign was only part of a much broader strategy. MPs were courted and political parties were asked to pledge their support for a move to unleaded petrol if elected to power. This process of gathering support and creating a head of steam had the effect of isolating the Government and forcing it on the defensive. Ministers came under severe pressure to act. One person close to the whole campaign claimed that it resulted in

> letters circulating (around Whitehall and Westminster) saying "of course, they (the campaigners) are right. If we are not careful it is going to become an election issue."[25]

Informed opinion at the time felt that the Government would eventually be forced to find a compromise solution which would allow for a diplomatic reversal of its policies. That solution came about as a direct outcome of the Royal Commission on Pollution which sat in 1983.[26] Its decision to take up the issue of lead – itself a result of CLEAR's public struggles – was crucial. Although Wilson never expected the Commission to come out in favour of his campaign because several of its members had already pronounced against a move to lead-free petrol on grounds of insufficient evidence, it did in effect back his campaign.

However, the Commission's reasoned judgement gave Wilson a limited victory. It had based its decisions on the need to reduce 'the rate of accumulation of lead in the environment' – car emissions being a major contributor to this – rather than on the grounds of brain damage. In other words, its conclusions left room for a continuing debate about the effects of lead on children's IQ levels. This verdict gave the Government ample opportunity to change policy without conceding the argument and being seen to bow down to pressure. Within sixty minutes of the Commission publishing its results, the minister concerned announced the Government's intention to move towards the elimination of lead from petrol.

In the event, the campaign had achieved one of its objectives, albeit in a much watered down way, but it had failed to obtain the commitment that would have ensured that it had triumphed. Indeed, by 1988 the Government had still not announced a target date for the elimination of lead from petrol nor had it introduced the legislation which would ensure that all new cars manufactured from a certain date would run on lead-free fuel. Its commitment to date is, therefore, merely at the level of intention rather than action.

In view of this limited victory, how does one assess the value of a successful and sustained media campaign? Two possible means exist:

1. one can examine it in terms of the aims and objectives which the campaign sought to achieve;
2. one can compare the campaign with a low profile campaign which sought to achieve similar objectives.

In the case of CLEAR, both avenues are open.

1. CLEAR had campaigned for a move to lead-free petrol at the earliest possible instance 'and in any event by early 1985'. Although lead-free fuel is now available across the UK at selected garages – largely on account of European pressure – there is as yet

no policy to phase out cars which run on leaded petrol and to phase in the new types of engines. Until such time, one cannot realistically claim any measure of success. For whatever reasons – and they probably include industrial and financial ones – the campaign has failed to land the knockout punch. The issue is on the agenda, just, but curiously the Government's diplomatic manoeuvre to get it off the hook in 1983 has given it an indefinite breathing space. Though it has not gone back over its commitment, it has not made a concerted effort to bring about a radical change in its policy.

It may be that CLEAR fell into the trap commonly associated with environmental lobby groups:

> when an issue has passed from the realm of intense media interest and parliamentary scrutiny back into the administrative realm, environmental groups may once again find themselves at a disadvantage, unable to sustain pressure to ensure the full implementation of hard-won reforms.[27]

2. CLEAR's 'predecessor', CALIP, the Campaign Against Lead in Petrol, never shunned publicity but the circumstances of its origin and the state of its finances limited its ability to produce the glossy newsletters, reports, opinion polls and continuous stream of stories which marked CLEAR's progress.

CALIP, an offshoot of the Conservation Society, was set up in 1974 to concentrate on pollution in the environment. Between 1974 and 1977, it was able to highlight the dangers of lead in petrol and the need for a review of contemporary policy. Much of its time was spent on publicizing the scientific evidence and ensuring that lead in petrol hovered in the vicinity of the agenda.[28]

The issue had, in fact, surfaced regularly in the House of Commons from about 1973 onwards but the work of CALIP was to change markedly the nature of the debate in, and outside, the Commons. During 1978 it held its symposium on lead in petrol and published its report, 'The health effects of lead on children: A review of the literature published since 1976',[29] which challenged the official view that lead entered the body 'principally through food and drink'. It was as a direct response to the report that the (then Labour) Government set up the Lawther Committee to look at the issue of lead in petrol.

The Lawther Committee reported back in March 1980 and two

years later the Government announced a reduction of the permitted levels of lead in petrol from 0.45 g per litre to 0.15 g per litre. It was at this point that Wilson entered the fray with CLEAR.

The two campaigns differed in numerous respects. Whereas CLEAR adopted the high profile, CALIP – mainly for lack of funds – beavered away behind the scenes cultivating contacts within the administration. CALIP established very close links with civil servants and had sufficient knowledge of the workings of the establishment to be able to use it to its advantage. Not unlike CLEAR, it too was able to put the petrol companies on the defensive.

On the face of it, both campaigns managed to put the issue on the agenda. Wilson's high profile guaranteed him continuous access to most of the quality press; CALIP was much less fortunate in this respect though it too succeeded in capturing headlines. More significantly, and despite its low profile, CALIP was instrumental in bringing about a large reduction in the levels of permitted lead in petrol.

If anything, the contrasting styles of the two campaigns demonstrate that media attention of itself and on its own cannot overcome the obstacles to reform. Wilson's CLEAR – with the Yellowlees Letter, with the polls, with the Royal Commission – has still failed to introduce that final bit of reform to crown the campaign. CALIP, on the other hand, can claim a measure of real success and a real reduction in the level of lead in petrol.

SUMMARY

Publicity *is* a valuable asset but the issue of its 'effectiveness' still remains. Until we can find out more about how 'policy-makers' view the media and what they do with information culled from the media, our knowledge will be based on circumstantial evidence and informed guesswork. There are too many pieces still missing in the puzzle for us to be able to offer definitive statements about the 'politics of media pressure'.

Chapter Nine

POLITICAL COMMUNICATION: THE MASS MEDIA AND GENERAL ELECTIONS

INTRODUCTION

Few events typify the concern over the political importance and effect of the mass media more than the coverage of general elections. In these political struggles which are seen by many as the hallmarks of a democratic political system, one can detect at least two separate, though not distinct, sets of issues which in their quite different ways hint at the media's political importance. First, it is suggested that the work of the media, and particularly the presentation and coverage of political contestants, can affect voter behaviour and choices; second, it is claimed that the journalistic practices, for example the nature of television's never-ending thirst for moving pictures, have an impact on the nature of the political struggle and political debates.

The first, and by far the older set of issues, focuses on whether the mass media can influence and change political choices. This research area has been investigated by many and, to date, the conclusions are by no means clear-cut. The empirical evidence derived from studies which focus on election campaigns is open to conflicting interpretations (see below) and the controversy is further compounded by major reservations about the validity of only focusing on electoral campaigns rather than the longer term. Unlike American presidential election campaigns which start many months before the actual election date, British general election campaigns usually last three to four weeks. During that period, political activity increases enormously as all attention is turned to the outcome of the election race. In spite of this increased activity, the period in question is a very short one and by concentrating on the campaign, one risks ignoring the period preceding the campaign: a period which may be equally, or more, significant.

Although political preferences probably do change for some people during the period of the campaign, and some of these changes may be directly linked to the mass media, it is possible to argue that long-term social, political and economic change *between* elections is more significant for predicting the election result. It is worth noting that in recent elections the final result corresponded very closely to opinion poll data obtained *before* the start of the campaign proper (see Table 9.1, p. 184). This would suggest that it is necessary to look closely at long-term change *between* elections rather than the short election campaign itself.

Despite these reservations, there are some real and important questions that need to be tackled even if there are no precise answers. Do the media have an effect on voting behaviour? Does the predominance of a Conservative press affect the fortunes of other political parties? Does television, with its newsmaking practices and its preferred neutrality, force it to occupy the political middle ground? What is the political significance of that? Such questions, and there are many others, only touch the surface of the debate about the impact of the mass media on voting behaviour.

Less problematic is the second area of concern identified above, namely, what changes have the media brought upon the nature of politics and the political process itself during, but also outside of, election campaigns? Inevitably, such questions take it for granted that of all the existing media, it is television that has had the greatest impact. Its immediacy and universality and the belief in the potency of the image have caused all political actors to direct their work towards gaining its attention. This behavioural change is not only an acknowledgement of television's importance but is itself an example of the way in which television has made a 'difference' to the process of political communication. In this approach one avoids the 'assumption that *the effect of the media is limited to the potency of the message*'.[1] In other words, the media perform a whole host of functions and have a variety of effects other than simply swaying voters. It is these functions and effects that illustrate the way the media have changed the nature and meaning of political communication and have, therefore, made a *difference* to British politics.

For example,

> one cannot talk sensibly of a national campaign at all in the
> absence of mass media. . . The national campaign is formed by a
> continuous interaction between the behaviour of party leaders
> and managers and that of the mass media.[2]

Speeches are arranged for the benefit of television; walkabouts
and photo-opportunities are set up to catch the television camera
and even leaders are moulded to suit the television medium.
Michael Foot's campaign in 1983 failed to recognize the implicatios
of this. His

> schedule was less geared to gaining visual coverage, or 'photo-
> opportunities'. . . His discursive style of speaking and his
> unwillingness actually to use the words in the speech handouts
> given to the media was also a handicap.[3]

His 'failure', in media terms, was a lesson to others: in the age of
television, a party leader must court television and become televisual. Television has thus changed the requirements for leadership,
the work and priorities of politicians and their managers, and the
nature of political communication itself. To quote Blumler,
'[M]odern election campaigns have to a considerable extent
become fully and truly television campaigns'.[4] But television's very
extensive coverage of elections in news and current affairs has also
given it a major role in defining and shaping the national election
campaign and contest. Its wall-to-wall coverage not only shapes
the contests but it brings them directly into the living room, so
bypassing local party organizations, peers, opinion leaders, and
other traditional mediators of political communication.

Television helps to shape and define the national campaign by
acting as a funnel: broadcasters collect the material and rearrange
it for the benefit of the national audience. Broadcasters strive

> to impose a structure on the materials flowing into the 'factory'
> (the television election control room), which reflects *their*
> perception of how the most outstanding elements can be fitted
> into the day's election jigsaw.[5]

As we shall see, these practices inevitably have an effect on the
parties' campaigns and on the ways in which they strive to reach
the public.

These two fairly distinct ways of looking at the part the mass media play in election campaigns – influencing voters and defining the nature of election campaigns – highlight the range of possible meanings that can be attached to terms such as 'influence', 'effects', and 'impact'. In reality, these terms can cover a multitude of interpretations; the broader the interpretation, the more one is likely to appreciate the full range of 'effects' which the media can have upon events.

This chapter will explore some of the different areas of research which have contributed to our knowledge about the role of the mass media in general elections. The first section looks at the role of the mass media in the political communication process; the second section will focus on existing media practices in both the press and television and it will discuss the interaction of the media with politicians and political parties. The third section looks at the development of Party Political Broadcasts (PPBs) and their counterparts during elections (PEBs), and the final section focuses on the press. All four sections will draw on examples from recent British general elections.

1: THE MASS MEDIA AND POLITICAL COMMUNICATION

With television becoming such a dominant medium for political communication, it is sometimes easy to overlook the range of mass media available to the public. This complicates the problem of determining whether, and which, media have an impact on electoral behaviour. A voter has access to the press, television, VCRs, radio, and a host of other specialist journals. Isolating one medium for the purpose of analysing causality has numerous drawbacks; one of these is that it can distort the nature of the real media environment which the voter inhabits.

The audience for, and the readership of, different media varies enormously (see Chapter 1, Table 1.2). Questions about the media's impact also need to take account of audience size and particularly the small audiences for 'political content'. With an 'overkill' of election broadcasting, even the audiences for television news programmes are likely to decline. During the 1987 election, the audience for 'BBC 1's extended *9 O'Clock News and Election '87* fell by nearly 3 millions, and *News at Ten* ratings were down by half-a-million on the previous month'.[6] Although seasonal factors probably contributed to this drop, the figures emphasize the reaction to the surfeit of political news (see Table 9.7, p. 195).

Difficulties in determining the influence of different media, in charting the impact of these media, and in isolating short periods for analysis should not be taken as a denial of the media's importance. Television election campaigns are, for most people, 'the major learning experience of democratic polities'[7] and through television the public is 'exposed to a larger body of rational evidence on which to base their electoral choice than ever before'.[8] Nevertheless, there are some very real problems in attempting to explain electoral change.

1. The media environment is only one of many in which an individual participates. An individual is part of a larger social whole and the influence of one's peers at work, of one's perceived social class, or of one's perception of the economic well-being of the country may contribute greatly to one's political voting preference. Even if we are no longer directly open to the influence of community leaders, church or political organizations, and we are more directly exposed to the work and content of television, our lives are buffeted by a variety of, sometimes conflicting, media *and* non-media influences.

2. As the Introduction suggested, a general election is only a small part of a political and historical process. To study three or four weeks in the life of a government and an electorate may be to attach undue importance to a fraction of the process. Sometimes elections are preceded by events which have a significant impact on the outcome of those elections themselves – so much so that the result is never in doubt. This happened in 1979 and also in 1983.

The May 1979 election was preceded by the 'winter of discontent' – a period of public service pay disputes – which greatly damaged the Labour Party and ensured that the Conservatives entered the election campaign 21 percentage points ahead in the public opinion polls. The election gave the Conservatives a 7.2% lead over the Labour Party. A similar pattern of leading in the polls prior to the commencement of the campaign, and of retaining that lead throughout the campaign, was in evidence in 1983.

Prior to the Falklands conflict in 1982, the Conservative Party's popularity had slumped; its support stood at 28%, behind

Labour's 30% and the Alliance's 42%. Margaret Thatcher was 'the most unpopular PM since polls began', with 64% dissatisfied with her leadership. By June 1982 – after cessation of hostilities in the South Atlantic – the party's support stood at 47% and Thatcher's satisfaction rating was up to 51%.[9] The Conservatives entered the campaign 15.8 points ahead and won with a 15.2% lead over the other parties.

In 1987, just as in 1979 and 1983, the Conservative Party entered the election period in the lead. Before the election date was announced, the five major national polls reported that the Conservatives averaged 42% of the vote with Labour at 30.5% and the Alliance at 25.5%.[10] The actual election figures were:

Table 9.1 Opinion polls predictions prior to some recent election campaigns[11]

Election	
1987	Average of five major polls before the campaign began: Conservative share 42%; Labour 30.5%; Alliance 25.5% Result: Cons. 43%, Lab. 32%, Alliance 23%
1983	The Conservative Party entered the campaign 15.8% ahead of Labour. The election result gave it a 15.2% lead over Labour.
1979	During the last few days of the Labour Government (late Mar. and early April) and some five weeks prior to the election, the Conservatives were 10+ points in the lead. Gallup, on March 28, put them at 49%, Labour 38.5% and Liberals at 14.1%. The actual vote was: Cons. 44.9%, Labour 37.7%, Libs. 14.1%
1974	(Feb) On 9 Feb, a Marplan poll put: Cons. 45%, Lab. 39%, Libs. 12% The final result was: Cons. 38.8%, Lab. 38%, Libs. 23.6%
1970	May 21 Gallup poll put: Cons. 42.5%, Lab. 49.5%, Libs. 6.5% Result: Cons. 46.5%, Lab. 43.5%, Libs. 13.5%

Conservatives 43%, Labour 32%, and the Alliance 23% (Table 9.1).

3. Although shifts during elections and between elections are produced by a whole series of events, these events *and the reporting* of these events will impact differently on different population groups: women, young voters, those in public versus those in private employment, and so on. The 'impact' or 'influence' of the media – which medium? – is not a unitary one affecting all sections of the population in a similar way. It then becomes even more difficult to suggest that the media – in their totality or singly – are critical factors in these shifts.

Such a mosaic of changes cannot be accounted for by a single cause, nor could the media be introduced as the cause of them all. The variety is too rich to subsume under one heading and it is necessary to keep an open mind as to the range of possible causal factors. The academic evidence on the media's influence on voting behaviour is not strong and it has only detected minor changes or shifts. It is unable to explain large-scale shifts, neither is it able to pinpoint a single or significant medium of communication, though television is the obvious candidate. As Blumler admits 'the magnitude of measured communication effect has typically proved modest and unlikely to be able to override strong countervailing forces'.[12] Nevertheless, he has documented a variety of media 'effects' which suggest that the media do more than simply reinforce existing predispositions.[13] What are these 'effects'?

(a) Blumler and McQuail's study of the 1964 general election hypothesized that 'exposure to campaign messages would have a different effect on those members of the audience who view out of political interest, from those who watch political programmes' simply because they are heavy television viewers. Amongst the less interested electors they found 'a strong and progressive relationship between pro-Liberal change and party broadcast exposure'.[14] As levels of exposure increased so did the rate of shift towards the Liberals.

A similar case can be made out in relation to the Social Democratic Party's position in the 1983 general election. For the SDP, as for Labour, television is *the* solution to the problems of a press committed to the Conservative Party. No national newspaper gave it full support and no newspaper covered it in more than a cursory fashion. Its coverage ranged from 9% of the total space devoted to the political parties in the *Mirror* to 19% in the *Guardian*. However, when one takes account of the paucity and superficiality of news in the tabloids, even such percentages are misleading since 'on most days it was a case of a few column inches and occasionally nothing at all'.[15]

Table 9.2 The campaign's effect on vote choice, 1983

Reason for vote choice	All voters	Late Deciders	Loyalists	Switchers
Because of a:				
Cons. broadcast on TV	6%	14%	5%	8%
Lab. broadcast on TV	5%	12%	5%	7%
Alliance broadcast on TV	9%	26%	6%	22%
Newspaper advertisements and personal influences – either in the family or at work – do not elicit responses of a similar magnitude. Thus, because I was persuaded by:				
my wife/husband	2%	2%	2%	3%
my parents/children	3%	4%	3%	1%

Source: BBC TV/Gallup survey, June 8–9, 1983, quoted in Crewe, I, Table 3, Appendix.

Overall the Alliance's coverage in the press was in the ratio of 2 to the major parties' 5. This was not as good as the 5:5:4 division of television and radio air-time and television gave, therefore, not only a broader picture of the electoral contest but it may also have influenced the outcome of the Alliance's share of the vote. With the majority reading newspapers which advocated a Conservative victory, it is highly probable that television's more open window was the means through which potential voters learnt of the Alliance's campaign. It was certainly one important way in which the Alliance's supporters could find out about the Alliance itself. As Ivor Crewe notes, the Alliance was the only party to gain support during the campaign (Table 9.2), and the Alliance's Party Election Broadcasts had a significant impact on late deciders (Table 9.3). The same was broadly true in the 1987 general election (Table 9.4).[16]

(b)   Blumler and McLeod set out to explore why certain first-time voters (aged 18–24) abstained and in so doing changed their original intentions to vote. They looked at 11 possible factors which would account for the change, including parental influence, class position, prior political dispositions, i.e. amount of political interest, knowledge, exposure to campaign in the mass media, newspaper readership and evaluation of the campaign.

Their findings suggest that whether the young people in their sample would vote or not depended on:

Table 9.3 Partisan impact of the three parties' TV broadcasts among late deciders, 1983

	Decided how to vote in the last few days and was influenced by		
	Cons. TV Broadcast (%)	*Lab. TV Broadcast (%)*	*Alliance TV Broadcast (%)*
Voted			
Conservative	16	4	6
Labour	3	15	5
Alliance	14	11	52
Per cent finally voting for party that made TV broadcast	48	50	83

Source: as for Table 9.2.

Table 9.4 The impact of parties' election broadcasts (PEBs), 1987

% saying vote influenced by	*switched to*			*decided during the campaign to vote for*		
	Con	*Lab*	*All*	*Con*	*Lab*	*All*
Cons PEB	16	2	5	21	4	6
Lab PEB	8	23	6	9	26	9
All PEB	4	1	26	8	4	30

(i)   the extent to which they discussed the campaign; the more they discussed the campaign, the more likely they were to vote;

(ii)   their readership: reading a newspaper which opposed their political views reduced their likelihood of voting. Conservatives taking Labour newspapers suffered in particular.

(iii)   their evaluation of the campaign: 'Labour supporters who rated the campaign a dismal event. . .were. . .more likely to abstain.'[17]

Though class position and prior political dispositions were more important variables, the communication variables had an 'explanatory power' which was no less significant than the explanatory power of other variables.

(c)   Studies of media agenda-setting suggest that the news media structure the main political issues of the day and prioritize them by virtue of the processes of selection and presentation. One contemporary British example would be the villification of the 'Loony Left' in British politics.

The agenda-setting function of the media can also be observed in relation to events and circumstances surrounding the 1983 general election. Throughout the years 1979–1983 the Government's policies were justified in terms of TINA – There Is No Alternative. Political parties which argued to the contrary were usually pilloried in the press. In fact, the effect of the TINA philosophy was so great as to deny the possibility of alternatives even though such alternatives were seen as sound and laudable. This paradox was at its clearest over the issue of unemployment, a key feature of TINA.

In 1979 [the Labour Party's] edge over the Conservatives as the party for jobs was 15%; after a tripling of unemployment in 4 years of Conservative Government, its edge was 16%.

But despite the public's concern over unemployment 'no more people (in 1983) than before were convinced that Labour would be better than the Conservatives at shortening' the dole queues. What was in doubt was 'not Labour's concern over unemployment, but its ability to do much about it'.[18]

Had the public at large accepted Conservative Party accounts that the world recession was the root cause of increases in the levels of unemployment? Had the public accepted the Conservative Party view that governments could not create jobs? Had the Conservative Party's strategy effectively deflected interest away from any possible consideration of alternatives? Private polls for the Conservative Party showed that its message of lower expectations of growth and prosperity was getting through to the public; 'people thought it would be a long time before there would be a substantial improvement in the economy, with less unemployment and lower rates of tax.'[19] In such circumstances, alternative proposals could be discussed openly but they would never sound convincing.

One can only puzzle over the source of these perceptions of Britain's economic fortunes. At a time when academic and business critics pointed out the inadequacy of government policy and when indicators contradicted the up-beat messages the Government produced, where and how did the public learn of their fortunes and of the need for economic self-sacrifice? Television and the press are the obvious answers.

(d) Another study which confirms the importance of television is Patterson's work on the 1976 American presidential elections.[20] According to Patterson, the public's perception of who 'won' the debates between the candidates depended upon whether or not they had watched political commentators and broadcasters analysing the candidates' performances.

His sample was asked to rate the performances of Gerald Ford and Jimmy Carter in the 1976 presidential election debate. Respondents who were interviewed within 12 hours of the debate thought Ford had 'won'. Those who were interviewed 12 hours or more after the debate, i.e. who were interviewed in plenty of time for the media assessments to reach them, gave very contrasting opinions of who had 'won' the debate. Respondents in this second

Table 9.5[21]

Which candidate did respondent feel won the debate	Time elapsed between interview and second debate	
	12 hours or less after debate	*12 to 48 hours*
Ford	53%	29%
Undecided	12%	13%
Carter	35%	58%

group mirrored the media's judgement that Ford had lost on the grounds that he had 'mishandled' the East European question (Table 9.5). This reversal of opinion was particularly marked among 'regular news users'.[22]

(e)   Responses to the question 'Did television influence your vote?' suggest that 'floaters' are more likely to answer positively than those who remain loyal to their preferred party. Thus, Alliance voters, new voters and 'floaters' were more likely to answer the question positively in 1983 (Table 9.6)[23] than others.

Table 9.6a Has the television coverage of the election helped you in deciding about who to vote for in the election?

	May 24	*June 8*	*June 13*
Yes	18%	21%	18%
No	80%	76%	79%
Don't Know	3%	3%	3%

When broken down into different groups of voters – those voting for the same party as in 1979, those who were voting for a different party, and 'new' voters – the results are more dramatic.

Table 9.6b Has television coverage helped you in deciding?

		Stability of vote	
	Same as 1979	*Different from 1979*	*'New' voters*
Yes	13%	25%	31%
No	85%	73%	63%
Don't Know	1%	2%	6%

Source: BBC Broadcasting Research, Special Report. The 1983 General Election: Special Survey, Aug. 1983, pp. 19–20 Also Harrop, p. 57.

These studies identify a number of ways in which the media are important:

- voters can increase their knowledge of the parties and their leaders and this may play a part in determining their choices at election time;
- when party loyalties are weak, the media may contribute to voters' decisions about choices. The more 'believable' or credible the medium the more the attention that is likely to be paid to it;·
- when the traditional political anchor points of class, party and community decline in importance or are removed, the influence of the media, if only in allowing for gains in information, is likely to grow. Though the evidence is far from conclusive, television's reporting of the campaign and its *direct* access to the individual are likely to reinforce its dominance and influence on individual electoral choices.

2. THE MASS MEDIA AND POLITICAL COMMUNICATION: MEDIA PRACTICES AND MEDIA CONTENT

Although the national press continues to give extensive coverage to political parties and political analysis during election campaigns, it is television that has come to dominate the thinking and actions of political party strategists. But British political parties cannot buy broadcast air-time to propagate their views and so they rely on the broadcasters for their coverage.

The politicians' dependence on the broadcasters for coverage contrasts with their political power over the broadcasting institutions. One result of this is conflict: politicians seek, in the main, favourable publicity whilst broadcasters seek to hold politicians to account. During election campaigns, this conflict becomes more pronounced as political party strategists work to obtain as much favourable television coverage as possible and to ensure that the setting and the content of that political coverage is determined by them rather than by the broadcasters.

Broadcasters though have long abandoned any pretence that their main role during election campaigns – and in political communication generally – is to replay the political struggle without comment. Their suspicions that political parties and politicians would seek to control the political debate and agenda *to the detriment of* a proper informed public debate have fired their oppositional, public service, stance. This inherent tension between two sets of actors with quite different objectives has been in evidence ever since television began to report general elections in the late 1950s. Blumler's study of television producers during the 1966 general election – a mere 8 years after Granada TV first reported electoral politics – reveals their already well developed perceptions of their duties. Broadcasters wanted to achieve 'a more *revealing* campaign than the political parties were likely to provide through their own unaided efforts'.[24]

This objective has guided television producers ever since and it does account for the broadcasting organizations' continued efforts to develop new forms of political television in order to better explain the election contest to the public. The variety of formats so developed – the 'phone-in', the 'election forum', and the interview with politicians amongst others – all represent ways through which television seeks to open up the political debate *for* the public, and these are additional to the party political/election broadcasts which give the politicians direct unmediated access *to* the public. All these formats, be they 'windows' through which the voter gets a view of the political arena or 'platforms' for the rhetoric of political parties,[25] are developed within the constraints which regulate the relationship of the broadcasting organizations to the political process generally. They therefore represent a series of solutions to the problem of how to deal with political television and, at the same time, preserve the delicate balance of power between broadcasters and politicians.

What lies behind these 'solutions' and the forms of political communication? Four factors stand out. The first is the tradition of public service broadcasting which emphasizes the need to inform and educate. Second, the broadcasting organizations are required to treat all political comment in an impartial and fair way. This ensures a degree of balance in political reporting, particularly during television elections, and it also ensures that emerging political parties can gain access to television. This is discussed more fully below in relation to the birth of the Social Democratic Party.

The third factor are the legal requirements such as the Representation of the People Acts. Under the Acts, reports on a constituency must, for example, make reference to all the candidates concerned and all the candidates must be invited to participate in discussions. As with the injunctions to observe impartiality, these guarantee a degree of equality of access to all politicians. The final factor is the relationship which has developed between the broadcasting authorities and the political parties (see Chapter 6).

Although these regulations ultimately ensure that the major political parties are 'fairly' treated, they do not explain either the nature of television's coverage or the overall perspective within which elections are treated. These explanations can be found in the broadcasters' *perceptions* of the importance of *a certain form of politics and political debate*. Television's coverage stresses the supremacy of elections and the importance of the vote and of politics as a mirror of the Parliamentary arena. It thus legitimates the Parliamentary process and electoral contest and gives them considerable ideological backing to the detriment of other, e.g. class, perspectives of politics.[26]

Television thus elevates the status of political parties above those of other institutions, including broadcasting, so that although broadcasters are willing to confront politicians and devise forms for such confrontations, they continue to define their role as spectators on the scene and as subservient to the politicians. It is the politician who 'defines' the issues and it is television which follows. Whether this produces the best possible form of political debate is open to question. One prominent school of thought has long argued that the public wants, and is best served by, broadcasters taking on a 'more active' confrontational and inquisitional role towards the politicians. But since politicians will not voluntarily agree to this, it is up to the broadcasters to take a lead.[27] Such a view has its critics; critics who maintain that as politicians and political parties are at the *centre* of the democratic process, it is they who should be dominant rather than the unaccountable and unelectable broadcasters.[28]

It would be false to claim that television broadcasters have completely abdicated their responsibilities as journalists. In the various formats that television now uses regularly numerous issues *are* covered and the politicians *are* quizzed. Programmes such as *Panorama* and *Election Call* create a framework for issues to be raised and discussed. But does television do enough? Does it explore the issues critically and in sufficient depth? Does it stick too closely to the general agenda that is set by the political parties? The detailed analysis of television's coverage of the 1983 election campaign shows that it largely followed the political parties' agenda: though there were minor variations with regard to priorities and ranking, there was a large degree of agreement as to what the issues were, and these were set out by the political parties.[29] Opportunities were consequently missed,

> there was scope for tougher questions in the news conferences or from reporters on the campaign trail. . .there was room for more policy briefing reports. . .for more active, enterprising and imaginative election reporting, and for a wider spread of coverage of issues and individuals.[30]

David Butler has also argued that during the 1983 election, television concentrated too much on the 'presidential' features of the campaign and not enough on the issues. Both points were rejected by senior broadcasters. Alan Protheroe, then in overall charge of the BBC's news and current affairs output, and Sir Robin Day insisted that the issues *had* been covered and also that it was the politician's duty, not the media's, to raise issues. As Protheroe asked, somewhat rhetorically,

> Is it really the role of TV and radio to set the agenda. . .our job as public service broadcasters is to reflect the continuing debate, to help the public understanding. It would have been easy for the BBC in *Panorama* or *Newsnight* to say quite simply, 'This morning the press conference discussed the NHS, the National Coal Board, the position of the nationalised industries. . .', and to then have said 'but let's forget all that, let's really talk about defence'.
> . . . I don't think actually that is the role of the public service broadcasters; the public service broadcaster is a reflector of what is going on in the country.[31]

TV's election coverage

Given the extensive nature of election coverage, and the variety of settings in which it is presented, it is difficult to pass any final judgement on its performance. There is no shortage of political television though one can ask whether it is of the right sort. The public appears to be generally satisfied with the coverage[32] but not with the quantity (Table 9.7). This section will concentrate on certain important features of that coverage.

Table 9.7 Attitudes to TV election coverage over five campaigns (%)[33]

	1970	1974(M)	1974(O)	1979	1983
Far too much	17	31	28	32	43
Too much	47	67	63	65	69
A bit too much	30	36	35	33	21

Television devotes a large part of its journalistic resources to the task of covering general elections. News bulletins are usually extended to incorporate election coverage, current affairs programmes are rearranged so as to deal with election issues and personalities, special programmes are placed in the schedules to deal with election issues, voters are invited to meet and question politicians, and so on. The result is that the election is replayed from a number of different angles.

Nevertheless, that continuous replay is by no means entirely satisfactory. One problem for the broadcasters is how to treat election news items in *news programmes*: should they be treated as ordinary news items and so be allowed to compete for space with other news items, or should ordinary news values be abandoned and election items be given some coverage irrespective of their worth? This problem is best illustrated by referring to two major features of electoral coverage: 'walkabouts' and personalities.

In all recent elections, party strategists have spent a considerable amount of time and energy setting up 'photo opportunities', namely, settings in which a politician could be photographed in such a way as to convey a 'positive' image. One such memorable image from the 1979 election was a photograph of Margaret Thatcher holding a new-born calf. 'Walkabouts' are another version of the 'photo opportunity': the media are presented with an 'opportunity' to watch and film or photograph the party leader, say, walking and meeting the great British voter. Yet, and this is the key point, such 'events' are 'pseudo events'[34] created for the media but with the needs of the political party in mind. They have little intrinsic news value since, by and large, political strategists ensure that nothing adverse will happen throughout their duration. Despite their very questionable newsworthiness, they take up a substantial proportion of election news coverage (Table 9.8).

Table 9.8 Walkabout on TV news[35]

	1983		1979
BBC 1	10.9%	20.7% (early news) and	14.2% (main news)
ITV	13.8%	35.3%	16%
C4	7.0%		

The problem is compounded by the injunctions that broadcasters be impartial: it forces them to balance the un-newsworthy with the opposing political party's un-newsworthy walkabout! A similar criticism can be levelled against television's infatuation with personalities and, in particular, political leaders (Table 9.9).

Table 9.9 Coverage of leaders as % of total party coverage on TV news (1983)[36]

Thatcher	48% of Cons. coverage		but 28% on C4
Foot	43% of Lab. coverage		but 30% on C4
Jenkins	29% of Alliance coverage ⎫	71%	but 52% on C4
Steel	42% of Alliance coverage ⎭		

It may be that television news just cannot ignore party leaders but, because such walkabouts and other set pieces are prearranged and predictable, their status as news items isclearly suspect. Not only do these practices 'presidentialize' the process of political communication but it also gives the electoral contest a

> highly concentrated character. That is, the places (and faces) from which the news personnel secured raw campaign material were few in number and were repeatedly revisited on an almost predictable basis.[37]

One other consequence of this infatuation with leadership is that it greatly increases the importance of the 'packaging' and the marketing of the leader. If they are likely to appear on television nightly, then it is equally important to ensure that they appear in the proper setting, saying and doing the proper things. Although the use of packaging and marketing techniques goes back many years,[38] they have become more prominent in recent general elections.

Until the very recent past, it was only the Conservative Party which had employed agencies to market politics but in 1987 the Labour Party eagerly embraced the full panoply of marketing techniques in such diverse settings as the Kinnock-Hattersly launch of the manifesto and the Kinnocks' party election broadcast. The former was a show piece of music and lights – described by a *Guardian* columnist as possessing all the properties of a 'gay wedding' – whilst the latter was a superbly directed film about a caring couple surveying a piece of the British countryside on a beautifully sunny day. Overall, the Labour Party's concern with the television medium was so great that it ignored the needs of the press and of print journalists to a much greater extent than Margaret Thatcher's campaign had done in 1983.

The increasing emphasis on imagery, possibly to the detriment of content, was the cause of immense interest and concern in the period 1978–9 when Saatchi and Saatchi was first employed by the Conservative Party to run its publicity campaign. This appointment confirmed the party's commitment to the use of 'established techniques of commercial marketing on the British political scene'.[39]

Unlike its predecessors, though, Saatchi and Saatchi was given almost complete access to all the information available concerning party policy and research; its task was not simply to market the political party but to create a marketing strategy: it did not 'sell [politicians] like soap, but . . . produce[d] the cohesion needed, first, to create a professional communication strategy and then, secondly, to make it work'.[40]

Under these circumstances, the Labour Party could no longer afford to ignore the onslaught from the new image makers. Not only did the Labour Party have to reconsider its image but it had to be clearer about its constituency. It too needed to realize that 'the name of the game has changed. You can no longer cut to a picture of a man at a lathe every time you talk about industrial relations. . .'.[41]

Though much of the agencies' work went into the controlled environment of the press and poster advertisement campaigns and of the Party Political and Party Election Broadcasts, their presence merely confirmed the extent to which 'the game had changed'. Other examples drawn from the 1983 campaign illustrate not only this point but also the way that all aspects of politics were touched by the hands of the marketing men. Three such men come to mind: Gordon Reece was retained as Director of Public Relations and he played a great part in tutoring Margaret Thatcher in voice and television techniques; Harvey Thomas was taken on to use skills acquired as a producer for Billy Graham's evangelical meetings in the context of party conferences and other set pieces and, finally, Chris Lawson was taken on as Director of Marketing. Lawson had previously worked for Mars Inc. and he was involved in a number of areas, including the design of a new logo to resemble the Olympic flame, a Thatcher campaign song, a Youth Rally in which a host of showbiz personalities paid homage to the leader, and a Thatcher campaign tour totally geared to the demands of the television cameras and the press photographers.

The close attention which the marketing section paid to detail can also be seen in the use of alternative sets of curtains as backdrops for the Conservative Party's morning press conferences.

> The main aim was to be able to create different moods. . . Light blue was for the relaxed mood, dark blue was for the resolute approach. The morning the Conservatives launched their manifesto stirring Musak was piped through the speakers . . . including 'Land of Hope and Glory' and 'The Dambusters' March'.[42]

Examples from the 1987 general election campaign would not be hard to find since it has become a truism of television elections that they need to be fought, and presumably won, on television. Such examples would merely confirm a very basic point, namely, that all these techniques are employed in order to ensure that the right 'message' and the right 'image' get across to the public via television. The campaign is, thus, orchestrated by marketing professionals, and the broadcasters, in their duty as reporters, are forced into reporting the orchestrated event. The danger is that broadcasters would then abandon their public service duties.

The present trends are likely to persist in the future. Television will continue to try different formats in which to explore politics in an entertaining televisual way and political parties will continue to utilize the now commonplace techniques of marketing. In short, television elections will continue to dominate our screens.

The one feature of television elections that will not disappear is the Party Election Broadcast. Their origin, and their significance, are explored in the next section.

3. PARTY POLITICAL BROADCASTS (PPBs) AND PARTY ELECTION BROADCASTS (PEBs)

The injunction that broadcasting institutions should treat the major competing political parties fairly has long been acknowledged as a key feature of British political broadcasting. Another feature is the requirement of balance between the political parties. These injunctions ensure that emerging political parties such as the SDP can gain access to the airwaves. Rather than acting as a restraint, such injunctions offer support to broadcasters who wish to open up the political debate. This applies to the case of ministerial broadcasts (see Chapter 6, p. 121) as well as to election practices.

An agreement between the BBC and the political parties – recorded in an *aide-mémoire* and later published as an Appendix to the 1949 Beveridge Committee report – establishes the pattern for party political broadcasting. Each year a limited amount of time is offered by the BBC to the major political parties for their use. These PPBs are the editorial responsibility of the political parties and they can use these time slots as they wish. The PPB thus guarantees a political party direct access to the public.

The allocation of time between the political parties is agreed annually by the Committee on Party Political Broadcasts – a body made up of representatives of the broadcasting institutions and the political parties. Their decisions are based on a formula which takes account of a party's share of the popular vote in the previous general election. Prior to the 1983 election and the emergence of the SDP, the allocation of time between the Conservative, Labour and Liberal Parties was in the ratio of 5:5:3. This ratio was usually retained for the duration of a general election campaign though political parties fielding more than fifty candidates would also be given access to the airwaves. During the election campaign, these broadcasts are known as Party *Election* Broadcasts.

These rules can be adapted to meet changing circumstances, as happened in 1983. When the SDP came into prominence in 1981, it presented major problems for broadcasters. For although it had a handful of MPs, all but one of these had defected to the SDP from the other political parties. Furthermore, as it had not been in existence when the previous general election took place in 1979, it was difficult to judge if, and whether, it could be granted a bloc of broadcast time. The rules did not appear to deal with such occurrences. This difficulty was exacerbated when the SDP joined the Liberals to form the Alliance in the 1983 election contest.

After a lengthy and sometimes acrimonious period of discussion, the BBC decided that the allocation of time between the major political parties should be in the ratio of 5:5:4. The major political parties accepted this decision.

Two points are worthy of note. First, it was the BBC which was forced to take the initiative since the political parties could not agree amongst themselves about the proper allocation of time. This was in line with the view that, strictly speaking, the allocated time was not the political parties' but the BBC's. 'It (the BBC) had the responsibility to ensure that such time was fairly shared and properly used.'[43] The BBC thus imposed its own view of the nature of the political system and judged the parties accordingly. Second, this particular outcome may have given undue prominence to a political grouping that had never previously contested an election. Given its large share of the vote in the election, it is worth pondering whether the extensive publicity accorded the Alliance had an impact on its vote. The BBC's decision undoubtedly helped the SDP build up support and credibility.

The Alliance's performance in the 1983 election underpinned its demands for greater access to broadcasting. By the 1987 election, and after threatening legal action, the Alliance was granted parity with the two other major parties. The 1987 election was, therefore, fully a three-cornered fight.

In recent years there have been attempts to change the long established pattern of the 10-minute PPB or PEB so as to increase their effectiveness. As Saatchi's Tim Bell admitted, in 1979

we put in a strong plea for two-minute PPBs . . . Ten minutes is really the most ludicrous length of time; it is a nightmare for a

Table 9.10

Viewing of PEBs in Great Britain (1987)[45]	
'Avoiders' (of PEBs)	13%
'Passives' ('because the set was on')	35%
'Seekers' (of PEBs)	39%
'Addicts' ('watched as many as they could')	13%

professional to have to produce to this length. Ten minutes on the same subject is bound to be boring. [44]

Despite their drawbacks, PPBs and PEBs continue to play a part in election campaigns (Table 9.10) – they do give parties the opportunity to rally the faithful and they do offer ideological ammunition to the politically committed. It is unlikely, therefore, that they will disappear though with the advent of new media, their dominance will surely be challenged.

4. ELECTION CAMPAIGNS AND THE BRITISH PRESS

What is the impact of the Conservative press on the fortunes of the political parties? In 1983, the majority of the national Sunday and daily press supported the Conservative Party's election campaign and it was left to the *Mirror* to give its lukewarm support to the Labour Party; the *Guardian* and the *Observer* dithered but eventually declared themselves against a Conservative victory rather than in favour of either the Labour Party or even the SDP.

By the 1987 general election there had been some slight change in allegiances across the British press, largely on account of the emergence of some new newspaper titles. *Today*, for example, preferred a combination of tactical voting and votes for the SDP over any other options. The same could be said of the *Independent*. Like the *Guardian* and the *Observer*, it remained unconvinced about the Labour Party's policies in general and its defence policy in particular. Only the Maxwell newspapers put forward the case for the Labour Party although this time round their commitment was in no doubt. The *Mail*, *Express*, *Sun* and *Telegraph* – and their Sunday equivalents – continued to offer their wholehearted support to the Conservative Party.

201

By and large, the qualities attempted to show some consideration to all the contestants though even they did not completely abandon their specific political perspectives in reporting the election. Some were fairer than others; the *Independent*, for instance, was more balanced in its coverage of all the parties than, say, the *Telegraph*, but all gave extensive coverage to specific areas or topics. However, as always, it was the tabloid press that offered the most interesting styles of journalism. In this respect there were few major differences between the coverage in the 1983 (or 1979) election and in the 1987 election.

In the 1983 election, as in elections before and since, the *Daily Mail* pursued the Labour Party with a vengeance: it did not even pretend to be fair to it. It produced the usual scare stories and it reproduced Conservative Party press releases as news items. By 1987 all these tactics had become very familiar and predictable. On 5 June its front page was dominated by 'Labour's lies over taxation', a story which has little substance to it since the Labour Party had not actually set out its plans in detail. Four days later, it carried on its front pages Thatcher's views that the defence chiefs would neither accept nor work with a unilateralist Labour Party, under the banner headline 'How Could They Work With Kinnock?'.

That particular story shared the front page with a picture and a story on a series of strikes led by civil servants protesting about their pay and conditions *under* a Conservative Government. The *Mail*, loyal to the end, saw this as a good opportunity to hark back to the days of 'the winter of discontent' *under* Labour. Was this, it asked, 'The shape of things to come?' and just in case readers were confused about the similarities between these events, it devoted its centre pages to pictures from 1979 under a headline 'Do we REALLY want to go back to all this?'.

If the *Mail* kept up a barrage of stories against the Labour Party, it was the *Daily Mirror* which thrust its sharply crafted stories into the Conservative Party. (In this respect, it differed greatly from its rival, the *Sun*, which was content to lead with non-election stories on most days of the campaign.)

- In the 1 June issue, it devoted some 10 pages to the election under such headlines as: 'Divided Britain', 'Whose Life, Whose Future. She doesn't care for them, DO YOU?' (Fig. 9.1), 'Our

Figure 9.1 Whose Life, Whose Future

Disunited Kingdom', 'Pain and Privilege' in the NHS, and 'Despair'.
- On 9 June, its front page screamed 'Dirty Liars', an attack on both Conservative politicians and the *Sun*. That day it carried a 1½ page feature on unemployment.
- the day preceding the election, its front page was devoted to an attack on the Conservative Party under the headline of

Figure 9.2 Privilege and Poverty

'Privilege and Poverty. The Conservative Party exists to preserve is privileges...that is its historic role.' (Fig. 9.2). Three other pages were devoted to unemployment, education, homelessness, crime, and the NHS in 'Thatcher's Britain'.

- on election day, its front page carried a picture of a smiling Kinnock and the words 'You Know He's Right – *Chuck Her Out!*' (Fig. 9.3).

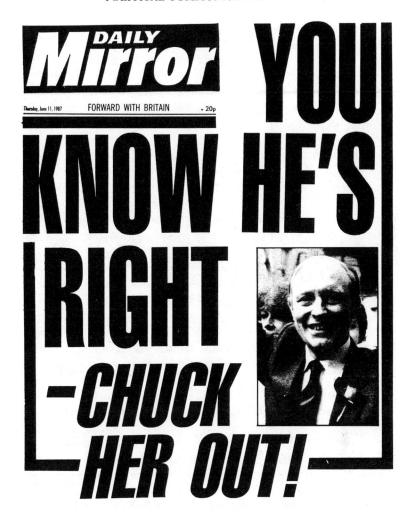

Figure 9.3 You Know He's Right

With newspapers eager and willing to volunteer their commitment to political parties, such excesses – if these are indeed excesses – are not surprising. But does this sort of coverage have an impact on readers? Does it have an impact on changes of voting behaviour? As with television, the concern of many politicians (and academics) is not simply with the kind of coverage which political parties get but with the effect of that coverage on voters. And, as with television, the answers are by no means clear cut.

Most recent studies confirm that the influence of the press can best be seen in terms of its ability to reinforce political choices. According to Harrop, newspapers 'exert at most a small *direct influence on changes* in voting behaviour among their readers'.[46] But in phrasing this conclusion in terms of 'changes of voting behaviour', one is masking what is potentially the most significant influence of the press; namely, its long-term ability to capture and sustain support for the Conservative Party. The press, therefore, reinforces political allegiances. In the 1983 election, the 'Conservative vote and the Conservative lead over Labour are highest amongst readers of the Tory press and the next highest amongst other press (but Conservative) readers'.[47] However, the Conservative vote was lower amongst people 'primarily exposed to non-Tory messages than it is amongst readers of the Tory press. . .'.[48]

But do people choose newspapers because they reflect their own politics or do they buy newspapers and then their politics? The difficulty of resolving this problem naturally leads to some kind of reinforcement thesis and, indeed, there is a very strong correlation between readership and voting behaviour. The exception to this general observation or statement is the readership of the *Sun.* Despite its strident political stand and its own brand of Conservative support, the political affiliations of its readers were divided between the three parties: in the election of 1983, 34% voted for Labour, 40% for Conservative, and 26% for the Alliance.

Nevertheless, with the Conservative press dominating the print media and with Fleet Street and the broadcasters adopting similar news values a 'critical' Labour campaign would be ridiculed in the press and in broadcasting. This happened to an extent in 1987; the Conservative press focused on the Labour Party's weakest points such as defence and the 'Loony' tendency and broadcasting played along with these themes albeit in less strident tones. The point that one must stress, and it is one that appears at several points throughout this book, is the difficulty of opposition when there is no way of gaining public support for it.

It is easy to exaggerate the influence of the press and to underestimate the importance of television when there is no easy way to determine the relative power of either. Certain trends may increase the influence of the press. As the Labour Party press declines, there are fewer sources for competing ideologies. New titles have failed to give the Labour Party anything but lukewarm support and remain content to dabble in the politics of the middle ground. Another trend which may be significant is the increasing volatility of the electorate alongside the increasing partisanship of the press. In these circumstances, the press may give electors anchor points of some significance. But for the majority of the newspaper reading public, television is seen as the more credible medium and it may therefore be that the influence of the tabloid press is mediated by the growing importance, and universality, of television.

5. SUMMARY

The absence of empirical evidence makes it difficult to substantiate the belief that the media are important influences on voting behaviour. The arguments put forward in this chapter address much broader issues which, in themselves, illustrate the power of the media to change the nature, and content, of British election campaigns. This is clearly seen in the close attention that is paid to television and the increasing use of techniques which emphasize imagery to the detriment of content. Such moves increase the importance of the press and television as sources of *critical* political analysis. It is for this reason that journalists should pursue their targets with greater relish. If they fail to do so, and if their journalism becomes no more than a rehash of political addresses, it is the voter who is at a disadvantage.

For such reasons, the ownership and control of the press and television are important issues. If there are imbalances in the press's political allegiances, where will the alternative ideologies find a platform? Television, and radio, are the obvious answers and so every effort should be made to ensure that they continue to play an impartial role so as to assist the public to scrutinize those who seek public office.

Chapter Ten

'THE NEW MEDIA': CABLE TELEVISION, SATELLITE BROADCASTING AND THE FUTURE OF BRITISH BROADCASTING

INTRODUCTION

For many countries, the 1980s will be regarded as a watershed in the development of broadcasting systems. The traditional dominance of broadcasting institutions has been undermined by two related developments: on the one hand, there has been a development of new means of signal origination and distribution and, on the other hand, there has been a readiness to question the existing broadcasting institutions' 'monopoly' of the airwaves. Although this chapter will focus primarily on the 'new media' of cable and satellite broadcasting, it is important to recognize the potential changes to broadcasting systems that can be engendered from within the political system.

France, for example, has recently experienced a tremendous overhaul of its broadcasting system. Yet none of these changes has been directly related to the growth of 'new media'. Changes in administration and political colouring led to the 1987 'privatization' of TF1, the main national public service channel, as well as to the creation of a number of other broadcasting channels. In 1980, the French viewer had access to 3 television services but by the end of that decade, there were at least 6 to choose from, with the prospect of more via cable systems or France's own Direct Broadcasting Satellite TDF1.

The collapse of the centralized and tightly controlled system in favour of a commercial, market-driven one has not yet taken place in Britain. Much of the contemporary debate about the future of broadcasting in Britain focuses on the 'new media' but there are, nevertheless, some strong indications to the effect that the much cherished ecology of broadcasting is far from immune from political and economic pressures for fundamental changes. Recently, a proposal was floated to the effect that a fifth television channel might be licensed;[1] this proposal, like those put forward by the Peacock Committee[2] in favour of 'floating off' Channel Four from the ITV companies and introducing some form of subscription television, possibly on BBC 2, contain within them forces which would undoubtedly fundamentally alter the principles of broadcasting. In short, the idea of the market-place in broadcasting could easily displace the heavily regulated, sometimes paternalistic, public service tradition of broadcasting.

Whether any of these proposals will be contained in the 1988 White Paper on broadcasting is impossible to say. What is clear, however, is that Margaret Thatcher and her colleagues are in favour of change. The central issue, then, is what changes should take place and in whose interest should those changes be? Should some notion of the 'public good' prevail? Should market forces direct decisions in broadcasting? Is culture and communications a sphere where the 'national interest' should be paramount? None of these questions is easy to answer though they are precisely the sorts of questions that should be asked.

THE 'NEW MEDIA'

From about 1980 onwards, interest in the 'new media' has grown tremendously. Cable television and satellite broadcasting – once only of interest to idiosyncratic researchers and futurist scientists – began to occupy more and more space on the agenda of 'the future of broadcasting'. It was not so much that the technologies had themselves changed radically from their earlier technical or social forms, say, in the 1970s, but that their potential for radically altering the face of domestic broadcasting services began to be appreciated.

The example of the American Home Box Office (HBO), a film channel, illustrates this point. HBO was the first company to use satellites as a means of delivering television signals to cable systems and it was soon followed by others. Whereas in 1977 there were about 500 cable systems with suitable satellite receiving dishes, by 1982 there were just under 5000.[3] Also, the number of households linked to cable systems doubled to 28 million between 1978 and

1982; by 1987, that figure stood at around 44 million subscribers. Finally, by 1985, there were some 55 national video services available to cable operators.[4]

These changes have altered the face of American broadcasting. They had an enormous impact on the three main networks, ABC, CBS and NBC. From a position of omnipotence in the 1970s, they have seen their share of the audience cut quite dramatically. Though the networks remain dominant, they have felt the 'impact' of the new media.

The diffusion and popularity of the 'new media', particularly of cable television, in the United States has had both a physical and a psychological effect on Europe generally. Not only did it make Europeans – and their governments – aware of possible new areas for industrial/technological expansion and growth but it also made them aware of impending change: it would only be a matter of time before satellite services would be available across Europe and these were not likely to be hemmed in by national regulatory and cultural considerations. Europe would no longer be able to keep satellite services (or their backers) out: Murdoch's Sky Channel (born in 1982), Ted Turner's Cable News Network, even the US Information Service's Worldnet, cross national boundaries with the greatest of ease. Domestic regulatory mechanisms would, in the long run, prove ineffective in their efforts to oversee or supervise these new channels.

The potential influence of the 'new media' gave rise to a number of concerns. Some were primarily focused on 'traditional' broadcasting and cultural issues:

- would the American experience be replicated in Britain and across Europe more generally?
- what would be the consequences of this for British, and other European domestic broadcasting systems?
- would the European tradition of a limited number of state controlled, (mainly) publicly funded, public service broadcasting institutions survive in an enormously competitive environment?
- was there a threat of an invasion of foreign and unwanted material, a 'Coca-Colanization' of European broadcasting?

The answers to these questions were inevitably complex. Much depended on the diffusion of the new media, on costs, on cultural perceptions of television and even on the availability of satellite launchers. Optimists predicted the advent of real choice in television entertainment, pessimists spoke of 'wall-to-wall *Dallas*' and one could select a set of predictions from the range which lay in between these two extremes. What was clear in the European context, though, was that the 'new media' of cable and satellite broadcasting would take much longer to establish themselves in Britain and France as well as in West Germany. In this respect, the American experience was unique and not a good predictor of future change in Europe. Nevertheless, the 'new media' had arrived and by their very existence had prised open the all too often closed and heavily regulated systems of broadcasting.

Other concerns were focused on the industrial and technological implications of the 'new media'. Briefly, although the term 'new media' usually refers to cable and satellite broadcasting, these novel means of video signal distribution are only the most visible parts of a fundamental transformation of the communications and telecommunications systems. In effect, a whole series of technologies were 'converging'. Computers, telecommunications systems, telephones, satellites, television and videotex were no longer separate and distinct entities but connected or related in some way and now subsumed under the heading of 'information technology'. Thus a telephone call, a television programme, a stockbroker's video display unit, or a teletext picture were all different information uses of a common communications system.[5]

For individual governments, the implications of 'information technology' were enormous. Britain, like France and Germany, had a very limited number of outdated cable systems and it could, at least in theory, redesign its telecommunications system around the construction of a sophisticated fibre optic cable network which would carry a whole range of information services. This would herald the coming of 'the wired nation' (Fig. 10.1).

Such an interventionist industrial strategy would not only generate industrial growth, research and development and other economic benefits but it could also lead to exports of technologies and software as Britain gained a lead over other countries. It was this dimension of 'information technology' rather than simply the 'new media' which was to find so much favour with governments and cable and satellite broadcasting soon became part of an industrial strategy which also had cultural implications (rather than the other way round).

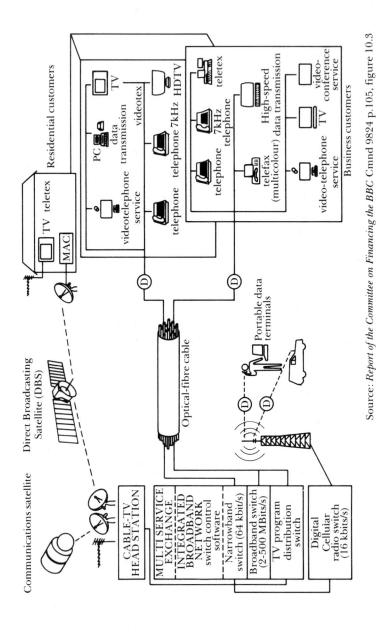

Source: *Report of the Committee on Financing the BBC* Cmnd 9824 p.105, figure 10.3

Figure 10.1 Telecommunications in the 21st century[6]

This duality led to many contradictions in public policy. For example, should cable systems be publicly funded, centrally directed and led, or should they be privately funded and led? Should they be primarily telecommunications networks or entertainment networks? Should satellite broadcasting be 'British' or could it rely on imported hardware? As one decision rapidly followed another, it was soon clear that under the Thatcher Government, 'new media' policy comprised a whole series of twists and turns which could never produce a coherent telecommunications infrastructure to exploit the opportunities presented by 'information technology'. Indeed, the piecemeal approach encouraged further contradictions.[7]

Although the Thatcher Government was never likely to adopt an interventionist strategy, it was also reacting to forces which were gradually gaining strength across the world. There was growing pressure to 'privatize' and 'deregulate' communications systems so as to allow private competition into hitherto regulated, national and public systems. The overall effect of moves towards 'privatization' and 'deregulation' (and this would apply to cable, satellite *and* terrestrial broadcasting) was the opening up of communications to private competition and interests and the reduction of controls on information flows. British broadcasting was no longer going to be protected from external forces.

As all these considerations were thrown into a global melting-pot, it became difficult to deal with specific aspects of 'information technology' in a compartmentalized and distinct way. The interrelations between the technologies produced cumulative effects: a decision regarding BT had consequences for Mercury Communications, for cable systems, for satellite broadcasting, and so on. Nevertheless, for the sake of ease and clarity, this chapter focuses primarily on the implications of cable and satellite broadcasting for the structures of broadcasting in Britain.

A BRIEF GUIDE TO THE 'NEW MEDIA'

The 'new media' refers to a number of different systems by which audio-visual signals are distributed to individual households. Terrestrial broadcasting, e.g. the BBC, broadcasts its signals over-the-air. These can then be picked up by ordinary television aerials. By contrast, cable television relies on a physical link – a co-axial or fibre optic cable – as the channel of distribution. Households must therefore be attached to cable systems to receive the signals. In practice, the cable system's 'control centre' or head-end can collect both terrestrial and satellite transmitted signals and/or originate signals which are then 're-diffused' or redistributed along the cable network to individual households. The capacity of the network will depend on the type of cable used, its configuration, the types of switches it uses and the software employed at the head-end.

Satellite broadcasting systems are yet another way of diffusing or distributing the audio-visual signal. The satellites are usually placed some 36,000 kilometres above the Equator and in this orbit – the geostationary orbit – the satellite 'appears to hang over roughly the same spot on the Earth's Equator at all times. The stationary nature of the satellite relative to the Earth is what makes this orbit so important, since the earth station antenna does not have to move to track the satellite'.[8]

Audio-visual signals are then beamed up to the satellite where

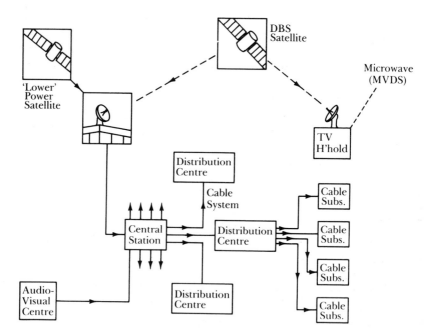

Figure 10.2 'New media' distribution systems: cable and satellite

they are amplified and then re-transmitted to ground receiving stations. The strength of the re-transmitted signal determines the size of the ground receiving station: a low-power satellite requires a large (1.2 metre or over) dish whereas a high-power satellite requires a much smaller dish. The satellites presently in use across Europe are usually low-power systems and so require large dishes, though the more powerful DBS satellites currently proposed would only need small dishes. This latter category of satellite systems are usually designated Direct Broadcast Satellites (DBS) or quasi-DBS since they are designed for direct-to-home (dth) reception. Low-power satellites, in contrast, are usually intended for reception by cable system head-ends and for cable distribution (Fig. 10.2).

Although all these systems present different ways of reaching the audience, it is their *combination* that is of immense significance. The marriage of physically separate cable television systems and a satellite broadcast service such as Sky Channel creates a new international 'network' instantaneously. By 1988, for example, Sky Channel was available in over 11 million homes across the whole of Europe. For existing broadcasters, the real threat of the new media was that their 'wall-to-wall *Dallas*' programming – a term for cheap American imports – would eventually erode the public service tradition in broadcasting and lead to 'lowest common denominator' type programming with no regard for quality, education or information.

Cable television

Current interest in cable television can be traced directly to the Information Technology Advisory Panel 1982 report, CABLE SYSTEMS.[9] The panel was set up in 1981 by Margaret Thatcher to look at issues in 'information technology'. Its first report contained a series of recommendations which were to become the Government's policy towards the development of cable systems in Britain.

For the panel, cable systems could become the telecommunications infrastructure of tomorrow: 'the main role of cable systems eventually will be the delivery of many information, financial and other services to the home, and the joining of businesses and homes by high capacity data links.'[10] Its major recommendations were aimed at achieving these objectives speedily. Two key recommendations were to determine the nature and the direction of developments.

First, cable systems were to be developed within the private sector. Private funding would be attracted to these ventures not by the prospect of the 'future communications system' but by *estimates of the revenue (likely to be obtained) from additional popular programming channels*.[11] This was the crux of the 'entertainment-led' policy: popular programming would eventually pull through the other components of the future communications system. This approach not only denies the possibility of a centralized, government directed and publicly funded strategy but it also puts the emphasis on privately led development in the hope that the latter will lead to the creation of a sophisticated communications network. This strategy of private funding was only feasible, though, if cable television was 'deregulated' and permitted to carry that which was popular and profitable.

Second, and in keeping with its view of the technological potential of cable systems, ITAP recommended that licences be awarded to those cable operators who would construct technologically advanced switched systems. Such systems could be used for both telecommunications and television purposes and they would also provide facilities for interactive services, that is, services such as teleshopping and voting which can benefit from the ability of cable systems to carry data not only from the head-end to subscribers but vice versa as well. These systems would then be able to make the most of the state-of-the-art technology and they would, in due course, become part of Britain's telecommunications infrastructure providing both video and data facilities.

Within two years of the report – and following a number of related inquiries in the intervening period – the Government had begun the licensing process. Eleven cable franchises were awarded in December 1983 and in the (interim) period prior to the setting up of the Cable Authority in 1985. Once in place, the Authority began to issue licences at fairly regular intervals. By the end of 1987, 22 cable systems had been licensed, although less than half were in service. These systems covering such areas as Westminster, Coventry, Glasgow, Aberdeen, Guildford, and Swindon *when fully constructed* will pass some 2.5 million homes. At the time of writing (Autumn 1987), the systems which are now in service are still at a very early stage of development and only have some 210,000 subscribers. In this respect, cable's progress has been remarkably slow. The estimates touted in the early 1980s of millions and millions of subscribers to cable systems by 1990 have proved to be vastly exaggerated. Most operational systems have a penetration rate in the region of 20%, i.e. only 20% of those able to subscribe do. However, it is expected that the total number of subscribers will increase as more systems are licensed and as the existing systems develop.

One important reason for the rather slow progress in the construction of broadband cable systems is that they require an enormous financial outlay. A franchise covering an area of around 100,000 homes would cost between £30m and £50m to construct with over half of that outlay spent on civil engineering works such as digging up and reinstating roads. Such funds are difficult to find at the best of times but the uncertainty surrounding cable's real profit potential – would it ever succeed in Britain? – put it at an ever greater disadvantage. Many financial institutions still see it as too risky a venture to dabble in unless, and until, there is real evidence that levels of penetration can rise substantially.

In addition to licensing these new cable systems, the Government also licensed the *existing* cable operators, a not insubstantial group of interests since they passed well over 1 million homes. These 'upgrades' are of limited channel capacity and the licence merely permitted their operators to 'upgrade' the systems so as to take advantage of some of the new channels which were becoming available. In effect, these 'upgrades' only offered a fraction of more than a dozen non-terrestrial channels such as SKY, Première, CNN, Bravo, SuperChannel, Screensport, available on broadband cable systems. Furthermore, they would never be able to offer telecommunications or interactive services.

Subscribers to cable systems – whether broadband or upgrades – pay a one-off installation charge and a monthly charge which varies according to the services bought. Basic services are usually covered by a charge of about £10 per month; premium channels such as film channels cost extra (about £8 per month). The precise mix of channels available and the pricing of these various tiers varies from system to system. Under the new liberalized and market oriented cable régime, one gets what one pays for and, mercifully for the cable industry, subscribers seem willing to pay in the region of £20 plus per month for their entertainment needs.[12]

Regulating the 'new media'

As cable systems are both telecommunications and cultural entities, they require two licences. In addition to granting franchises to construct cable systems, the Cable Authority also issues a licence for the provision of cable programmes on those systems. This licence is complemented by a telecommunications licence from the Department of Trade and Industry (DTI). In effect, the Authority grants franchises and licences and oversees, broadly speaking, the programming side of cable systems, whilst the DTI concerns itself with the technical requirements for cable systems and the manner of their installation. Some of these latter duties are also carried out by the Office of Telecommunications (OFTEL).

Although the Authority is a regulatory body, it adheres to the philosophy, first formulated by ITAP, that cable systems should be 'lightly regulated' so as not to thwart or slow down the development of the industry. The direct effect of that philosophy is that cable operators are burdened with few of the regulatory restrictions that apply to either the BBC or ITV companies.

Cable operators are only required to carry the existing broadcasting services plus the proposed DBS services (see below). Few other restrictions apply. Operators can carry any (satellite or other) television channel they desire provided that these channels or programmes on those channels do not infringe laws relating to decency, accuracy and impartiality (in British news services), issues of violent content, and so on. There are no quotas on foreign programmes – the BBC and ITV companies work with a 14% quota on foreign programmes – and there are no requirements that material must be of British or European origin; nor are there any requirements that cable systems carry a mix of 'entertainment, information and educational' programmes. In effect, there are no regulatory directives on either the *range or the sources* of programme material (see Fig. 10.3 and Table 10.2).

It is this liberalized approach to cable systems that has made them so threatening to the existing framework of broadcasting. For if there are no requirements to serve the British public with home produced news and current affairs, drama or light entertainment, cable operators can fill their channels with entertainment programming only. That could either consist of cheap imported programmes

– Rupert Murdoch's SKY Channel epitomizes this with its mixture of pop music shows, old American situation comedies, some children's programmes, old films, and sports programmes – or premium material such as films, as on Première. Programmers will have, as it were, audience pulling 'power without any responsibility'.

In such a television environment, competition for audiences pushes broadcasting organizations to look for large audiences and the lowest common denominator. Confronted by an erosion in their share of the audience, the BBC and the ITV companies may be forced to compete more vigorously. For the BBC, a significant reduction in its share of the audience may impact on its justification of the licence fee: if more and more households get their entertainment from satellite delivered or cable distributed television services, why should they continue to pay the licence fee? For ITV the problems are slightly different, though again they derive from the reduction in the size of its audience share. As fewer watch ITV, its advertising rates decline and this could lead to a decline in its total revenue. In both cases, there is a consequent loss in both the quality, and the range, of programmes produced.

This 'scenario' of the impact of the 'new media' on the existing structures of broadcasting makes the critical assumption that cable systems (and DBS) are successful and do eat into the terrestrial broadcasters' share of the television audience. The evidence to support this assumption is rather mixed. In the US where cable systems proliferate – about one half of all TV households are cabled – the networks have seen a decline in their audience share. Data for 1985 suggests that cable's share of weekly viewing in *cable households* was some 30% of total viewing. The networks had a share of 53% and independent broadcasters 21%.[13] In Britain, there is evidence that a similar pattern can be detected. In cable households, 'new media' services take a larger share of total television viewing than the terrestrial services.[14] The problem for the cable industry, though, is that there are not many of those households: only some 15% to 30% of all homes passed by cable systems actually subscribe to cable. Unless that figure improves, cable may be a limited threat to terrestrial broadcasting. One current forecast estimates that by 1991 cable systems will pass some 3m to 4m homes but that there will be only just over 1 million subscribers.[15] Other forecasts see even these figures as optimistic: the Cable Authority predicts some 600,000 homes connected to cable systems by 1990. Significantly, though, at these levels, the cable audience will remain a minority of the 20 million TV households in the United Kingdom and this would still leave the terrestrial broadcasters in a dominant position.

The significance of cable systems goes beyond its direct threat to the status quo. Cable systems introduce a completely different conception of the duties of the broadcasting media. Broadcasting and cablecasting become directly linked to the market principle. Those who wish to subscribe do, those who wish to buy extra services can, and those who want to avoid the fruits of the Reithian philosophy can. Like the press, the viewer can buy that which he/she desires. To some, this introduces freedom of choice, to others it brings an erosion of choice since competition ultimately produces 'sameness', not variety. Again, the evidence to support this is mixed. In the US, the number of channels available has greatly increased but there has not been a commensurate increase in the range of material presented. Some offer the same sort of material previously available though others are moving into specialist areas to suit specialist markets. Furthermore, cable has not entirely undermined the power of the advertiser since only the subscription or pay-channels, a minority, are free of advertising, nor has the development of cable been able to sustain either 'cultural' or community channels.

There are other areas of public concern and public policy where the Authority has shown itself to be closely allied to the development of the industry. Under the Cable and Broadcasting Act 1984, the Authority has to ensure that certain groups or individuals do not become holders of licences. For example, licences can only be awarded to British or EEC nationals. Foreign nationals, local authorities, political and religious bodies, are specifically excluded. Yet the Authority has campaigned for a relaxation of those rules so as to permit foreign nationals to invest in British cable systems. Similarly, it has sought to reform regulations concerning limits on advertising, the 'must carry' rule, cross-ownership of media, and the use of microwave systems by cable operators. This last move would permit an expansion of choice via microwave transmissions without forcing the cable operator to construct a cable system.[16]

In all these instances, the Authority has ceased to act as a true regulatory body as that term would apply to BBC, IBA or even

OFTEL. It is carrying the industry standard rather than pursuing any notion of a public interest. All these reforms favour private development and the exploitation of cable systems for private profit rather than for public benefit. Whilst that may be the proper role of an industry body, it is difficult to argue that it is the role that a public regulatory body should adopt, particularly as its work impacts on the public sphere of communications and culture.

Cable systems inject a whole new set of issues into discussions on the future of the British media but they are themselves dependent on the proliferation of satellite-delivered channels. Most cable programme services available in Britain are also available across Europe. As a result, the 'new media' is having an impact not only within one country but across a continent. It is this broader set of issues that is explored below.

Broadcasting by satellite

Existing European cable systems, like their British counterparts, depend on the numerous television programme services broadcast by satellite across Europe. The first such service was Murdoch's SKY Channel (1982–) and it made use of an Orbital Test Satellite to reach cable systems across the continent. The OTS satellite, like many of the satellites currently in use, e.g. Telecom-1, EUTELSAT, etc., was essentially a telecommunications satellite. Some of its capacity was, however, leased to satellite broadcasters but recently, and with the growing interest in the 'new media', telecommunications satellites have become the satellite broadcasters' main means of reaching European households. One indication of this is the phenomenal increase in the number of satellite to cable channels currently (Autumn 1987) available across Europe: when SKY started up there were 2 (the other was a German language service), by 1987 there were 18 – 8 English language, 8 German language, 1 French and 1 Dutch.[17]

These low-power satellites provide a signal that is adequate for reception by the large dishes available to cable head-ends. It is then through the cable systems that satellite broadcasters can extend their reach. As parts of Europe – in particular, the Low Countries and Scandinavia – are heavily cabled, it is possible for broadcasters to reach enormous audiences. Even so, a large audience base does not guarantee profitability; SKY's 11 million households are still inadequate to return a profit.

Many countries have not welcomed SKY's intrusion into their heavily regulated broadcasting systems. Countries which limit or do not permit advertising on their terrestrial broadcasting systems objected to the advertising content and other countries objected to the unbridled presence of commercial broadcasters. It was abundantly clear, however, that the objections and obstacles to these services could not keep them out indefinitely and that they

Table 10.1 British interests in the new media[18]

	Arts Channel	Children's Channel	Lifestyle	MTV	Premiere	Sports Channel	Sky Channel	Super Channel
British Telecom		22%		24%	30%			
Central TV		22%						17.5%
Columbia					10%			
Commercial Union	28%							
DC Thompson		22%	15%				3%	
Equity & Law	28%							
Granada Group								23.2%
Home Box Office					10%			
John Griffiths	21%							
London Weekend TV								11.7%
Mirror Group				51%	30%			
News International							83.5%	
Showtime					10%			
TV South	7%		18.5%					11.7%
Thames TV		22%						
Thorn EMI		12%						
20th Century Fox					10%			
Viacom Int'l			25%					
Virgin Vision								15%
WH Smith	14%		48.7%		91%			
Yorkshire TV			18.5%					6.9%

would eventually all be available for reception in most European countries. Not only would one not be able to keep them out, but their international status put them outside national regulatory mechanisms. Whereas cable systems could be regulated by national 'Cable Authorities', satellite broadcasting services could not because they were not always based in the country of reception. Thus, Britain would not be able to regulate CNN, TV5 or certain other services since they originate outside the UK. The legal, regulatory and political consequences of this are only now being appreciated and there are now moves at the European level to try to co-ordinate policies towards such transnational media.[19]

Perhaps the most surprising aspect of the 'new media' is the existence of so many satellite delivered channels ready to exploit a revolution that has yet to take place in three major European markets, namely Britain, France, and Germany. Indeed, although cable systems have yet to establish themselves in Britain, one finds British interests heavily involved in satellite delivered channels (Table 10.1). One probable reason for this is the success of English language media across Europe, not only in television but in music and films also.

The other 'threat' from the skies is the Direct Broadcast Satellite (DBS) and the quasi-DBS system. DBS is usually thought of as an extension of the existing terrestrial broadcasting system. DBS systems are internationally agreed satellite systems which, in theory, respect national cultural sovereignty. Thus the problem of trans-border television eroding national boundaries does not arise; furthermore, DBS systems are nationally regulated.

When a British DBS system was first proposed in 1981–2, it was conceived of as a way of introducing more channels into the British broadcasting system without brusquely upsetting the ecology of the system. A high-power DBS satellite directed at Britain would not only cover the whole of the country but its signal would be of such a strength as to be receivable by all households in possession of a small (about 30 cm in diameter) dish. This combination of properties – universality, spread and availability – made it an ideal public service medium and it therefore comes as no surprise to find that the original DBS franchises were awarded to the BBC. The BBC planned to offer two additional channels – one based on subscriptions and one not – so extending the choice of programmes but without threatening fundamental structures as well as introducing a degree of market responsiveness to the television sector.

For a variety of complex reasons, mainly related to the cost of the British-built satellite that the government insisted the BBC ought to buy, the BBC pulled out. Years later, the DBS plan was revived and it has now surfaced in a quite different form. In 1986, British Satellite Broadcasting (BSB) was awarded the franchise to operate three channels on a DBS satellite. BSB, a consortium consisting of Anglia TV, Granada, Pearson, and Virgin and many more, plans to transmit four television services, including a premium film channel, a news channel, and a children's channel. Unlike the earlier DBS plan, BSB will be regulated by the IBA and its satellite will be bought from the American manufacturers Hughes Communications. As the Hughes satellite will be of a lower power than the original (BBC) DBS specifications it will be necessary to use a dish larger than 30 cm in diameter, possibly one of 45 cm.

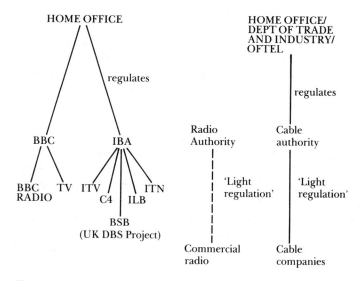

Key

--- Proposed change from IBA regulation

Figure 10.3 Regulating the 'new media'

The DBS satellite will be launched in late 1989 and the mixture of subscription and advertising channels will present the IBA, the regulators, with a unique regulatory problem: how will it be able to reconcile its duties to protect the ITV structure with its task of regulating ITV's competitor DBS?

In fact, the 'new media' highlight the inadequacy of the British regulatory and policy-making process. As Fig. 10.3 illustrates, the maze of bodies and duties is too complex to give rise to a co-ordinated policy towards culture and communication, particularly *in a period of rapid change*. For not only will viewers be confronted by cable and DBS, but they will also be presented with an even more extended menu from DBS's direct competitor, quasi-DBS.

Quasi-DBS is a more powerful version of the existing satellite broadcasting services available across Europe. Like DBS, however, the signal will be strong enough to be picked up by owners of small receiving dishes (about 85 cm in diameter). Unfortunately for BSB, the competitiveness of quasi-DBS does not stop there. Whilst BSB will offer four television channels, Luxembourg's ASTRA project has 16 channels at its disposal. Significantly, ASTRA hopes to win over currently popular satellite delivered services – such as SKY and Super Channel – so as to become the dominant 'bird' in Europe. The importance of dominance becomes immediately clear when one realizes that a satellite dish can only pick up signals from the satellite towards which it is pointed. A dish pointing towards ASTRA is a dish that is pointing away from BSB!

The competition between these two satellite services is likely to be intense as each attempts to convince the consumer of its superiority. Crucially, receiving dishes cannot easily and inexpensively be adapted for both uses so the race to be the market leader in the 'small and basic' receiving dish market is a significant one. The key to success is likely to be the capture of the householder who is prepared to make a small outlay – about £300 – to acquire another entertainment device. The reason the dish must be fairly inexpensive is twofold: first, it must be within easy financial reach of the majority of the population and, second, a dish owner will have to pay other charges such as subscription charges, licence fees, and possibly also charges for decoders for encrypted or scrambled services. In other words, the cost of the dish, the selection of channels on offer, and *the cost of these channels* will, more than likely, determine the viability of these two satellite systems and, indeed, any others *as well as their competitive edge over cable systems* and their ability to deliver both 'entertainment' and telecommunications services.

For Britain, then, the next decade will be of immense significance. A householder will be able to increase his/her choice of entertainment by adding a VCR – a much neglected revolutionary new medium since it puts householders in control of their own entertainment – and then choosing the appropriate 'new medium'. Subscribing to a broadband cable system will provide another 15 to 30 channels of entertainment (including terrestrial and DBS services). If the householder decided not to subscribe to a cable system, he/she could buy a small dish, or several dishes, and so choose from amongst BSB's 4 channels, ASTRA's 16, and EUTELSAT II's 16, though some of these channels will most likely carry French, German and Scandinavian services. As always, the willingness to part with one's money will determine the precise choice of packages.

THE POLITICAL SIGNIFICANCE OF THE 'NEW MEDIA'

Changes in broadcasting structures inevitably impact on the institutions of broadcasting concerned. To this extent, it is inevitable that the changes brought about by the 'new media' will be both widespread and deeply felt. Some of those changes have already been discussed: there is likely to be a threat to the BBC's monopoly over the licence fee, advertising revenue for ITV may also be affected and both institutions might have to reconsider their public service duties and responsibilities in the face of an onslaught from cheaper but popular television entertainment. All are aware of the fact that without 'public service' obligations a commercial broadcasting organization would be forced to favour the most popular, the cheapest, and therefore the most profitable fare regardless of its cultural merit.

When threatened, the broadcasters have never been very reluctant to use such arguments against radical reform. Such a defence is understandable even though it is somewhat dishonest and shortsighted. British television, for example, swallows up a tremendous amount of American imports. The 14% quota on foreign programmes operated by British broadcasters does not take into account the *scheduling* of that content, with the effect that prime time television may consist of nothing but American imports. Furthermore, some of that programming may be of the type so often decried by British broadcasters, namely, the *A-Team*, *Dallas*, and the 'shopping catalogue' cartoon such as *He-Man*.

These programmes are usually popular and reach substantial audiences. They are also relatively cheap compared to home produced drama and light entertainment. However, they do not occupy the Top Ten programmes slot very often. Home-made programmes – usually soaps – are always well placed. This suggests that the 'new media' have been too readily condemned for engaging in practices which are endemic in British broadcasting organizations and that British broadcasters, amongst others, have failed to take on board some of the major implications of the 'new media', namely, that there is always likely to be a demand for both (American imported) entertainment and 'quality' British programming.

Similarly, those who have made proposals for change in the British broadcasting industry have based their proposals on an extension, rather than a restriction, of choice. In a freer broadcasting climate, the viewers will determine their choices and if British programmes are worthwhile they will remain dominant. They should not be dominant merely because they are British and because other programming is restricted.

The idea that viewers should be able to exercise greater control over their choices of programming is not new but it has gained currency with the advent of the video cassette recorder (VCR) and the promise of the 'new media'. Although attention is often paid to the 'new media', it is the VCR which has had an enormous impact on broadcasting, if only in terms of putting viewers in control and of releasing some of the pent-up desire for extra premium television. In effect, VCRs have created a 'fifth channel' of television; over 50% of households have VCRs and that population spent some £419m on pre-recorded cassettes, that is, a sum that is equivalent to about one-third the total advertising revenue earned by the ITV companies.[20]

Terrestrial over-the-air television will remain a nationally important entity. The *Coronation Street/Eastenders* type of programme will continue to be nationally popular and will give a cultural cohesion to the nation. One danger, though, is that the less popular programmes will either not be made because they are economically unprofitable or, if made, they will be relegated to a ghetto-ized public service broadcasting sector.

The other danger is only just becoming apparent. While satellite television currently depends upon cable subscription for its audience, and is therefore in effect regulated by the Cable Authority, direct-to-home reception via small dishes will bypass cable altogether, thus bringing the viewer channels which are not controlled by any regulatory body in Britain. It then becomes an issue whether, in an age of direct-to-home satellite broadcasting, it is even possible for a country to exercise control over the content of channels transmitted from beyond its national boundaries, and what actions can be taken when programmes are deemed to be politically sensitive or harmful?

News coverage is one looming area of controversy. In the past, foreign television news coverage of British events had posed little difficulty to the British Government since foreign news programmes were never received directly by the British public. With satellite broadcasting this will no longer be the case. Cable News Network (CNN), an American news channel, and Worldnet, the US Information Agency's channel, are already available in the UK and they will be joined in the near future by others.

Foreign news coverage beamed directly to Britain may result in some tricky situations. If a sensitive news item, such as the MI5 allegations in the banned memoirs of Peter Wright, *Spycatcher*, were to achieve prominence in America as a news story, its coverage on CNN, for example, would be assured. The problems that this would pose for the British Government would be acute since CNN is essentially an American broadcaster and, therefore, not restricted in the same way as domestic media are. In these circumstances, how would a British Government exercise its control over media content?

In practice, the British Government would soon find that its options are very limited. It could, for instance, attempt to influence the programmer or reach an agreement concerning sensitive content but, as the Peter Wright affair demonstrated, its powers overseas are fairly limited. Another option would be to put pressure on British Telecom, the 'middleman', the agency in charge of the uplinking and downlinking operation. This could prove a strong possibility. All of these possible courses of action are, at the time of writing, purely speculative although they do point to the way future difficulties may arise.

BROADCASTING IN THE 1990s

The impact of the 'new media' will take many years to work its way into the crevices of the long established broadcasting structures in Britain. It may be 1995 before the full significance of the new distribution systems is appreciated. Yet change is likely to come to Britain well before that date. Some of that change is an indirect result of the 'new media'; the moves towards giving viewers a greater choice underlines the appeal of cable and satellite broadcasting. But there are other significant trends towards accepting more openness and competition in the broadcasting system. These include the proposal to float off Channel 4 from the IBA, the requirement that the BBC and ITV companies place some 25% of their broadcasting time in the hands of independent producers, the possibility of a fifth channel, the introduction of a form of subscription TV on existing systems, and the 'auctioning' of the ITV franchises in 1992.

Whilst all of these proposals are speculative, they point to a fundamental change of attitude towards broadcasting. The Thatcher Government is intent on putting its philosophy into practice so as to introduce choice and free the television viewer, nowadays seen as a consumer, from the strait-jacket of the BBC and ITV.

The eventual outcome of all these changes will almost certainly point away from the past and to a quite different future. It behoves the broadcasting institutions to argue why that future should be shunned and dreaded; it also demands of opposition political parties a coherent and alternative future strategy. The risk is that once the changes are being implemented – barring accidents, this Conservative Government will be in power until 1992! – it will be too late to retrace our steps and recapture the Reithian ideal.

None of these reasons are sufficient arguments against the introduction of the 'new media' or against reform. For, despite the admirable record of quality and consistency in British broadcasting, there has always been much to criticize. Britain has had its monopoly, its quiz shows, soap operas, and repeat programmes; there have also been many occasions when the television companies have not delivered what they had promised. Furthermore, the last three decades have seen an expansion in the broadcasting services (in both radio and television) which has, in part, reflected a changing social and political context. Few would, for example, wish to return to the BBC monopoly or to television without Channel Four. In change, then, there is both good and bad and Britain has been lucky enough to ensure that there is more of the former than of the latter.

Why there should be no further change in British broadcasting may then be the central question in the 'new media' debate. One reason could be that it could detrimentally affect the programming on BBC and ITV. The case for this is not fully proven, though there are obvious dangers. However, protecting the status quo suggests that new services ought not to develop; but such restrictions on new services of national and even local character appear bureaucratic and censorious.

A more powerful reason for not permitting wholesale 'new media' developments is that the new services will neither provide different services nor extend the range of control and ownership. This is a powerful argument; most of the organizations involved in the 'new media' are commercial institutions and it is therefore probable that their moral, social, or public responsibilities will be dwarfed by the economic logic of their organizations.

For the future, there is one issue that has not received much comment. If the nature of the 'new media' revolution has already been determined and the usual institutional players are now occupying the most favourable places, what happens if, or when, their plans do not measure up to the full potential of the 'new media' and the 'wired nation'? If, in other words, the economic logic does not touch upon the social and political benefits that broadband systems can deliver. Will the speed at which 'new media' developments had been pursued prove worthwhile? Will the policy to favour private developments and not national ones have proved unwise? Will the 'wired society' be dismissed as an illusion rather than perhaps an illusion if developed in private hands? Finally, will the public, in whose name so much has been promised, be able to reclaim the 'new media' revolution for itself and for a better society?

DO WE NEED A MEDIA POLICY?

The concern over the future of British broadcasting and the likely impact of the new media has often been translated into a desire for a more coherent and imaginative policy towards the media as a whole. With rationality and coherence, so the argument goes, one can plan for a better broadcasting future. This would not only ensure that the best is retained but that the policy inconsistencies which have been the hallmark of the Thatcher Government's approach to cable and satellite broadcasting are eliminated: cable television was encouraged in one year (1983), only to be badly affected in the following year (1984) when the same Government allowed the Treasury to phase out capital allowances. This slowed down its development considerably. There was similar confusion in the satellite broadcasting field. The British DBS project was initially designed as a British project and the Government insisted that the BBC should buy the British Aerospace Unisat craft. After the BBC (and others) withdrew on account of the high cost of the satellite, the Government awarded the franchise to BSB and permitted it to buy an American satellite.

These contradictions emphasize the lack of coherence that one can find in the *media* field.[21] Cable, satellite, and terrestrial television, though related, are dealt with not only by different agencies but under different rules (see Table 10.2). To take a contemporary example, the IBA has to ensure that the ITV companies are owned and controlled by British interests; but the proposals put forward by the Cable Authority would remove that stipulation with regard to control of cable operations. This would bring cable *television* in line with the regulatory régime which affects the British *press*.

Such anomalies populate the media field and they do so for three main reasons. The first reason is an historical one. The media in Britain, like elsewhere, were established at different times and so rules and regulations developed incrementally. The second reason is that as the different media developed they were 'allocated' to the most appropriate department of government. This created an additional difficulty in that the media became embroiled in the governmental policy process with its myriad departmental, political, and financial struggles. Thus, the Treasury – a department not traditionally associated with media affairs – often plays a crucial part in policy by determining financial targets or by affecting financial strategies as it did with cable television in 1984.

Finally, and this is of fundamental significance, the term 'the media' is a very loose term. It refers to an indeterminate range of facilities, distribution systems and organizations. This book deals

Table 10.2 Regulations, duties and obligations of different media (1987)

provide programmes of:	BBC/IBA	DBS	QDBS*	CABLE
● High quality/standard	YES	YES	NO	NO
● information, education, entertainment	YES	YES*	NO	NO
● proper balance and wide range in subject matter	YES	NO	NO	NO
secure showing for prog. of merit	YES	NO	NO	NO
prog. must not offend good taste or decency	YES	YES	YES*	YES
there must be a sufficient time for news	YES	NO	NO	NO
news progs must be impartial and accurate	YES	YES	NO*	YES (for UK news)
'due impartiality' in matters of controversy	YES	YES	NO*	YES**
quota of foreign prog.	YES	NO	NO	NO
there must be a suitable matter for regions	YES	NO	NO	NO*?
progs covered by Obscene Publications Act	NO	NO	NO	YES
control of operation must be in British hands	YES	YES	NO	YES***

*Strictly speaking, there are no mechanisms by which to regulate programme channels which originate outside the United Kingdom but are beamed into it. If those channels are available via cable systems, however, it would be possible to regulate the cable systems with a view to exercising some indirect control on satellite delivered services. Alternatively, the Cable Authority may ask foreign programmers to refrain from broadcasting a particular programme because it is considered offensive. This has, in fact, happened and the programmers complied.

**The obligations are diluted in some way or other. For example, although the BBC and the ITV companies have to observe 'due impartiality', cable operators are required to ensure only that 'undue prominence is not given to the views and opinions of particular persons or bodies. . .on matters of political or industrial controversy or relating to current public policy'. (Section 11(3)(a))

***Although the Act restricts control of UK or EEC nationals, participation by other groups is also permitted. This also applies to ITV. Currently (1987), the Cable Authority is arguing for a relaxation of this, and other, rules contained in the 1984 Cable and Broadcasting Act.

with television, the press, and the 'new media', it does not deal with VCRs, records, films, and many others. One result of this selectivity is that discussions of media policy are often conducted without reference to a clear definition of 'media' themselves; another is that discussions are conducted as if there was a common and universal agreement about which media were being covered. Arguments in favour of a single coherent media strategy to cope with the development of the 'new media' and their relationships with the 'old media' of terrestrial television do not usually deal with the press, records, films, radio, or books. But is there a rational case for their exclusion?

One outcome of this process of incrementalism and compartmentalization over time is not an absence of policies towards the media but the absence of a *single*, coherent, co-ordinated and visible[22] media policy.

What are the features of the existing media policies? Three stand out. In the first place the emphasis has usually been on the structural, organizational, financial, and technological aspects of the media rather than on content or audiences.[23] Second, there has been a preference for 'minimalist legislation and the voluntary principle'[24] of self-regulation. The former refers to the rather brief documents which establish regulatory bodies with enormous discretionary powers and the latter to a desire on the part of governments that the industries should regulate themselves, as in the case of the Press Council or the Advertising Standards Authority. In both cases, detailed analysis of the media and future developments are usually conspicuous by their absence.

Another important feature of the 'policy process' is that certain media, particularly the national mass media of television, radio, and the press, become sucked into the policy-making process at the Ministerial and Cabinet level. Examples of this abound. Newspaper mergers in recent decades have depended upon Ministerial and Prime Ministerial approval.[25] In recent years, developments in broadcasting have been initiated or closely examined at Cabinet level. This applies to cable policy[26] and, even more recently, to the setting up of the Peacock Committee to look at the funding of the BBC. Finally, in September 1987 Margaret Thatcher called a meeting of senior broadcasters and Ministers to Downing Street to review the present, and future, state of television in Britain. 'Consequently, "Downing Street" in practice becomes the main locus of British media policy-making. Media policy is largely made in Britain by senior ministers in and around major Cabinet Committees.'[27]

Nevertheless, the features identified above reinforce the view that British Governments have not been consistent in their dealing with different media. With thirty or more agencies dealing with 'the media' or media related matters,[28] a degree of consistency would have been surprising but this administrative and regulatory compartmentalization begs a more general question as to whether consistency is ever possible. Can there ever be *a* media policy as opposed to several media policies?

Unfortunately, it is not possible to treat these questions in a purely administrative, rationalist way as if in a political/ideological vacuum. Indeed, the questions cannot be answered unless one is guided by a clear conception of the objectives of such a singular – or plural – media policy. And these objectives are, inevitably, normative and ideological. It is one thing to identify, say, excessive monopoly or centralization as contemporary concerns but it is another to determine what precisely *ought* to be done *about* that issue. They can only be resolved *politically*; there are no objective bench marks which will produce non-political answers.

The political dimension is but one aspect of media policy-making and there are others which suggest that it is, in fact, an area fraught with difficulties. Those who argue for consistency and coherence across different media, for a single media policy or strategy, take it for granted that such a thing is possible; that despite their different characteristics, markets, organizations, ownerships, and 'functions', there can be some underlying unity or bond which would allow all media to develop hand-in-hand and co-operatively. Yet the opposite is probably the case. Cable and satellite broadcasting are complementary systems but cable and DBS are competitive systems. More generally, cable and satellite broadcasting together compete against terrestrial television.

The other difficulty that soon becomes apparent is that it is not possible to regulate on the basis of the medium's technical characteristics. The medium of television well illustrates this problem. Cable television is, more or less, regulated on the same lines as ITV with regard to content of programmes and the ownership of cable systems. The assumption is that because there is a monitor it is close to that other medium which uses a monitor, namely terrestrial television. But cable television is actually very different from television as it presently exists. It does not suffer from a scarcity of channels, the subscriber can actively select from a wide range of programme channels (including different sources of news), the subscriber can also select from video libraries, the subscriber has access to data banks, and the subscriber can shop or bank from home. It is not surprising, then, that fervent advocates of cable liken it more to 'electronic *publishing*' than to television.

What may appear as an anomaly in a policy may in fact be the result of an uncertainty over the nature of the medium and the problem of deciding whether one ought to make policy regarding structures – how cable is organized, how television or radio is run – or on content – what cable carries, what television or radio carries. The problem is most acute with regard to the 'new media' precisely because the television monitor can be used in such radically different ways. Treating cable systems as television is inconsistent with their properties as telecommunications yet, paradoxically, although they are lightly regulated as 'television' services they are heavily regulated as telecommunications systems since they are not permitted to offer telephony services for fear of upsetting the evolving duopoly of BT and Mercury.

Although the desire for an overall coherence is deeply felt, those who express such a desire may be labouring under the misconceived assumption that coherence *can* be achieved. It is probable that this could only be achieved if the very nature of the separate media were somehow distorted to suit the regulatory objectives of the regulators. How would one compromise the 'promise' of the 'new media' – choice and plenty – with the 'threat' that it poses to the 'old media': would one sacrifice the former for the latter? Why should one halt a 'revolutionary' process to maintain the status quo? Why should one object to 'consumer-driven' media?

None of these questions has easy answers and they are all fundamentally about the sort of society which we desire and the processes of change which we may have to direct in order to reach that goal – and these are political considerations.

POSTSCRIPT:

BROADCASTING IN THE '90s

The long-awaited Government White Paper on broadcasting, *Broadcasting in the '90s: Competition, Choice and Quality* (Cm 517) was published on 7 November 1988. In addition to outlining major plans for reforming British broadcasting, it also sets out a legislative timetable. Since many of the proposals for reform are still open to discussion, consultation, and review, comments on the White Paper will be accepted until the end of February 1989. Following this period of consultation, the Government will bring forward the legislation which will frame the future of British broadcasting.

The various themes and proposals which are developed in the White Paper can be traced back to earlier reports. Two are particularly important in this context. These are the Peacock Committee report on financing the BBC and the commissioned report on Subscription Television (see Chapter 10 for a discussion of these). Most importantly, the White Paper appears to accept the philosophical argument for greater broadcasting freedom and consumer choice which is articulated in the Peacock Report.

There is, however, another 'influence' on the White Paper which must not be overlooked. That 'influence' is best described as the realization that technological change cannot be contained any longer for the sake of the duoply and that this, of itself, makes the reform of broadcasting inevitable (see Chapter 10 for a discussion of these broad issues). As the White Paper observes:

> The government places the viewer and listener at the centre of broadcasting policy. Because of technological, international and other developments change is inevitable. It is also desirable:

only through change will the individual be able to exercise the much wider choice which will soon become possible. . . . The Government is also clear that there need be no contradiction between the desire to increase competition and widen choice and concern that programme standards of good taste and decency should be maintained.

(para 1.2)

It is this approach which guides the proposals in the White Paper; proposals which are designed to open up the structures of broadcasting to the forces of the market-place and to the power of the consumer. In this respect, one can identify three sets of proposals which are likely to produce the desired change. These are:

1. A major reform of the duopoly and the introduction of choice via new video delivery systems;

2. A reform of the present methods of funding broadcasting services. Such reforms will allow for greater competition for advertising revenue and for any revenues which can be obtained directly from consumers, e.g. via subscription payments;

3. The general loosening up of the regulatory framework of British broadcasting so as to allow the commercial television sector to compete in a more competitive and more truly commercial broadcasting environment.

THE PROPOSALS

The BBC

The BBC will remain 'the cornerstone of British broadcasting'. Like the commercial television sector, it will be free to raise finance through subscription payments and sponsorship. It will be up to the BBC to judge 'the extent and pace of the move towards subscription' but this should be done with a view to the 'eventual replacement of the licence fee' (para 1.3 and para 3.10).

A 'natural starting point for subscription would be during the night hours' and the government thus proposes that the BBC introduce such a service on one of its two channels. The night hours on the other channel will be assigned to the commercial sector (para 3.12).

237

The Independent Television sector

ITV should no longer be considered in isolation but as part of a developing and expanded commercial television sector. The Government proposes to create 'a liberalized enabling framework for the development of new services, subject to the necessary consumer protection requirements' (para 4.2). This framework should allow 'entrepreneurs and viewers, subject to the minimum necessary regulation, to decide in the market place which technologies should play the most significant roles' (para 6.2).

To fulfil these aims, the Government proposes to reform the existing structures and to allow for the introduction of new services.

The IBA

It proposes that a new body, the Independent Television Commission, should replace the IBA and the Cable Authority. It will license and supervise the liberalized commercial sector and will use a 'lighter regulatory' touch though it will have tougher sanctions.

ITV

'The present ITV system will be replaced by a regionally based Channel 3 with positive programming obligations but also greater freedom to match its programming to market conditions' (para 1.3).

Licences will run for ten years. Applicants 'for licences would have to pass a quality threshold. They would have to satisfy the ITC that they . . . are qualified to take on a Channel 3 licence.' They would also have to meet the ownership tests which will be introduced. Once satisfied that applicants can meet these requirements, the ITC 'would have to select the applicant for each licence who had submitted the highest tender' (para 6.17). These procedures will be open to public scrutiny.

The performance of these companies will be reviewed periodically by the ITC and it will have the power to issue formal warnings and to remove the licences if company performances are deemed unsatisfactory (para 6.19).

The government also proposes that under the new liberalized commercial régime, commercial television companies should no longer be protected from commercial takeovers. However, the Government 'is determined that ownership. . . should be, and remain, widely spread' (para 6.48). It is therefore 'considering what further rules . . . are needed to restrict concentrations of ownership' (para 6.53). These would apply across the whole of the commercial television sector.

Channel Four

The Government believes that Channel Four should retain its remit. However, it should sell its own advertising time and should be 'constituted differently than at present'. The White Paper invites comments on its possible future structure.

New servies: Channel 5

The Government proposes that a fifth commercial television service be set up by 1993. This will serve some 70 per cent of the population and it will use the UHF frequency. It will be funded by a mix of advertising and subscription revenue. A sixth channel may be authorized if technical studies show that it is feasible.

Channels 3–5 will have to meet certain 'consumer protection' requirements. These include that news be imparital and accurate, that content should not offend standards of good taste and decency and that controversial matters be dealt with impartially (para 6.10). Channel 3 will additionally be required to show regional programming, to show high quality news and current affairs material and to provide a diversity in its programme service (see Table P1).

Other proposals which will increase viewer choice include:

DBS

The two remaining DBS channels will be allocated by 1990. These channels would be exempt from the sorts of programming requirements imposed on Channels 3–5. In view of this, the Government is also ready to discuss with BSB, the current holder of three channels, whether it would wish to alter its 'programming and other obligations' (para 6. 30).

Local services

Using microwave transmissions (MVDS) will be encouraged. These will be established (from 1991) alongside cable systems and could provide a multiplicity of channels. One advantage of MVDS is that such systems are considerably less expensive to construct than cable systems. Operators will therefore 'be free to decide upon the best mix of technologies' as between cable, MVDS or a combination of both. In effect, the Government has abandoned the high technical requirements it had previously imposed upon cable operators. Operators 'will now be free to build to the standards they choose. The extent to which they lay down cable facilities physically capable of functioning as a fully interactive tele-communications network will be a matter for their judgement; not one for Government or regulators' (para 6.33).

Such local services will be based on 15-year franchises awarded by the ITC.

Other proposals in the White Paper include:

- the further encouragement of independent productions
- the deregulation and expansion of independent radio
- putting the Broadcasting Standards Council on a statutory footing
- taking steps to ensure that the programme content of all satellite services is supervised either by UK regulations or by regulations drawn up by European bodies.

Table P1: Proposed programme obligations for independent sector television services (p. 33)

	Channels			DBS	Saturday local services	
	3	4	5			
Consumer protection	yes	yes	yes	yes	yes	yes
News and current affairs	yes	yes	yes	no	no	no
Diverse programme content	yes	yes	yes	no	no	no
Regional programming	yes	no	no	no	no	no
Educational programming	no	yes	no	no	no	no
Minimum 25%of prog. from independents	yes	yes	yes	yes	no	no
Proper proportion of material of European Community origin	yes	yes	yes	yes	no	no

Reactions to the White Paper have highlighted a number of concerns. Firstly, there are fears that a plethora of services – BBC, C3, C4, C5, cable, MVDS and satellite services – all competing against one another for subscription and advertising revenue will have a significant effect on the available funding for any one service. For example, competition for advertising revenue may reduce the funds available to any one commercial television enterprise with consequent effects on its chances of survival and its ability to produce content of a high quality.

Secondly, and more generally, there is a concern that the Government's preference for a competitive television environment is being pursued to the detriment of programming considerations. The view that 'quality television' would suffer in the commercial free-for-all of deregulation has been voiced by many.

Finally, there are many questions about the precise details of the arrangements which the Government has proposed. In this respect, the White Paper is only a short step in the long haul of reforming and restructuring British broadcasting. Nevertheless, if the broad strategy of the Government remains unchanged, British broadcasting will change dramatically in the next five years.

NOTES

PREFACE

1. Seymour-Ure, C. K. 'Media policy in Britain: now you see it, now you don't', in *European Journal of Communication*, Sage, London, Autumn 1987.

1 POLITICS AND THE MASS MEDIA

1. IBA, *Attitudes to Broadcasting in 1985*, London, 1986, p.5.
2. Jowell, R. and Witherspoon S. (eds) *British Social Attitudes, The 1985 Report*, Gower, Aldershot, 1985.
3. ibid., pp.46–7
4. Dunleavy P. and Husbands C., *British Democracy at the Crossroads*, Allen & Unwin, London, 1985.
5. See D. Held in G. McLennan, D. Held and S. Hall (eds) *The Idea of the Modern State*, Open University Press, 1984, p.235.
6. Blumler, J. *The Political Effects of Mass Communication*, Open University Mass Communication and Society Course, Unit 8, Open University, 1977, p.24.
7. ibid., p.24.
8. C. Wright Mills quoted in E. Said, *Covering Islam*, Routledge and Kegan Paul, London, 1981, p.42.
9. Lippmann, W. *Public Opinion*, The Free Press, New York, 1965.
10. T. Gitlin, *The Whole World is Watching*, University of California Press, 1980, p.2.
11. S. Hall, 'The determination of the news photograph' in S. Cohen and J. Young (eds) *The Manufacture of News*, Constable, London, 1973, p.183.
12. E.R. Murrow quoted in Batscha, 'Foreign affairs and the broadcast journalist', Praeger, New York, 1975, p. 53.
13. C. K. Seymour-Ure, *The Political Impact of Mass Media*, Constable, London, 1974, p.62.
14. Gitlin, op cit.,pp. 8–9.

15. Seymour-Ure, op cit., p.42.
16. Seymour-Ure, op cit., p.16.
17. Seymour-Ure, op cit., p.43. Emphasis supplied.
18. Seymour-Ure, op cit., p.21.
19. Seymour-Ure, op cit., p.62.
20. Seymour-Ure, op cit., p.44.
21. Seymour-Ure, op cit., pp.44–8.
22. Kurt and Gladys Lang, 'The unique perspective of television' in B. Berelson and M. Janowitz (eds) *Public Opinion and Communication*, The Free Press, New York, 1966.
23. Kurt and Gladys Lang, ibid., pp.289–90.
24. Kurt and Gladys Lang, *Television and Politics Re-Viewed*, Sage, London, 1982, p. 198.
25. Kurt and Gladys Lang, ibid., pp.201–2.
26. Kurt and Gladys Lang, ibid., p.220.
27. H. Wainwright, the *Guardian*, 23 September 1987.
28. Martin Walker, the *Guardian*, 19 November 1985.
29. N. Jones, *Strikes and the Media. Communication and Conflict*, Blackwell, London, 1986.
30. Linklater, M. and Leigh, D. *Not With Honour. The Inside Story of the Westland Scandal*, Sphere, London, 1986.
31. H. Gans, 'Broadcaster and audience values in the mass media' in *The Image of Man in American TV*, 1965. And R. Bauer, 'The communicator and the audience' in L. Dexter and D. White (eds) *People, Society and the Audience*, The Free Press, New York, 1964.
32. I am grateful to André Goodfriend for this contribution.
33. S. Chibnall, *Law and Order News*, Tavistock Publications, London, 1977.
34. M. Cockerall, M. Walker and P. Hennessey *Sources Close to the Prime Minister*, Macmillan, 1984. See also J. Blumler and M. Gurevitch, 'Politicians and the press. An essay in role relationships' in Nimmo, D. and Sanders, K. (eds) *Handbook of Political Communication*, Sage, London, 1981, pp. 467–93.
35. Becker, McCombs and McLeod quoted in Blumler, op cit., p.24.
36. Cumberbatch, G., McGregor, R., Brown, J. and Morrison, D. *Television and the Miners' Strike*, Broadcasting Research Unit, May 1986, p.5.
37. Cumberbatch, G. *et al.*, ibid., p. 133.
38. See McCombs, M.E. and Shaw, D.L. 'The agenda-setting function of the press', *Public Opinion Quarterly*, 1972, **36**: 176–87; Becker, L. 'The mass media and citizen assessment of issue importance: A reflection on agenda-setting research' in Whitney, D. E. *et al. Mass Communication Review Yearbook*, Sage, London, 1982, Vol. 3; Kraus, S. and Davis, D.K. *The Effects of Mass Communication on Political Behaviour*, Pennsylvania State Univ. Press, 1976.
39. Hartmann, P. and Husband, C. in McQuail, D. *Sociology of Mass Communications*, Penguin, London, 1972.
40. Golding, P. and Middleton, S. *Images of Welfare*, Blackwell and Martin Robertson, Oxford, 1982.

41. See especially Cohen, S. *Folk Devils and Moral Panics*, MacGibbon and Kee, London, 1972.
42. J. Blumler and M. Gurevitch, 'Politicians and the press. An essay in role relationships', in Nimmo, D. and Sanders, K. (eds) *Handbook of Political Communication*, Sage, London, 1981, p. 477.
43. J. Blumler and M. Gurevitch, ibid., p. 489.
44. See R. Miliband, *The State in Capitalist Society*, Quartet, London, 1972.
45. G. Murdock and P. Golding, 'Capitalism, communication and class relations' in J. Curran, M. Gurevitch and J. Woollacott (eds) *Mass Communication and Society*, Edward Arnold, London, 1978.
46. G. Murdock and P. Golding, ibid..
47. T. Bennett, T. Mercer and J. Woollacott (eds) *Popular Culture and Social Relations*, Open University Press, 1986, Preface p. xiv.
48. T. Bennett *et al.* (eds) ibid., p.xiv.
49. J. Thompson, *Studies in the Theory of Ideology*, Polity Press, Oxford, 1985, p. 132.
50. See S. Lukes, *Power. A Radical View*, Macmillan, London, 1974, esp. pp. 24–5.
51. G. Blumler and M. Gurevitch, 'The political effects of mass communication', in M. Gurevitch, T. Bennett, J. Curran and J. Woollacott (eds) *Culture, Society and the Media*, Methuen, London, 1982, p.65.

2   THEORIES OF THE MEDIA

1. *Report of the Committee on Financing the BBC* (Chairman: Prof. A. Peacock), HMSO, Cmnd. 9824, July 1986, paras. 16–27. Henceforth The Peacock Committee.
2. Milton, *Aeropagitica* (1644), quoted in A. Lee, *The Origins of the Popular Press, 1855–1914*, Croom Helm, London, 1976, p.23.
3. Milton quoted in Lee, ibid., p.23.
4. Alexis de Tocqueville quoted in Lee, ibid., p.24.
5. T. Burns, 'The organisation of public opinion' in J. Curran, M. Gurevitch and J. Woollacott (eds) *Mass Communication and Society*, Edward Arnold, London, 1978.
6. G. Boyce, 'The fourth estate: The re-appraisal of a concept' in G. Boyce, J. Curran and P. Wingate (eds) *Newspaper History: From the 17th Century to the Present*, Sage/Constable, London, 1978, p.26.
7. K. Middlemass, *Politics in Industrial Society*, André Deutsch, London, 1979, p.131.
8. Middlemass, ibid., p.367.
9. J. Bentham quoted in Lee, *The Origins of the Popular Press*, p.23.
10. J. Curran and J. Seaton, *Power Without Responsibility*, Methuen, London, 1985, pp. 27–52.
11. F.S. Siebert, T. Peterson and W. Schramm, *Four Theories of the Press*, University of Illinois Press, 1956.

12. D. McQuail, *Mass Communication Theory. An Introduction*, Sage, London, 1983, p. 94.
13. S. McBride *et al.*, *Many Voices, One World*, Unesco, Kogan Page, London, 1980.
14. McQuail, op cit., p. 96.
15. McQuail, op cit., p.96.
16. See H. Schiller, *Mass Communication and American Empire*, New York, 1969; Tunstall, J. *The Media are American*, Constable, London, 1977; Nordenstreng, K. and Varis, T. *Television Traffic – A One-Way Street?*, Unesco, Paris, 1974; Golding, P. 'Media professionalism in the third world' and Boyd-Barrett, O., 'Media imperialism' both in Curran, J., Gurevitch, M. and Woollacott, J., *Mass Communication and Society*, Edward Arnold, London, 1978; Lee, C.C. *Media Imperialism Reconsidered*, Sage, London, 1979.
17. I. Gough, *The Political Economy of the Welfare State*, Macmillan, London, 1979, pp.45–47.
18. R. Norton Taylor, the *Guardian*. For a good example of manipulation of media, see Veitch, A. 'How you have been hearing only one side of the stories', the *Guardian*, 13 August 1986.
19. W. Shawcross, *The Quality of Mercy*, André Deutsch, London, 1984.
20. ibid., p.12.
21. Royal Commission on the Press, 1974–7 (Chairman: McGregor), HMSO, Cmnd. 6810, 1977.
22. Curran and Seaton, op cit., p.297.
23. Curran and Seaton, op cit., pp.343–4.
24. Curran and Seaton, op cit., p.343. Emphasis supplied.
25. Curran and Seaton, op cit., p.345. Emphasis supplied.
26. S. Brittan, 'The fight for freedom in broadcasting', *Political Quarterly*, 1987, Vol. 1.
27. The Peacock Committee, Introduction.
28. Curran and Seaton, op cit., pp. 335–47.
29. Brittan, op cit., p.8.
30. The Peacock Committee, para. 547.
31. Brittan, op cit., p.16.
32. The Peacock Committee, para. 598.
33. The Peacock Committee, para. 701.
34. The Peacock Committee, para. 696.
35. Brittan, op cit., p.20.
36. Brittan, op cit., p.19.

3   THE BRITISH PRESS

1. Koss, S. *The Rise and Fall of the Political Press in Britain*, vol 1, Hamish Hamilton, London, 1981, p. 431.
2. Lee, A.J., *The Origins of the Popular Press 1855–1914*, Croom Helm, London, 1976, p. 198.

3. Seymour-Ure, C. K., 'National daily papers and the party system' in *Studies on the Press*, HMSO, London, 1977, p. 166.

4. Seymour-Ure, C.K., *The Political Impact of Mass Media*, Constable, London, 1974, pp. 157–9.

5. John Whale quoted in Seymour-Ure, C. K., 'Parliament and government' in *Studies on the Press*, HMSO, London, 1977, p.101.

6. Koss, S. *The Rise and Fall of the Political Press in Britain*, vol 1, pp. 3–4.

7. See Culture and the State, Open University, U203 Popular Culture, Unit 28, p.24.

8. Lee, A.J., op cit., p. 279.

9. Lee, A.J., op cit., p. 287.

10. Koss, S. *The Rise and Fall of the Political Press in Britain*, vol 1, p. 48.

11. ibid., p. 9.

12. ibid., p. 3.

13. Lee, A.J., op cit., Tables 5,6 p.279 and Table 24 p.287.

14. Lee, A.J., op cit., Table 34, p.296. In his tables, Lee has attempted to differentiate between 'proprietors' and other related categories such as 'publishers'. These distinctions disappear in more recent publications. See ref. 16 below.

15. Seymour-Ure, C. K., op cit., p. 185.

16. *The Times Guide to the House of Commons, 1979*, Times Newspapers, London, 1979. It is difficult to be very precise about these figures because the distinctions between occupations are not clear cut. The category of 'journalists and authors' is a flexible one. This is particularly evident in Andrew Roth's book on the *Business Background of MPs* (Parliamentary Profiles, 1982). His categories include 'Journalist/Authors', 'Author/Journalist', 'ex. Journalist', 'ex.broadcasters'. Furthermore, who fits into which category is open to some debate. He gives well over 80 MPs with journalist related occupations. There is a similar problem with the categories of 'publisher' and 'proprietor'. Many MPs have minority shareholdings and directorships but these in no way amount to controlling interests. Also, the category publisher includes journals, business magazines, etc. Perhaps the MP with the most prominent media interests would be Jonathan Aitken whose interests in both Beaverbrook Newspapers and TV-am are extensive.

17. Criddle, B., 'Candidates' in Butler, D. and Kavanagh, D. *The British General Election of 1983*, Macmillan, London, 1984, pp. 236–7.

18. Boyce, G., 'The fourth estate: the reappraisal of a concept' in Boyce, G.,Curran, J. and P. Wingate (eds), *Newspaper History: From the 17th Century to the Present Day*, Constable, London, 1978, p. 26.

19. Koss, S., op cit., p. 10.

20. Curran, J. and Seaton, J. *Power Without Responsibility*, Fontana, London, 1981, pp. 43–62.

21. Koss, S. op cit., p. 15.

22. Boyce, G., op cit., p. 27.

23. Lee, A. J., 'The structure, ownership and control of the press: 1855–1914', p. 118 in Boyce, G.,Curran, J. and P. Wingate (eds), op cit.

24. Koss, S. op cit., p. 10.
25. Koss, S. op cit., vol 1, p. 12.
26. Lee, A.J. op cit., p. 105.
27. Lee, A.J. op cit., p. 121.
28. Lee, A.J. op cit., p. 125.
29. Lee, A.J. op cit., p. 130.
30. Taylor, A.J.P., *Beaverbrook*, Penguin, London, 1972, p. 95.
31. ibid., p. 214.
32. Boyce, G., op cit., p. 32.
33. *The Times*, London, 17 March 1931.
34. *The Times*, 18 March 1931.
35. Koss, S. op cit., p. 18.
36. Seymour-Ure, C. K., op cit., 1977, p. 190.
37. Seymour-Ure, C. K., op cit., 1977, p. 192. Emphasis supplied.
38. Koss, S. *The Rise and Fall of the Political Press in Britain*, vol 2, p.628.
39. Seymour-Ure, C. K., op cit., 1977, p. 194.
40. Hollingsworth, M. *The Press and Political Dissent*, Pluto, London, 1986, Ch. 7.
41. Seymour-Ure, C.K., op cit., 1974, pp. 172–3.
42. Dealler, S. *The SDP and the Press*, MA Dissertation, City Poly, (unpublished), 1983, p.11.
43. Butler, D. and Kavanagh, D. *The British General Election of 1983*, p. 217.
44. Curran, J. and Seaton, J., *Power Without Responsibility*, Methuen, London, 1985, pp. 342–3.

4 THE BRITISH PRESS: OWNERSHIP, CONTROL, ADVERTISING, AND RESTRUCTURING

1. Read, D. *Press and People 1790–1850: Opinion in Three English Cities*, Edward Arnold, London, 1961.
2. Schudson, M. *Discovering the News*, Basic Books, New York, 1978, Ch. 1.
3. Briggs, A. *Mass Entertainment: the Origins of a Modern Industry*, 29th Joseph Fisher Lecture in Commerce, Adelaide, Griffin Press, 1960.
4. ibid..
5. Royal Commission on the Press 1947–9 Report, 1949, HMSO, London, Cmnd 7700.
6. Lee, A. *The Origins of the Popular Press*, Croom Helm, London, 1978, p. 293.
7. Royal Commission on the Press, op cit., para 18, p. 4. Emphasis supplied.
8. See Murdock, G. and Golding, P. 'Capitalism, communication and class relations' in Curran, J., Gurevitch, M. and Woollacott. J. *Mass Communication and Society*, Edward Arnold, 1978, and also Murdock, G. 'Large corporations and the control of the communications industries' in Gurevitch, M., Bennett, T., Curran, J. and Woollacott, J. *Culture, Society and the Media*, Methuen, London, 1982.

9. Murdock, G. and Golding, P. 'Capitalism, communication and class relations', p. 15.
10. ibid., p. 15.
11. ibid., p. 28. Emphasis supplied.
12. ibid., p. 33.
13. Tunstall, J. *The Media in Britain*, Constable, London, 1983, pp. 186–188.
14. Murdock, G. and Golding, P. op cit., pp. 32–3.
15. Tunstall, J. op cit., 1983, p. 173.
16. Tunstall, J. op cit., 1983, p. 183.
17. Tunstall, J. *Journalists at Work*, Constable, London, 1971.
18. Tunstall, J. op cit., p. 182.
19. Jones, N. *Strikes and the Media*, Blackwell, Oxford, 1986, p. 115.
20. ibid., p. 193.
21. Hollingsworth, M. *The Press and Political Dissent*, Pluto, London, 1986, p. 215.
22. Tunstall, J. op cit., 1983, p.78.
23. Curran, J. 'Advertising as a patronage system' in Christian, H. (ed) *The Sociology of Journalism and the Press*, Sociological Review Monograph 29, University of Keele, Staffs, 1980, p. 78. Emphasis in original.
24. ibid., p. 92. Emphasis supplied.
25. Tunstall, J. op cit., 1972, pp. 92–94.
26. Dyer, G. *Advertising as Communication*, Methuen, London, 1982, pp. 184–185. See also Williamson, J. *Decoding Advertisements*, Marian Boyers, London, 1978, and Berger, J. *Ways of Seeing*, Pelican/BBC, London, 1972.
27. Hirsch, F. and Gordon, D. *Newspaper Money*, Hutchinson, London, 1975, p.42.
28. ibid., p. 19.
29. ibid., p. 36.
30. Chibnall, S. *Law and Order News*, Tavistock Publications, London, 1977, pp. 21–22.
31. Curran, J. op cit., p. 105.
32. Seymour-Ure, C. K. *The Press, Politics and the Public*, Methuen, London, 1968, p. 29.
33. Curran, J. op cit., p. 104.
34. Curran, J. and Seaton, J. *Power Without Responsibility*, Fontana, London, 1981, pp. 123–125.
35. ibid., p. 123. Emphasis supplied.
36. Curran, J., Douglas, A. and Whannel, G. 'The political economy of the human-interest story' in Smith, A. (ed) *Newspapers and Democracy*, The MIT Press, London and USA, 1980, pp. 288–349.
37. ibid., p. 295.
38. Pegg, M. *Broadcasting and Society 1919–1939*, Croom Helm, London, 1983, p.218.
39. Figures from the *Royal Commission on the Press 1947–9*, HMSO, Cmnd 7700, 1949, and Curran, J., Douglas, A. and Whannel, G. op cit.

40. Curran, J., Douglas, A. and Whannel, G. op cit., p. 343.
41. Cleverley, G. *The Fleet Street Disaster*, Constable, London, 1978, p.27. See also Sisson, K. *Industrial Relations in Fleet Street*, Blackwell, Oxford, 1975.
42. Winsbury, R. 'Introduction' in Cleverley, G. *The Fleet Street Disaster*, p. 10.
43. This account is drawn from Goodhart, D. and Wintour, P. *Eddie Shah and the Newspaper Revolution*, Coronet, London, 1986.
44. ibid., p. 63.
45. ibid., p. 64.
46. SOGAT *New Technology: The American Experience*, 1985, p. 3.
47. Melvern, L. *The End of the Street*, Methuen, London, 1986.
48. Annual Financial Report, the *Guardian*, 16 September 1986.
49. *Royal Commission on the Press 1974–7*, HMSO, Cmnd 6810, London, 1977, Final Report, p.42.

5 BROADCASTING IN BRITAIN

1. A. Gouldner, *The Coming Crisis of Western Sociology*, Heinemann, London, 1971, p.342.
2. P. Eckersley, *The Power Behind the Microphone*, Cape, London, 1941, p.18.
3. Crawford Committee of Enquiry, 1926, quoted in the *Report of the Committee on the Future of Broadcasting* (Chairman, Lord Annan), HMSO, Cmnd. 6753, 1977, p.9.
4. *The Annan Report*, p.33.
5. R. Negrine, 'From radio relay to cable television: an historical approach', *The Historical Journal of Film, Radio and Television*, Vol. 4, No. 1, 1984.
6. T. Burns, *The BBC: Public Institution and Private World*, Macmillan, London, 1977, p.41.
7. H.H. Wilson, *Pressure Group: The Campaign for Commercial Television*, Secker and Warburg, London, 1961.
8. *Report of the Committee on Financing the BBC* (Chairman: Prof. A. Peacock), HMSO, Cmnd. 9824. Henceforth referred to as The Peacock Committee.
9. ibid., especially Ch. 3.
10. ibid. and S. Brittan, 'The fight for freedom in broadcasting' in *Political Quarterly*, 1987, Vol. 1; see also *Subscription Television*, A study for the Home Office by CSP International Ltd., HMSO, May 1987.
11. *Report of the Committee on Broadcasting* (Chairman: Pilkington), HMSO Cmnd. 1753, 1962.
12. The Peacock Committee, para. 30.
13. BBC Royal Charter and Lord Normanbrook's letter.
14. Lord Normanbrook's letter.
15. IBA Act 1973. Quoted in *The Annan Report*, para. 100.

16. *The Annan Report*, para. 5.6.
17. Broadcasting Research Unit, *The Public Service Idea in British Broadcasting – Main Principles*, Broadcasting Research Unit, 1985/6.
18. K. Kumar, 'Public service broadcasting and the public interest' in C. MacCabe and O. Stewart (eds) *The BBC and Public Service Broadcasting*, Manchester University Press, 1986, p.58, p.59.
19. ibid., p.59.
20. The Peacock Committee, para. 213.
21. The Peacock Committee, para. 211–17.
22. The Peacock Committee and S. Brittan, 'The fight for freedom in broadcasting', 1987.
23. The Peacock Committee, para. 3.
24. The Peacock Committee, para. 7.
25. *The Annan Report*, op cit., p.14.
26. Morgan, J., in Hoggart, R. and Morgan, J., (eds) *The Future of Broadcasting*, Macmillan, London, 1982, p. 64.
27. Annan Committee, p.14.
28. Briggs, A., 'Governing the BBC' in Hoggart, R. and Morgan, J. (eds), op cit.
29. Milne, A., *The Communicators*, BBC Radio 4, 1981.
30. Smith, A., Evidence to the *Annan Committee*, p. 231.
31. *Broadcasting Bill*, February 1980, HMSO, London, Clause 3.
32. For a discussion of some of these proposals, see Prof. A. Ehrenberg and P. Barwise 'What are the alternatives for Channel 4?' in *Broadcast*, 2 October 1987 and Prof. A. Budd, 'Give C4 its liberty' in *Broadcast*, 23 October 1987.

6   THE POLITICS OF BROADCASTING: 'LIBERTY ON PAROLE'

1. Hoggart, R., 'Preface' in Glasgow University Media Group, *Bad News*, London, Routledge and Kegan Paul, 1976, p.x.
2. Gitlin, T., *The Whole World is Watching*, Berkely, University of California Press, 1980, p. 10.
3. A. Smith, *The Politics of Information*, Macmillan, London, 1978, p.98.
4. S. Hall, 'External influences on broadcasting: the external-internal dialectic in broadcasting. Television's double bind', Occasional Paper, Centre for Contemporary Cultural Studies, Birmingham, 1972, p.8.
5. BBC Yearbook 1976, BBC, London, p.272. Five 'directions of a general kind' have been issued. Only two are currently in force. One deals with the Authorities' duty to refrain from broadcasting or publishing their own opinions and the other requires the broadcasters not to broadcast material which uses subliminal techniques. The other directions which have long since been abandoned were: a 1927 direction to the BBC to refrain from broadcasting on matters of political, industrial, or religious controversy; the 1955 '14 day rule'

which prevented broadcasters dealing with issues within a 14 day period of them being raised in Parliament and, lastly, broadcasters were once prevented from 'broadcasting controversial party political broadcasts other than those arranged in agreement with the major political parties'. See Annan Report, para. 5.10.

6. T. Burns, *The BBC: Public Institution and Private World*, Macmillan, London, 1977, p.16.

7. J. Reith quoted in Stuart, *The Reith Diaries*, p. 96. Entry dated 10 May 1926, Collins, London, 1975.

8. ibid. p.96.

9. Tracey, M. in Aubrey, C. *Nukespeak*, Comedia, London, 1983.

10. Burns, op cit., p.20.

11. BBC evidence to *The Annan Report*, p.268.

12. A. Smith, *Television and Political Life*, Macmillan, London, 1979, p.21.

13. Goldie, G.W., *Facing the Nation: Television and Politics*, The Bodley Head, London, 1977.

14. Some recent examples include material from the Falklands (see the *Guardian*, 11 January 1983) and on foreign reporting (see the *Guardian*, 31 January 1981). Reports on the security services also came under scrutiny.

15. *The Annan Report*, p. 269.

16. The *Observer*, London, 18 and 25 August 1985.

17. BBC, *CCO Media Monitoring – The BBC Response*, 5 Nov. 1986.

18. Critchley, J., quoted in the *Observer*, 20 September 1987.

19. L. Curtis, *Ireland and the Propaganda War*, Pluto Press, London, 1984, Appendix.

20. The item concerned was to appear in the Bandung File in Nov. 1987. The IBA objected to part of the item and it was pulled out of the programme.

21. B. Hosking, IBA, the *Guardian*, 13 February 1982.

22. R. Gott, 'A Greek tragedy to haunt the old guard', the *Guardian*, 5 August 1986 and the *Guardian*, 10 and 17 July 1986.

23. *The Annan Report*, para. 13.7.

24. *The Annan Report*, para. 13.10.

25. Sendall, B. *Independent Television in Britain, Expansion and Change, 1958–1968.*, Vol. 2, Macmillan, London, 1983, p.295.

26. ibid., p.306. Emphasis supplied.

27. *The Times*, London, 25 April 1980.

28. R. Negrine, 'The press and the Suez Crisis: A myth re-examined', *The Historical Journal*, December 1982.

29. A. Briggs, *Governing the BBC*, BBC, London, 1979, p.211. Emphasis supplied.

30. ibid., p.213.

31. ibid., p.215.

32. ibid., p.214.

33. Quoted in the *Guardian*, 2 January 1987.

34. G. Cox, *See It Happen. The Making of ITN*, The Bodley Head, London, 1983, pp. 71–4.

35. BBC 2, *Newsnight*, 2 May 1982 and BBC 1, *Panorama*, 10 May 1982.
36. Margaret Thatcher, 6 May 1982.
37. *Sunday Times*, London, 30 January 1983.
38. R. Harris, *Gotcha! The Media, the Government and the Falklands Crisis*, Faber and Faber, London, p.80.
39. J. Reith quoted in Stuart, *The Reith Diaries*. Entry dated 11 May 1926.
40. *The Times*, 29 July 1985.
41. L. Brittan quoted in the *Guardian*, 30 July 1985. Emphasis supplied.
42. M. Tracey, *The Production of Political Television*, Routledge and Kegan Paul, London, 1978, Ch. 10.
43. The *Guardian*, 7 August 1985.
44. The *Observer*, 4 August 1985.
45. The 'Zircon Affair' concerned one programme in a series *The Secret Society* by Duncan Campbell which was stopped by the Special Branch in 1987. For details, see *The Zircon Affair*, NCCL, London, 1987.
46. Smith, A., *The Shadow in the Cave*, Quartet, London, 1973, Appendix 1.
47. *The Times*, 30 July 1985.
48. The *Guardian*, 15 July 1985.
49. See Kuhn, R., 'France: The end of the government monopoly' and Sassoon, D., 'Italy: The advent of private broadcasting' in Kuhn, R. (ed) *The Politics of Broadcasting*, Croom Helm, London, 1985.

7   NEWS AND THE PRODUCTION OF NEWS

I am grateful to Mr Howard Tumber for his help in the writing of this chapter.

1. Lippmann, W., *Public Opinion*, The Free Press, New York, 1965, p. 223.
2. Gans, H., *Deciding What's News*, Vintage Books, New York, 1980, p.80.
3. Golding, P. and Middleton, S., *Images of Welfare*, Martin Robertson, 1982, p. 113.
4. ibid., p. 153.
5. Hall, S., Critcher, C., Jefferson, T., Clarke, J. and Roberts, B., *Policing the Crisis*, Macmillan, London, 1978, p.55.
6. Hall, S., 'A world at one with itself' in Cohen, S. and Young, J., (eds) *The Manufacture of News*, Constable, London, 1973, p. 86.
7. Lippmann, op cit., p. 216.
8. Lippmann, op cit., p. 226.
9. Galtung, J. and Ruge, M. 'The structure of foreign news' in Tunstall, J. (ed) *Media Sociology*, Constable, London, 1969.
10. ibid., pp. 262–264.
11. Tunstall, J., *Journalists at Work*, Constable, London, 1972, pp. 20–2.
12. Golding, P. and Elliott, P., *Making the News*, Longman, London, 1979.

13. ibid., 1979, p.123.
14. Hetherington, A., *News, Newspapers and Television*, Macmillan, London, 1985, p.8.
15. ibid., p. 8.
16. Golding, P. and Elliott, P.,op cit., p. 208.
17. Golding, P. and Elliott, P., op cit., p. 209.
18. Gans, H., op cit., p.81.
19. Whale, J., 'News' in *The Listener*, 15 October 1970.
20. See Epstein, J., *News from Nowhere*, Basic Books, New York, 1972. Also Schlesinger, P., *Putting Reality Together*, Constable, London, 1978.
21. Boorstein, D., *The Image*, Penguin, London, 1961, pp. 22–23. See also Lippmann, op cit., p. 218.
22. Schlesinger, P., op cit., p. 69.
23. Golding, P. and Middleton, S., op cit., p. 123.
24. Golding, P. and Middleton, S., op cit., p. 124.
25. See Tunstall, J., *Journalists at Work*, Constable, 1972.
26. Cockerell, M., Hennessey, P. and Walker, D., *Sources Close to the Prime Minister*, Macmillan, London, 1984.
27. Golding, P. and Middleton, S., op cit., p. 152.
28. Golding, P. and Middleton, S., op cit., p. 124.
29. White, M. 'A hundred years of seductive secrecy' in the *Guardian*, 18 January 1984.
30. Golding, P. and Elliott, P., op cit., p. 93.
31. Tunstall, J. 'News organisation goals and specialist newsgathering journalists' in McQuail, D., *Sociology of Mass Communication*, Penguin, London, 1972, p. 279.
32. Gans, H., op cit., p. 145.
33. Hall, S. *et al.*, op cit., p.58.
34. Sigal, L., *Reporters and Officials*, D.C. Heath, 1973, p. 144.
35. Gans, H., op cit., p. 144.
36. Gans, H., op cit., p. 49.
37. Cohen, S., *Folk Devils and Moral Panics*, MacGibbon and Kee, London, 1972, p. 9.
38. Hall, S. *et al.*,op cit. p. viii.
39. Hall, S. *et al.*,op cit., p. 29.
40. Golding, P. and Middleton, S., op cit., p. 206.
41. Golding, P. and Middleton, S., op cit., p. 229.
42. Golding, P. and Middleton, S., op cit., p. 230.
43. Golding, P. and Middleton, S., op cit., p. 231.
44. Golding, P. and Elliott, P., op cit., p. 208.
45. Lang, K. and Lang, G., 'The unique perspective of television' in Berelson, B. and Janowitz, M., *Reader in Public Opinion and Communication*, The Free Press, New York, 1966.
46. Glasgow University Media Group, *Bad News*, Routledge and Kegan Paul, London, 1976, p.1.
47. Sparks, C., 'Striking results?' in *Media, Culture and Society*, Vol. 9 (1987), pp. 369–377, p. 371. Emphasis supplied.
48. Glasgow University Media Group, *Bad News*, p. 258.

49. Harrison, M. *TV News: Whose Bias?*, Policy Journals, Berks., 1985, p. 94. See also Collins, R. 'Bad news and bad faith: The story of a controversy' in *Journal of Communications*, Autumn 1986.

50. Cumberbatch, G., McGregor, R., Brown, R., and Morrison, D., *et al.*, *Television and the Miners' Strike*, BRU, London, 1986.

51. Sparks, C., 'Striking results?', p. 376.

52. Cumberbatch, G. *et al.*, op cit., pp. 131–2.

53. Cumberbatch, G. *et al.*, op cit., p. 132.

54. Brown, J., McGregor, R. and Cumberbatch, G., 'Tilting at windmills: an attempted murder by misrepresentation' in *Media, Culture and Society*, Vol. 9 (1987), pp. 381–4.

55. ibid., p. 383.

56. Gans, H., op cit., p. 98.

57. McQuail, D., op cit., 1983, p. 146.

58. Golding, P. and Elliott, P., op cit., p. 207.

59. Bennett, T. 'Media, "reality", signification' in Gurevitch, M., Bennett, T., Curran, J. and Woollacott, J., *Culture, Society and the Media*, Methuen, London, 1982.

60. Tuchman, G. 'Objectivity as strategic ritual' in *American Journal of Sociology*, Vol. 77, Number 4, pp. 660–79.

61. See Golding, P. and Elliott, P., op cit., pp. 215–218.

62. Golding, P. and Elliott, P., op cit., p.218.

63. Cumberbatch, G. *et al.*, op cit., p.134.

64. See Harris, R. *Gotcha! The Media, The Government and the Falklands Crisis*, Faber & Faber, London, 1983. See also Defence Committee, House of Commons, 1st Report 1982–3, Vol. 1, 1982, and Morrison, D. and Tumber, H. *Journalists at War*, Sage, London, 1988.

65. Seymour-Ure, C.K. 'Government:The lobby correspondents' in *Studies on the Press*, HMSO, 1977, p. 117.

66. Aitken, I. 'The leaks that drip from a damned Whitehall source', in the *Guardian*, 16 March 1984. See also Tunstall, J., *The Westminster Lobby Correspondent*, Routledge and Kegan Paul, London, 1970; Margach, J., *The Anatomy of Power*, W. H. Allen, London, 1979.

67. See Seymour-Ure, C.K. op cit..

68. White, M. 'A hundred years of seductive secrecy'.

69. Aitken,I. 'The insecurity behind all the mudslinging' in the *Guardian*, London, 24 November 1986.

70. Seymour-Ure, C.K. op cit., p. 124.

71. 'The lobby report' in the *Guardian*, 9 December 1986.

72. See Cockerell, M. *et al.* op cit., Chapter 11.

8 'M IS FOR MEDIA': THE POLITICS OF MEDIA PRESSURE

1. Lowe, P. and J. Goyder, *Environmental Groups in Politics*, George Allen & Unwin, London, 1983, p. 79.

2. Jones, N. *Strikes and the Media*, Blackwell, Oxford, 1986, and McShane, D. *Using the Media*, Pluto Press, London, 1979.

3. Wilson, D. *Pressure: The A–Z of Campaigning in Britain*, Heinemann, London, 1985.

4. Davies, A. *The Politics of Pressure*, BBC, London, p. 149.

5. Lowe, P. and J. Goyder, op cit., p. 79.

6. Lowe, P. and Morrison, D, 'Bad news or good news: Environmental politics and the mass media' in *Sociological Review*, 1984, Vol. 32, No. 1–2, p. 79.

7. Wilson, D. op cit., pp. 79–80.

8. Harrison, P and Palmer, R. *News out of Africa. Biafra to Band Aid*, Hilary Shipman, London, 1986, p. 97.

9. ibid., p.129.

10. Barbara Castle, *The Castle Diaries* quoted in the *Sunday Times*, 5 April 1969.

11. Golding, P. and Middleton, S. 'Making claims: News media and the welfare state', *Media, Culture and Society*, 1979, 1, p.19.

12. ibid., p.19.

13. Sigal, L. *Reporters and Officials*, D.C. Heath, USA, 1973, p. 185. See also Blumler, J. and Gurevitch, M., 'Politicians and the press: An essay in role relationships' in Nimmo, D. and Sanders, K. (eds) *Handbook of Political Communication*, Sage, London, 1981, Ch. 17.

14. Sigal, L. *Reporters and Officials*, p. 133.

15. James Reston quoted in Cohen, B. *The Press and Foreign Policy*, Princeton University Press, New Jersey, 1963, p. 102. Emphasis supplied.

16. Halperin, M. *Bureaucratic Politics and Foreign Policy*, Brookings Institute, Washington, 1974, p. ix.

17. Banting, K, *Poverty, Politics and Policy*, Macmillan, London, 1979, p.73.

18. Lowe, P. and Morrison, D., op cit., p. 80.

19. Yellowlees Letter, *The Times* 13 February 1982.

20. Yellowlees Letter, *The Times* 13 February 1982.

21. Wilson, D. op cit., p. 135.

22. This account is drawn from Wilson, D. *The Lead Scandal*, Heinemann, 1983; Evans, H. *Good Times, Bad Times*, Coronet, London, 1984 and personal interviews.

23. ibid., p. 419.

24. Yelland, Managing Director of Associated Octel in a letter to *The Times* 10 February 1982.

25. Personal interviews.

26. Royal Commission on Environmental Pollution, Report 9. *Lead in the Environment*, T.R.E. Southwood (Chmn), London, HMSO, Cmnd 8852, 1983.

27. Lowe, P. and J. Goyder, *Environmental Groups in Politics*, p. 68.

28. Personal interview with Jill Runnette, CALIP, 1982.

29. 'The health effects of lead on children: A review of the literature published since 1976', CALIP, London, 1978.

9 POLITICAL COMMUNICATION: THE MASS MEDIA AND GENERAL ELECTIONS

1. Seymour-Ure, C. K., *The Political Impact of Mass Media*, Constable, London, 1974, p. 43.
2. ibid., p. 206.
3. Butler, D. and Kavanagh, D. (eds) *The British General Election of 1983*, Macmillan, London, 1984, pp. 271–2.
4. Blumler, J., Gurevitch, M. and Ives, J., *The Challenge of Election Broadcasting*, Leeds University Press, Leeds, 1978, p. 43.
5. Gurevitch, M. and Blumler, J., 'The construction of election news. An observation study at the BBC' in Ettema, J.S. and Whitney, D.C. (eds) *Individuals in Mass Media Organisations: Creativity and Constraint*, Sage Annual Review of Communication Research 10, London, 1982, p. 197.
6. Axford, B. and Madgwick, P. 'Indecent Exposure', Paper given at the Conference on Political Communications, Essex University, 1987, p. 1.
7. Katz, E., 'Platforms and windows: broadcasting's role in election campaigns' in McQuail, D.(ed) *Sociology of Mass Communications*, Penguin Special, London, 1972, p. 353.
8. Butler, D., 'The changing nature of British elections', in Crewe, I. and Harrop, M. (eds) *Political Communications: The General Election Campaign of 1983*, Cambridge, 1986, p. 16.
9. Crewe, I., *How to Win a Landslide Without Really Trying: Why the Conservatives Won in 1983*, Essex Papers in Politics and Government, Essex University, No. 1, April 1984, pp. 4–5.
10. Kavanagh, D., 'The timing of elections: The British case', Paper given at the Conference on Political Communications, Essex University, October 1987, p. 12.
11. Sources for polls are as follows:
    1987 – Kavanagh, D., 'The timing of elections: The British case', p.12.
    1983 – Butler, D. and Kavanagh, D., *The British General Election of 1983*, Macmillan, 1984, pp. 124–7.
    1979 – Penniman, H. R. (ed), *Britain at the Polls, 1979*, AEIPPR, London, 1981, pp. 196–9.
    1974 Feb. – Butler, D. and Kavanagh, D., *The British General Election of 1974*, Macmillan, 1974, p.278.
    1970 – Butler, D. and Pinto-Duschinsky, M., *The British General Election of 1974*, Macmillan, 1974, pp. 177–8.
12. Crewe, I., *How to Win a Landslide Without Really Trying*, p. 12.
13. Blumler, J., *The Political Effects of Mass Communication*, Open University, Course DE 353, Unit 8, 1977, p. 42.
14. Blumler, J. and McQuail, D., *Television in Politics*, Faber & Faber, London, 1968, quoted in Blumler, J., *The Political Effects of Mass Communication*, p. 27.

15. in Butler, D. and Kavanagh, D., (eds) *The British General Election of 1983*, Macmillan, London, 1984.

16. Crewe, I., *How to Win a Landslide Without Really Trying*, p. 11.

17. Blumler, J., *The Political Effects of Mass Communication*, p. 25.

18. Crewe, I., *How to Win a Landslide Without Really Trying*, pp. 20–25.

19. in Butler, D. and Kavanagh, D. (eds) *The British General Election of 1983*, Macmillan, London, 1984, p. 11.

20. Patterson, T.E., *The Mass Media Election*, Praeger, 1980.

21. ibid., p. 123.

22. ibid., p. 124.

23. BBC Broadcasting Research, Special Report. The 1983 General Election, August 1983, pp.19–20. See also Harrop, M., 'Voters' in Seaton, J. and Pimlott, B. (eds) *The Media in British Politics*, Avebury, Aldershot, England, 1987, p. 57.

24. Blumler, J., 'Producers' attitudes towards television coverage of an election campaign: A case study', in Tunstall, J. (ed) *Media Sociology*, Constable, London, 1970, p. 413.

25. Katz, E., op cit., p. 356.

26. See also Seymour-Ure, C.K. op cit., Ch. 8.

27. Katz, E., 'Platforms and windows: broadcasting's role in election campaigns', p. 370.

28. See Seaton, J. 'Politics and television' in *Economy and Society*, 1980, vol. 9, no. 1.

29. Harrison, M. 'Television news coverage' in Worcester, B. and Harrop, M. (eds) *Political Communications. The General Election Campaign of 1979*, George Allen and Unwin, London, 1982, p. 73.

30. ibid., p. 76.

31. Quoted in David Butler 'The case of the disappearing issues', Radio 4, 1983.

32. Gunter,B., Svennevig, M. and Wober, M., 'Viewers' experience of television coverage of the 1983 general election' in *Parliamentary Affairs*, vol. 37, 1984, p. 279.

33. ibid., p. 279; figures for 1987 are from BBC Broadcasting Research, Special Projects Report, *Public Reactions to BBC and ITV Coverage of the 1987 General Election* Nov. 1987, p. 6.

34. Boorstein, D. J. *The Image*, Penguin, London, 1962, Ch. 1.

35. Figures for 1983 from Harrison, M. 'Broadcasting' in Butler, D. and Kavanagh, D. (eds) *The British General Election of 1983*, p. 161; figures for 1979 from Harrison, M. 'Television news coverage' in Worcester, B. and Harrop, M. (eds), op cit., p. 72.

36. Harrison, M., 'Broadcasting' in Butler, D. and Kavanagh, D. (eds) *The British General Election of 1983*, p. 161.

37. Gurevitch, M. and Blumler, J., 'The Construction of Election News', p. 184.

38. See Lord Windlesham, *Communication and Political Power*, Cape, London, 1966.

39. Day, B., 'The politics of communications, or the communication of politics' in Worcester, B. and Harrop, M. (eds) op cit., p. 5.

40. Delaney, T., 'Labour's advertising campaign', in Worcester, B. and Harrop, M. (eds) op cit., p.29
41. ibid., p. 31.
42. Cockerell, M., Hennessey, P. and Walker, D. *Sources Close to the Prime Minister*, Macmillan, London, 1984, p. 209.
43. Curran, C., *A Seamless Robe*, Collins, London, 1979, pp. 342–3.
44. Bell, T., 'The Conservatives' advertising campaign' in Worcester, B. and Harrop, M. (eds) op cit., p. 15.
45. BBC Broadcasting Research, Special Projects Report, *Public Reactions to BBC and ITV Coverage of the 1987 General Election* Nov. 1987, p. 18.
46. Harrop, M., 'Voters', p. 57.
47. Dunleavy, P. and Husbands, C. *British Democracy at the Crossroads: Voting and Party Competition in the 1980s*, Allen and Unwin, London, 1985.
48. ibid.

10 'THE NEW MEDIA': CABLE TELEVISION, SATELLITE BROADCASTING AND THE FUTURE OF BRITISH BROADCASTING

1. *Subscription Television. A Study for the Home Office*, Study conducted by CSP International, HMSO, London, May 1987.
2. *Report of the Committee on Financing the BBC*, Chrm. Prof. A. Peacock, HMSO, London, Cmnd. 9824, 1986.
3. Hollins, T. *Beyond Broadcasting*, BRU, London, 1983.
4. Tunstall, J. *Communications De-regulation*, Blackwell, Oxford, 1986, p. 129.
5. Howkins, J. *New Technologies, New Policies* BRU, London, 1982, p.7.
6. *Report of the Committee on Financing the BBC*, p. 105.
7. See Negrine, R. 'Cable Television in Great Britain' in Negrine, R. (ed) *Cable Television and the Future of Broadcasting*, Croom Helm, London, 1985.
8. Williamson, M. in Negrine, R. (ed) *Satellite Broadcasting*, Croom Helm, London, 1987.
9. Information Technology Advisory Panel (ITAP), *Cable Systems*, HMSO, London, 1982. See also Negrine, R. 'Cable Television in Great Britain', 1985.
10. ibid., p. 7.
11. ibid., p.48.
12. *Subscription Television. A Study for the Home Office*, May 1987.
13. 'Television', *The Economist*, London, December 20 1986.
14. *Subscription Television. A Study for the Home Office*, May 1987, p.16.
15. *Screen Digest*, London, March 1987.
16. *Broadcast*, London, 6 November 1987.
17. *Screen Digest*, London, October 1987.
18. Goodfriend, A. 'Satellite Broadcasting in Britain' in Negrine, R. (ed)

Satellite Broadcasting, Croom Helm, London, 1987.
19. EEC, *Television Without Frontiers*, Brussels, 1984.
20. Richard Hooper, 'Super Channel', quoted in *Broadcast*, 9 October 1987.
21. Negrine, R., 'Great Britain: is there a policy towards the new media?' in Dyson, K. and Humphreys, P. (eds) *Politics, Policy and the New Media in Western Europe*, Croom Helm, London, 1988.
22. See Seymour-Ure, C.K. 'Media policy in Britain: now you see it, now you don't' in *European Journal of Communication*, Sage, London, 1987, Vol. 2, pp. 269–287.
23. ibid., p. 272.
24. Tunstall, J. *The Media in Britain*, Constable, London, 1983, p.237.
25. ibid., p. 265.
26. See Negrine, R., 'Great Britain: is there a policy towards the new media?'
27. Tunstall, J. op cit., 1983, p. 238.
28. Tunstall, J. op cit., 1983, pp. 244–5.

INDEX